Concurrent Programming
The Java Programming Language

Stephen J. Hartley
Math and Computer Science Department
Drexel University

New York   Oxford
OXFORD UNIVERSITY PRESS
1998

Oxford University Press

Oxford   New York
Athens   Auckland   Bangkok   Bogota   Bombay   Buenos Aires
Calcutta   Cape Town   Dar es Salaam   Delhi   Florence   Hong Kong
Istanbul   Karachi   Kuala Lumpur   Madras   Madrid   Melbourne
Mexico City   Nairobi   Paris   Singapore   Taipei   Tokyo   Toronto   Warsaw

and associated companies in
Berlin   Ibadan

Library of Congress Cataloging-in-Publication Data

Hartley, Stephen J.
    Concurrent programming : the Java programming language / Stephen J.
Hartley.
        p.   cm.
    Includes bibliographical references and index.
    ISBN 0-19-511315-2 (pbk.)
    1. Java (Computer program language).   2. Parallel programming
(Computer science).   I. Title.
QA76.73.J38H375   1998   97–42037
005.2'752—dc21   CIP

9 8 7 6 5 4 3 2

Printed in the United States of America
on acid-free paper

Contents

List of Figures

List of Tables

Preface

One can hardly open a magazine or newspaper these days without reading about the Java programming language, the World Wide Web, and the Internet. Java is an object-oriented, multithreaded programming language designed by Sun Microsystems. Its most popular use undoubtedly is writing "applets," programs that can be embedded in Web pages and downloaded to the client's browser to animate the Web pages or provide a graphical user interface for the user to interact with the Web server. Java is promoted endlessly as the best tool for programming the Internet and has been proclaimed "a tsunami that will sweep through the economy" [18].

In addition to Web applets, Java is used to write stand-alone programs, in particular those utilizing a graphical user interface or multiple threads of control sharing the same address space. Examples abound: Web browsers, Web servers, database access programs, on-line transaction systems, file servers, and computer games. These applications are examples of the client-server model of programming. This model was originally used in the design of operating systems for file servers and client workstations connected by a local area network (LAN). With the Internet, clients and servers need not be in the same room or even the same country. The popularity of the Internet has led to a mushrooming interest in client-server programming by all kinds of businesses and organizations. Many client and server applications benefit from being designed as object-oriented programs having multiple threads of control. Demand for programmers skilled in object-oriented design and concurrency will only grow. These factors clearly show the importance of concurrent programming and the applicability of Java.

This book is an introduction to the issues and concepts associated with concurrent programming, operating systems, the client-server model, and multiple threads. It can be used by instructors of concurrent programming and operating systems courses to give students experience writing concurrent programs in a cutting-edge, object-oriented language. It can also be read by software professionals desiring to develop competency in concurrent programming. Topics include shared data, race conditions, critical sections, mutual exclusion, semaphores, monitors, message passing, remote procedure calls, the rendezvous, and an introduction to parallel processing. The primary context for this material is operating systems and computer architecture, similar to the text *Concurrent Programming* by Alan Burns and Geoff Davies [13]. In contrast, Doug Lea's recent book *Concurrent Programming in Java* [27] is more focused on object-oriented programming and software engineering.

The Java language is used in many programming examples in this book to illustrate the concepts and issues. Java has many features and advantages that are relevant to instructors, students, and professional programmers:

Interpreter and virtual machine. The Java compiler transforms a program's source code into an intermediate language called "byte code," which is then interpreted in the context of a virtual machine (JVM).

Portability and platform independence. Once a Java compiler and interpreter have been ported to a particular architecture, any Java program will run there without change.

Multiple threads. Any Java program can start with minimal overhead additional threads of control that share the same address space and run concurrently with the main thread.

Automatic garbage collection. Memory "leaks" and "dangling" references are not possible because the Java garbage collector, running as a low-priority thread, reclaims unreferenced memory blocks.

No pointer arithmetic. The only operations permitted on object references are assignment and checking for equality or inequality.

Many compiler and interpreter checks. Java is strongly typed and the interpreter makes many run-time checks, such as null references and array indexes being in bounds.

The attractiveness of these features leaves no doubt that Java is a powerful and useful programming language. Despite recent skepticism and misgivings [20, 29], its strong typing, interpreter run-time checks, lack of pointer arithmetic, and garbage collection are particularly valuable in a teaching environment.

Focus and Features

A practical and demonstrative approach is used in this book: many example programs are presented to illustrate the concepts and guide the developing intuitive skill of the reader. The Java windowing tool kit is used to animate some of the important algorithms. No attempt is made at mathematical rigor, such as proving programs correct, or developing a logical foundation for concurrent programming. The same approach is taken in the Burns and Davies book. In an academic environment, the logical foundations can be introduced in a more advanced, follow-up course. An excellent text for this is Gregory Andrews' *Concurrent Programming: Principles and Practice* [1], also appropriate for the interested professional.

Prerequisites are proficiency in a high-level programming language like C or, better, C++; knowledge of data structures (lists, stacks, queues); knowledge of computer architecture (CPU, registers, memory, bus, disk, machine language instruction); some assembly language programming experience; and some familiarity with systems programming and operating systems concepts (processes, multiprogramming, system calls, memory management, device drivers, deadlock). Hardware basics are reviewed in Section 1.1. Programming experience with the sequential and object-oriented features of Java, covered in Chapter 2, is desirable but not strictly necessary. For Chapters 6 and 7, some knowledge of the TCP/IP networking protocol, port numbers, and Berkeley sockets is helpful.

There are several important features of this book.

- To facilitate its use as a supplement in an operating systems course, the material is keyed to five standard operating systems texts: Deitel's second edition *Operating Systems* [15], Silberschatz and Galvin's fourth edition *Operating System Concepts* [34], Stallings' second edition *Operating Systems* [36], Tanenbaum's *Modern Operating Systems* [41], and Tanenbaum's second edition *Operating Systems Design and Implementation* [43]. The relevant sections of these texts for the major concepts, such as semaphores and monitors, are indicated.

- Since most concepts and terms are defined, the book can be used as the text in an introductory concurrent programming course for students with some architecture and systems background, as well as read on its own by professional programmers possessing a similar background.

- The on-line appendix contains the complete source code of the many example Java programs used throughout the book. Each of the programs includes output from one or more sample runs to show how the program works. Relevant code fragments from the programs are presented and explained in the running text of the book. All of the example Java programs are stand-alone applications; there are no applets. Many of the concepts and techniques shown also apply to multithreaded Java applets.

- Algorithm animation using Java's windowing tool kit is described and used in several of the examples.

- Numerous programming assignments and other problems are provided in the Exercises sections. Students and professional programmers reading this book should do the exercises to enhance their understanding of the material.

Organization of the Book

Chapter 1 briefly describes the history of concurrent programming and the benefits of programming with threads. A review of hardware basics is included. Chapter 2 introduces the sequential programming features of Java: types, classes, objects, inheritance, flow of control, interfaces, and exceptions. One program, a genetic algorithm coded in Java, serves as a capstone example. The concept of algorithm animation is also introduced. The concurrent programming focus of the book starts in Chapter 3. Topics covered include Java threads, race conditions, and hardware and software solutions to the mutual exclusion problem. The next three chapters (4, 5, and 6) cover five major tools provided by operating systems and programming languages for thread synchronization and communication: semaphores, monitors, message passing, the rendezvous, and remote procedure calls. Many example Java programs illustrate these tools. Several algorithm animation examples are shown. The algorithm animation tool itself serves as a good example of a concurrent program with many synchronization issues. Even though monitors are Java's built-in synchronization primitive, semaphores are covered first. This is the conventional order followed by most operating systems books and Andrews' concurrent programming book. Semaphore classes for Java are straightforward to implement as monitors. Last, Chapter 7 is an introduction to parallel processing.

The example programs in this book are available by anonymous `ftp` from site `ftp.mcs.drexel.edu` in a `gzip`-compressed `tar` archive file: in binary mode, retrieve file `bookJavaExamples.tar.gz` from directory `pub/shartley`. A `zip` archive is also available in file `bookJavaExamples.zip`. The appendix containing the complete source code of all example programs was deleted from the book but is available on line as a `gzip`-compressed PostScript file, `bookJavaExamples.ps.gz`, in the same anonymous `ftp` directory (see also page 237). Some of the material in this book is accessible with a Web browser from URL `http://www.mcs.drexel.edu/~shartley/ConcProgJava/index.html`. An errata sheet will be linked there. For further details or to report any "bugs" in this book, contact the author by electronic mail at `shartley@mcs.drexel.edu`.

The Java compiler and interpreter (Java Development Kit or JDK) have been ported to Sun's Solaris 2.x (Sparc architecture), Apple's Macintosh (68K and Power PC architectures), and Microsoft's Windows 95/NT (Intel x86 architecture). They have also been ported to the Linux operating system, which runs on PC compatibles. These ports are available for free downloading from many sites, such as `ftp.javasoft.com`, `ftp.blackdown.org`, and `sunsite.unc.edu`. For further information, access the Web pages at `www.javasoft.com`, `www.blackdown.org`, and `sunsite.unc.edu`. All of the Java examples in this book have been tested on the Windows 95/NT and/or the Solaris 2.x platform, using JDK version 1.1.

Acknowledgments

I thank Drexel University for the time to prepare this book. Many Drexel students have had the opportunity to use early drafts of this material, including the programming assignments, and have provided useful feedback.

Sun Microsystems deserves special thanks for making its implementation of the Java compiler and virtual machine for Solaris 2.x and Windows 95/NT available for free.

Much of the material in this book was drawn from my SR programming language text [22]; many of the Java programs are translations of the corresponding SR examples. I admire the work of the SR team at the University of Arizona, Greg Andrews, Ron Olsson, Gregg Townsend, and many graduate students, for designing and implementing a versatile concurrent programming language. I thank my editors at Oxford University Press, John Bauco, Krysia Bebick, and Bill Zobrist, for their help and interest in this project. I appreciate the many frank and useful comments made by the reviewers of various drafts of the manuscript: David Clay (Florida

Institute of Technology), Jeff Parker (Agile Networks, Inc.), Harry Tyrer (University of Missouri at Columbia), Jack Tan (University of Wisconsin), Boleslaw Szymanski (Rensselaer Polytechnic Institute), and K. C. Tai (North Carolina State University).

This book was prepared using the LaTeX formatting system on a PC running the Linux operating system. My deepest gratitude goes to the authors of TeX, LaTeX, and the many user-contributed macro and style files; the amazing global design and development team of Linux; and Oxford University Press for loaning me the PC. I also want to thank John T. Stasko and Doug Hayes for designing and developing the XTANGO algorithm animation software package. Many of the figures were done with idraw, part of the Interviews package from Stanford University, and xfig, part of the contributed software to the X11 Window System.

My sincere appreciation is due to Lori Weaver for her understanding and support during the preparation of this book.

Philadelphia, Pennsylvania   S. J. H.
September 1997   mailto:shartley@mcs.drexel.edu
                                                                           http://www.mcs.drexel.edu/~shartley

Chapter 1

Introduction

Concurrent programming has its roots in operating systems and systems programming. In the 1960s, independent input-output (IO) device controllers, called channels, were added to computers, each programmable as a small computer itself. Operating systems were organized as a collection of concurrently executing processes, some in the channels and others running on the main CPU. Several of these processes shared memory. For example, in a tape-to-disk copy the tape drive channel wrote data from the tape into a main memory region typically organized as a collection of allocated and free buffers; the disk channel read data from the buffer pool and wrote them to the disk drive. Sharing the buffer pool raised the problem of *process synchronization*. The tape drive controller needed to make sure that it did not overwrite a full buffer that the disk controller had not yet read. Conversely, the disk drive controller needed to make sure that it did not read an empty buffer or the same buffer twice. Further, to avoid reading a meaningless mixture of old and new data, a buffer should not be read while being written.

A related synchronization problem arises from the management of a multilevel priority interrupt system. Suppose the operating system is handling an interrupt at a certain priority level and a higher priority interrupt is raised. If the code for handling the higher priority interrupt manipulates the same data structure as the first interrupt, then that data structure may become corrupted. Either the interrupt priorities need to be rearranged so this cannot happen or all further interrupts need to be left pending, effectively locking the data structure, until the first interrupt has been completely handled.

Writing programs that consist of multiple processes sharing memory is one form of *concurrent programming*. Synchronization is often a major concern in these programs. Various tools, both hardware and software, were developed by operating system designers and computer architects to solve synchronization problems. The test-and-set instruction (Section 3.5.3) can be used to lock shared data structures for exclusive use by one process at a time. Computer scientists and mathematicians treated the problem of process synchronization as an abstract problem. Dijkstra [16] designed semaphores (Chapter 4) as a tool to solve this problem. Semaphores can be added to the run-time library of many programming languages. Hoare [24] considered making synchronization part of the expressive power of a programming language in the form of a monitor (Chapter 5). Semaphores and monitors are designed for use by processes that share memory. For processes that want to exchange information but do not share memory, some form of *interprocess communication*, such as message passing (Section 6.1), is needed. Clients and servers can communicate and synchronize using message passing, another form of concurrent programming. Process synchronization in a shared memory environment is a kind of interprocess communication.

More recent developments in hardware and computer architecture have also influenced concurrent programming. As a result of the declining cost of microprocessor chips, many computers are now equipped with several central processing units, all sharing a global main memory, in a parallel architecture called a *shared-memory multiprocessor*. Using all available CPUs to execute a program more quickly requires the programmer to write the program as a collection of processes that communicate through shared global variables or by passing messages. The processes are distributed across the CPUs so that each CPU has one or more of the processes. However, creation of a new process by the operating system is an expensive and resource-consuming system call for a program to make. A new address space must be created and mapped into physical memory, the new process code and initial data copied there, and operating system tables updated. Context switching between the processes assigned to a CPU is also expensive since all registers must be saved and restored and the mapping from process address space to physical memory changed. These costs led to the design of *lightweight* processes or *threads*, all sharing the same address space. It is much less expensive to create a new thread in a process than create a new process and to switch the context of a CPU from one thread to another than between processes. Using multiple threads is another form of concurrent programming. The programmer faces the same synchronization issues in a multi-threaded program as those when several processes share memory. Fortunately, the same hardware and software tools can be used.

Regardless of how many CPUs are available, writing a program as a collection of threads sharing the same address space often simplifies its design. Many applications benefit from multiple threads of control, as the following two examples demonstrate.

- One of the most important uses of threads is in the client-server model. Using multiple threads in a shared address space makes it much easier to design and implement a server application, compared to purely sequential programming. A dispatcher thread handles incoming requests for service from clients. The dispatcher gives the request to a new or idle worker thread, freeing the dispatcher to wait for the next request. The worker thread gathers the information needed by the client and generates a reply.

- The windowing system of a graphical user interface (GUI) is more easily managed with threads, one thread per window, to handle the events associated with each window, such as mouse clicks and keystrokes.

The declining cost of microprocessors has prompted the marketing of inexpensive desktop shared-memory multiprocessor machines. This type of architecture supports the dedication of a CPU to each thread in a program, increasing the workload handled and the attractiveness of multiple threads of control in the program address space. Worker threads in a server handle client requests in parallel for greater throughput. A windowing system responds more quickly to each window's events.

This book is an introduction to the issues and concepts associated with concurrent programming, operating systems, the client-server model, and multiple threads. In the following chapters, we cover the important topics involved in concurrent process synchronization and interprocess communication: shared data, race conditions, critical sections, mutual exclusion, semaphores, monitors, message passing, remote procedure calls, and the rendezvous. The last chapter is an introduction to a closely related area, parallel processing. Many programming examples are provided to illustrate these concepts and issues. They are coded in the Java* language because it is popular, object oriented, and supports multiple threads of control. Chapter 2 is an overview of sequential Java; coverage of its concurrent programming features begins in Chapter 3.

We will see that critical sections must be identified to avoid race conditions in processes or threads that execute concurrently and share memory. Semaphores and monitors are used to enforce mutual exclusion. Other tools, such as message passing, the rendezvous, and remote procedure calls, implement interprocess communication between address spaces. These tools are used to solve the so-called classical process synchronization problems described in Chapter 4: the bounded buffer producer and consumer, the dining philosophers, the sleeping barber, and the database readers and writers.

In order to reinforce their understanding, students of operating systems and professional systems programmers need practical experience using these concepts in a programming language and running multithreaded programs on a computer. The Java language provides an excellent environment for writing and executing concurrent programs, giving students and professionals the opportunity to build their confidence and deepen their understanding. To facilitate this, many Java programming assignments appear in the exercises at the end of each chapter.

1.1 Hardware and Software Concepts

The following is a description of the hardware (CPU, registers, memory, bus, disk, machine language instruction) and software concepts (processes, multiprogramming, system calls, memory management, device drivers) needed to understand the rest of the material in this book. More information about these topics can be found in books on assembly language programming, computer architecture, machine organization, and systems programming, for example [5, 35, 40].

A conventional computing system, such as a mainframe or workstation, usually consists of a system bus to which are attached one or more central processing units (CPUs), several main (physical) memory modules (RAM), and devices like disks, printers, terminals, plotters, and network cards for one or more local area networks

---

*Java is a Registered Trademark of Sun Microsystems, Inc.

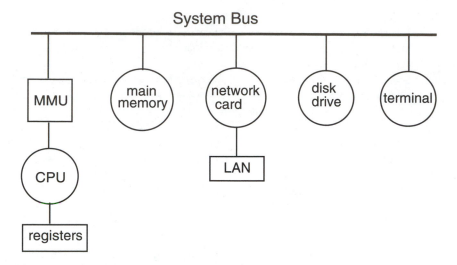

Figure 1.1: Computing System Components.

(LANs), as shown in Figure 1.1. The CPU typically contains a set of registers and a memory management unit (MMU) for address translation. Starting from low addresses, main memory normally contains interrupt vectors, memory-mapped device registers, and the operating system kernel. See Figure 1.2. The rest of memory contains operating system processes, such as network and file servers, and user-initiated processes, such as editors, compilers, and applications.

1.1.1   Processes

A *process* is program code that is in some state of execution. It has its own address space, some or all of which is mapped by the operating system into physical main memory. It has a single *thread* or *flow of control*. The program counter (PC) register in the CPU contains the address of the next instruction to be executed. In a multiprogrammed computer system, such as a mainframe or workstation, many processes are loaded into physical memory so they can execute concurrently, sharing the CPU and peripheral devices.

Sometimes the address space of a process corresponds byte-for-byte with a contiguous area of physical memory. Most current computing systems, though, implement *virtual memory*, using a memory management unit that is part of the processor. The parts of the process address space that are currently needed by the process to execute are mapped into one or more blocks (segments or pages) of main memory. As the process executes, its logical addresses are translated by the MMU into physical addresses. The entire process need not be resident in main memory for it to execute, nor does the memory it occupies need be contiguous.

The process logical address space, including most UNIX* implementations, is

---

*UNIX is a Registered Trademark of X/Open, Inc.

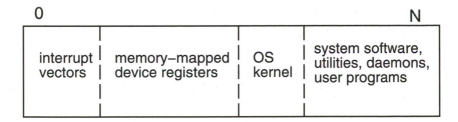

Figure 1.2: Computing System Physical Main Memory.

usually arranged as follows. Starting at the low addresses are the instructions or code of the program, usually read-only, also called the "text." Next come the program global data, both initialized and uninitialized, followed by the heap, from which dynamic memory allocation is done (malloc(*bytes*) in the C standard library), growing toward high addresses. Starting at the high end of the process address space and growing toward the low end is the process stack, containing storage for procedure local variables, passed parameters, and return addresses. See Figure 1.3.

A process has a current *state*: running, ready or runnable, blocked, or suspended. A more detailed description of the state of a process includes its CPU register values, program code variable values, open files, input data read, and output data written. A *running* process is currently using the CPU; a *ready* or *runnable* process is waiting to be scheduled to use the CPU; a *blocked* process is waiting for some service it requested from the operating system to be handled and until then is not scheduled for CPU cycles; a *suspended* process has been sent a "suspend" signal and until resumed is not scheduled for CPU cycles. A running process is changed to the ready state when it uses up its time slice, as described in Section 1.1.4 below; a running process becomes blocked when it issues a request to the operating system for some service that cannot be handled immediately. A suspended process becomes runnable when a "resume" signal is sent to it; likewise a blocked process becomes runnable when the service it requested has been performed by the operating system.

The operating system kernel keeps track of the state of all processes with a process table. Each existing process has an entry in this table, as shown in Figure 1.4, containing the state of the process (running, ready, blocked, suspended), the contents of the CPU registers from the last time the process was executing on the CPU, the process memory allocation, the process identifier (pid), the owner of the process (uid), the owner's group (gid), a list of open files, and accounting information. See ([15], Chapter 3), ([34], Chapter 4), ([36], Chapter 3), ([41], Sections 2.1), ([43], Sections 2.1) for more details.

1.1.2 Threads

Two processes can share data by requesting the operating system to map the shared data into both of their address spaces. Alternatively, a process can ask the operating system for more than one thread or flow of control in its address space. Operating systems that support this are called *multithreaded*. All the threads of a process share

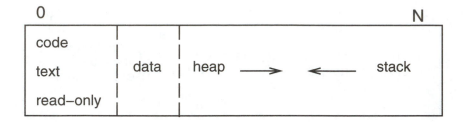

Figure 1.3: Process Logical or Virtual Address Space.

the same process address space and global variables; however, each thread has its own program counter, other CPU register values, and run-time stack for procedure calls, as shown in Figure 1.5. Because it is usually more efficient in terms of system time and resources to create one process with multiple threads than several processes that share some memory, threads are sometimes called *lightweight processes*. The same tools, semaphores and monitors, that are used for synchronization by processes that share memory are also used by the multiple threads in one process to synchronize their access to the process address space.

Birrell [7] motivates concurrent programming using threads with the following points:

- Shared-memory multiprocessors are becoming cheaper and more common so each thread can be allocated its own CPU.

- It is less expensive and more efficient to create several threads in one process that share data than to create several processes that share data.

- Input-output on slow devices like networks, terminals, and disks can be done in one thread while another thread does useful computation in parallel.

- Multiple threads can handle the events (e.g., mouse clicks) in multiple windows in the windowing system on a workstation.

- In a LAN cluster of workstations or in a distributed operating system environment, a server running on one machine can spawn a thread to handle an incoming request in parallel with the main thread continuing to accept additional incoming requests.

There are many types of situations more easily handled with a multithreaded program. A program that calculates something, say Fibonacci numbers, in a window with a "Stop" button at the top is much more easily written with threads than as a sequential program. Instead of periodically polling to see if the stop button has been activated while computing additional Fibonacci numbers, as would be done in a sequential program, one thread in a multithreaded program calculates numbers until stopped by the other thread. Meanwhile the other thread is blocked, waiting for the stop button to be activated. The Fibonacci number thread executes code that is

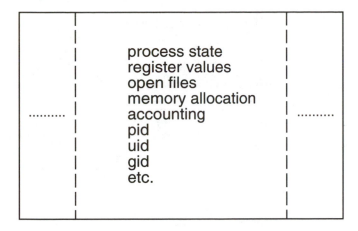

Figure 1.4: Process Table Entry.

completely independent of the button status-checking code; there is a clean division
of functionality. It is much easier to design, implement, and test the program.

Another situation where threads are used to great advantage is a server program
fielding requests from clients over a LAN. The server waits for the next client
request. When a new request comes in over the LAN, the server creates a new
thread to compute the results or retrieve from disk the data requested by the client.
In the meantime, the server is able to receive another client request even if the just-
spawned thread blocks. If threads were not available, the server would be executing
complicated polling-type sequential code to check the network for a new request,
check the status of a disk read issued earlier to retrieve data for a client, and in
spare CPU cycles compute numeric results requested by another client. Or the
server would need procedures to handle interrupts generated by devices to signal
the completion of IO system calls issued earlier. These procedures would record
state changes in variables that the server would have to check periodically, leading
to complicated error-prone code. Instead of complex polling or interrupt handling,
if the server used blocking IO to simplify the code, the server's performance would
be severely limited since it could handle only one client request at a time. The
sequential programming alternatives to threads (polling, interrupt-driven code, and
blocking IO) all have major disadvantages. To sum up, threads allow the increased
throughput of concurrency and parallelism while retaining the simpler coding style
of a single shared address space and blocking IO calls to the operating system. If
the multithreaded program is executing on a shared-memory multiprocessor, then
available CPUs can be allocated to runnable threads for an even greater increase in
concurrency and throughput.

The client-server multithreaded example just described uses a style of programming called the *dispatch* model. Another programming style using threads is the
pipeline model. Much like a manufacturing assembly line, each thread performs
some computation on a sequence of data items flowing along the pipeline.

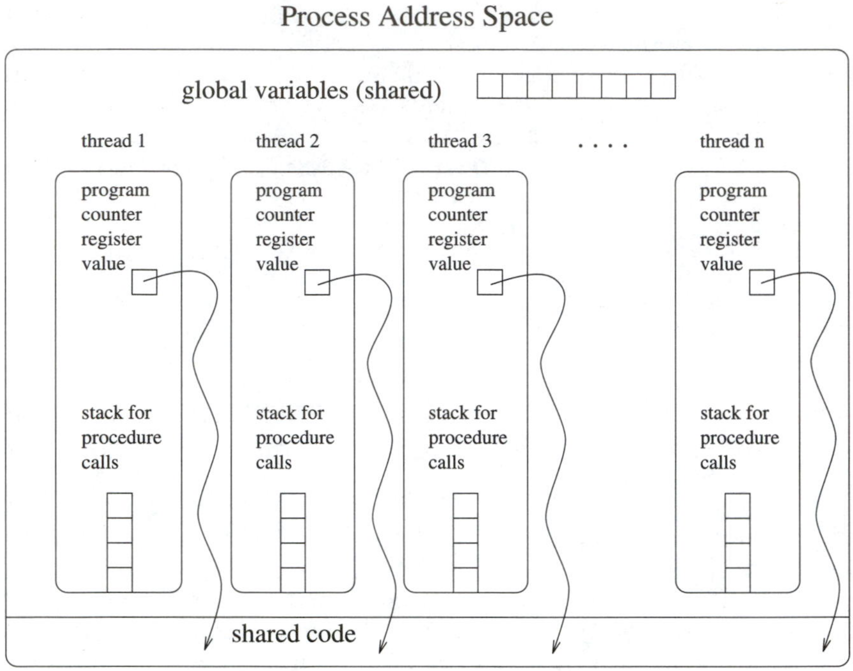

Process Address Space

Figure 1.5: Multiple Threads in a Process.

Threads are closely related to *event-driven* programming in GUIs. One thread in the windowing code is blocked, waiting for keystrokes and mouse clicks by the user. When such an event occurs, the thread is unblocked and calls a method designated by the programmer to be invoked every time the event occurs. There may be one such thread for each open window. Other threads in the program are performing computations whose behavior is modified by the window events. We return to this topic in Section 3.2.

1.1.3   Hardware and Software Interrupts

Hardware interrupts are generated by devices when they need service or have finished performing a service, for example, a disk controller after a requested IO operation has been performed or a network card controller when a packet arrives. Hardware interrupts are asynchronous, that is, unrelated to whatever process is currently executing on the CPU.

When a hardware interrupt occurs, it may be ignored or left pending if there is an interrupt priority system in effect, but usually the interrupt is handled. The CPU switches from user mode to kernel (supervisor or privileged) mode so that protected memory like operating system tables is accessible. Each device has an interrupt vector associated with it, which consists of a new program counter and status code word. The hardware loads the program counter and status register from the interrupt vector, causing the CPU to start fetching and executing instructions at the address of the interrupt handling code in supervisor mode. If handling the interrupt will result in a context switch, described below, the handler saves the register contents in the process table slot of the process that was executing when the interrupt occurred.

Depending on the device that generated the interrupt, the interrupt handler code in the operating system kernel performs such actions as

- saving the character typed by the user in the appropriate buffer,

- copying the incoming network packet from the network card to the appropriate buffer, or

- changing the state of a process from blocked to ready because a disk IO operation is now complete and the user process that requested the disk block can continue running.

The CPU scheduler now decides which process should run next, picking from among those in the ready state. It could be the one that was interrupted, or it could be the process that earlier requested a disk block and just had its state changed from blocked to ready during interrupt handling. The CPU scheduler sets a pointer to the process table slot of the process chosen to run next. The interrupt handler loads the registers from the process table slot. A return from interrupt is executed, causing a switch back to user mode of the CPU.

Software interrupts are generated by programs, such as user programs and system utilities, with the TRAP machine language instruction. Software interrupts are synchronous in nature since they are generated by the program currently executing on the CPU. For example, suppose a user program executes

```
dateAndTime = getDateAndTime()
```

or

```
count = read(file, buffer, nbytes)
```

Here **read** and **getDateAndTime** are library routines that execute a TRAP instruction after putting parameters, if any, in registers or on the stack. Because they execute a TRAP, **read** and **getDateAndTime** are called *system calls*. When a TRAP is executed, things proceed much like a hardware interrupt: TRAP has its own interrupt vector and a jump is made to the TRAP interrupt handler. The interrupt handler examines the parameters on the stack or in the registers. If the TRAP was from **getDateAndTime**, then the handler copies data from the clock registers into the return register and returns from interrupt. If the TRAP was from **read**, then the handler

1. Tells the appropriate device driver to load the disk controller's command registers for a disk read operation,

2. Changes the state of the process from running to blocked (the kernel maintains a list of processes that are blocked for various events),

3. Calls the CPU scheduler to pick a different process to run next, and

4. Returns from the interrupt.

Asynchronously, the disk seeks to the track containing the bytes requested by the **read**. The disk controller uses *direct memory access* (DMA) to copy the bytes into main memory ([43], Section 3.1.3), sharing the system bus with the CPU. The disk controller generates a hardware interrupt after the copy is complete; the interrupt handler then changes the state of the process that called **read** from blocked to ready.

The above is a simplified description of system calls and hardware and software interrupts. For a complete case study of an operating system, including the entire source code for the interrupt handlers, device drivers, and memory and file system management, see the "MINIX Overview" and "MINIX Implementation" sections of [43].

1.1.4   CPU Scheduling and Context Switching

To prevent a user program infinite loop from "hanging" the machine and to give each process on a multiprogrammed machine a fair share of the CPU, a hardware clock generates interrupts periodically, such as 60 times a second. This allows the operating system to schedule all processes in main memory to run on the CPU at regular intervals and to maintain time and date information for accounting.

Each time a clock interrupt occurs, the interrupt handler checks how much CPU time the process currently running has used. If it has used up its *time slice* or time quantum, then the CPU scheduling code of the operating system kernel picks a different process to run. The CPU scheduler uses one of many algorithms to allocate CPU time, such as round robin or multilevel feedback queues. See ([15], Chapter 10), ([34], Chapter 5), ([36], Chapter 8), ([41], Section 2.4), ([43], Section 2.4).

Each switch of the CPU from one process to another is called a *context switch*. The values of the CPU registers are saved in the process table slot of the process that was running just before the clock interrupt occurred, and the registers are loaded from the process table slot of the process picked by the CPU scheduler to run next. In a multiprogrammed uniprocessor computing system, context switches occur frequently enough that all processes appear to be running concurrently, each on its own slower "virtual" CPU. Thus the operating system implements *multiprogramming* with context switching: allocating the CPU in turn to each runnable process for a time slice of approximately 100 milliseconds. In a multiprocessor system, each process may have its own CPU if there are enough of them available.

If a process has more than one thread, the operating system can use the same techniques of context switching and time slicing to schedule the threads so they appear to execute in parallel, just as all processes appear to run in parallel under multiprogramming. This is the case if threads are implemented at the kernel level. Threads can also be implemented entirely at the user level in run-time libraries. Since in this case no thread scheduling is provided by the operating system, it is the responsibility of the programmer to yield the CPU frequently enough in each

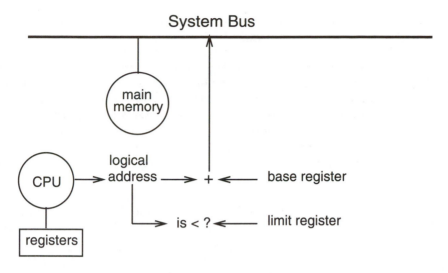

Figure 1.6: Base/Limit Register Hardware Memory Protection.

thread so all threads in the process can make progress. We return to this in Section 3.1.1. See also ([41], Section 12.1), ([42], Section 4.1).

1.1.5 Hardware Protection

In a multiprogrammed multiuser computing system, it is necessary to protect the main memory allocated to one process from access by another process. Otherwise one process could accidentally or maliciously corrupt the address space of another process. For the same reason, the operating system kernel code and tables, device controller memory-mapped registers, and interrupt vectors must be protected from access by user processes. In addition, to prevent disruption of the system, some instructions must be executed only by the operating system kernel code while the CPU is in a privileged mode, for example, setting accounting timers, halting the CPU, masking or disabling interrupts, locking the memory bus, and setting the base/limit registers described below. These protections can be implemented with (1) a dual mode of CPU operation and (2) a memory management unit (MMU) with an address translation scheme. The two modes the CPU executes in are user mode and supervisor (kernel) mode. In kernel mode, the CPU is able to reference all memory locations and execute all instructions; in user mode, the CPU cannot execute any privileged instructions and interprocess memory protection is enforced, such as with the base/limit scheme described next.

Operating systems texts discuss general memory protection and management schemes, such as multiple variable-sized partitions, segmentation, and paging ([15], Part 3), ([34], Chapters 8 and 9), ([36], Chapters 6 and 7), ([41], Chapter 3), ([43], Chapter 4). One very simple address translation and protection scheme uses a base register and a limit register in the CPU or MMU. A process executing on the

CPU generates addresses that reference logical address space (code, data, heap, and stack described above) in some range 0 to N, where N represents the size of the process. In the base/limit scheme, each process address space is loaded into some unique contiguous area of main memory. Whenever a process runs on the CPU, the starting address of its main memory allocation is loaded into the base register and the size of its main memory allocation is loaded into the limit or length register, as part of its context switch information. Before a logical address generated by the process executing on the CPU is placed on the address lines of the system bus, it is checked for validity and translated into a physical memory address. The logical address is compared to the value in the limit register. If the address is greater than the limit register, a memory protection violation has occurred and the process is aborted. If this check is passed, the value of the base register is added to the logical address to convert it to a physical address before it is placed on the bus. See Figure 1.6.

Summary

We looked at the history of operating systems and systems programming to see how concurrent programming started with processes that share memory. Creating multiple threads of control sharing one address space is a less expensive alternative to creating multiple processes. We saw the many advantages and benefits of designing a multithreaded program. For threads and for processes that share memory, synchronization is a major concern so that shared data are not corrupted. The following chapters discuss how critical sections must be identified to avoid race conditions. Semaphores and monitors are used for mutual exclusion and synchronization. Processes on different machines cannot share memory to exchange data. However, other facilities are available for interprocess communication, such as message passing, the rendezvous, and remote procedure calls.

Last, we reviewed the basic structure of a computing system. We defined the important concepts of a process, a thread, the states they can be in, and how they are scheduled for CPU cycles by the operating system with context switching. The operating system handles hardware interrupts from devices and software interrupts from user processes, the latter resulting from system calls for service. A computing system needs to implement various kinds of hardware protection to ensure the integrity of the operating system and user processes.

Chapter 2

The Java Programming Language

Java is a multithreaded, object-oriented, high-level language used to write both stand-alone programs and "applets," the latter for embedding in HTML (hypertext markup language) documents available on the World Wide Web. Applets give Web pages executable content accessible with a Java-enabled Web browser.

Java provides many advantages and useful features to the programmer.

- Once the Java compiler and interpreter have been ported to a new platform, any Java program will run there without change.

- Java is strongly typed: the compiler makes many checks, such as comparing the types of arguments passed to a method to make sure they match the types of the formal parameters.

- The interpreter makes many run-time checks, such as making sure an array index is in bounds and an object reference is not null.

- Memory "leaks" (a block of memory still considered allocated even though there are no references to it) and "dangling" pointers (a reference to a block of memory that has been deallocated) are not possible because the Java garbage collector reclaims the memory occupied by unreachable objects. There is no need for an error-prone free(*pointer*) procedure.

- There is no pointer arithmetic: the only operations permitted on an object reference are assignment by another object reference and comparison to another object reference. Thus the programmer cannot write error-prone code that steps a pointer variable through different areas of memory.

- Java comes with a windowing tool-kit class library (AWT) that applets and stand-alone applications use to implement GUIs.

Many books are available that describe the Java language, for example [2, 9, 14, 17, 28, 44]. Several come with a CD-ROM that contains the book's example programs and a copy of the Sun Microsystems' Java Development Kit (JDK). Most of these books concentrate on the sequential aspects of the language and on using the windowing tool kit to write applets. They all have a chapter or two describing Java threads. This book, starting with the next chapter, goes into much more detail about concurrent programming and using Java threads in stand-alone applications.

The JDK and associated documentation are available for free downloading from the archive at site `ftp.javasoft.com`, maintained by the JavaSoft subsidiary of Sun Microsystems. The JDK consists of the compiler, the interpreter (JVM or Java virtual machine), and the system class libraries. Available documentation includes a tutorial, a programming guide, and the Application Programming Interface (API), a description of Java's system class libraries. JDKs for Sun's Solaris 2.x OS, for Windows 95/NT on PCs, and for the Apple Macintosh (MacOS System 7.5, 68030 or better processor) are available. Information about new releases of Sun's JDK appears on the JavaSoft and Sun World Wide Web home pages, `http://www.javasoft.com` and `http://www.sun.com`.

This chapter describes the sequential features of Java and includes several example application programs illustrating their use. We look at command line argument processing, tokenizing keyboard input, and file input-output. The object-oriented features of Java (classes, objects, and inheritance) are explained. Some features unique to Java, packages and interfaces, are examined. We will see how Java uses exceptions to indicate run-time errors. One program, a simple genetic algorithm, contains examples of all the Java features in this chapter. The final section looks at the methods in a class designed for algorithm animation. After reading this chapter, you will be able to understand the sequential features of Java used in this book and write programs to solve the assignments in the exercises.

2.1 Sequential Features

Java draws many features from the C programming language and the C++ object-oriented language. To learn more about the object-oriented programming technique, see [8, 11].

Java programs are written as one or more classes, like programs in the C++ language. A *class* is a "template" or "set of architectural plans" or definition for constructing an object. Object-oriented languages like C++ have extended the idea of an abstract data type into a class, combining the features of C's user type definition, `typedef`, and record structure definition, `struct`. An *object* is an extension or enhancement of the ideas of variable and type in programming languages. In C and Pascal, a variable name is associated with one or more memory locations and has a type telling what the stored bits mean. As a Java program executes, objects are created from the classes and stored in dynamically allocated memory. An object's class specifies the meaning of the memory locations.

A class has variables, called *data fields*, and procedures to manipulate the data, called *methods*.

```
class Name {
```

```
        data fields
        methods
}
```

In code fragments like the above, we use a fixed-width font as in `class` for items that appear verbatim, a slanted fixed-width font as in *Name* for items of the correct form that vary in different examples, and italics as in *methods* for a description of blocks of Java statements appearing in fully coded examples. All the fields and methods of a class constitute its *members*. From a class, one or more objects can be constructed or instantiated at run time. Each such object *encapsulates* or hides its data, in general only allowing access to the data through its methods. The data fields of a class are global to the methods of that class. The variables declared in the body of a method are *local* to the method; storage for a method's local variables is allocated on the calling thread's stack for each invocation of the method.

Fields and methods can be declared with the keywords `public` or `private`. A public member can be accessed from anywhere outside the class, whereas a private member can be accessed only by the code inside the class. If neither public nor private access is specified, then the member can be accessed from outside its class, but only if the class is in the same package. This is described in more detail in Section 2.5. It is not always necessary to construct an object from a class in order to use the fields and methods of the class. If the keyword `static` is used in all member definitions, then the class can be used without instantiation. This is the case with the example programs in the next two sections. Java programs that consist of classes containing only static data fields and static methods are called *static programs* and correspond to code written in a procedural language like C or Pascal.

Java supports several standard data types: 8-bit `byte` integers, 16-bit `short` integers, 32-bit `int` integers, 64-bit `long` integers, 32-bit `float` reals, 64-bit `double` reals, 16-bit Unicode characters, strings, and Booleans. Any of these can be structured into an array with C-style indexing. (Strings and arrays are actually objects in Java.) The language includes an assignment statement, the while loop, the for-index loop, and the if-then-else statement, all using the C language syntax. Comments start with `//` and conclude with the end of the line; C-style `/*···*/` comments are also permissible. Java is a strongly typed language like Pascal and ANSI C: the compiler checks the types of arguments in method calls against the types of the formal parameters in the method's definition.

2.1.1 Single-Class Static Programs

Short or simple sequential programs can be written as a single class of the following form, where all fields and methods are static.

```
class Name {
    static fields ...
    static methods ...
    public static void main(String[] args) {
```

> *local variables* ...
> *executable statements* ...
> }
> }

In a single-class program, there is no need to declare members as public or private, except for the `main` method, which must be public. The `main` method is much like the `main` procedure in a C program: it is where program execution begins. The argument `args` to `main` is an array of strings, one string per command line argument.

The standard way to compile and run a Java program on a UNIX or Windows 95/NT platform using Sun's JDK is the sequence of two commands

```
javac file.java
java Name command line arguments...
```

where `file.java` is the file containing the Java source code and `Name` is the name of the class containing the `main` method (where execution begins).

The following examples illustrate some of the sequential features of the Java language. The complete source code for all the example programs in this book appears in the on-line appendix (see page 237 for access information) and includes one or more sample runs appended to the end of the code in the form of a comment. Program 2.1 reads a number from the command line and computes factorials from one to the number read.

```
class Factorials {
    static int computeFactorial(int k) {
        if (k < 0) return -1;
        else if (k == 0 || k == 1) return 1;
        else return k*computeFactorial(k-1);
    }
    public static void main(String[] args) {
        int n;
        n = Integer.parseInt(args[0]);
        for (int i = 1; i <= n; i++)
            System.out.println
                (i + " factorial is " + computeFactorial(i));
    }
}
```

A command line integer argument can be processed with the `parseInt` method of the Java library class `Integer`. The syntax of the `if` and `for` statements is the same as C. The index variable of a `for` statement can be declared in the first component, restricting the scope of the index variable to the body of the `for` statement. String constants are enclosed in double quotes. Output to `stdout` is done with the `println` method of the `out` field (a reference to a `PrintStream` object) in the `System` library class. Numeric items are converted to strings and concatenated (using `+`) with other strings to form a line of output.

Program 2.2 uses the "exchange" algorithm to sort numbers read from the command line. The **new** reserved word is used to allocate space for an array; the size expression can use variables whose value is not determined until run time (dynamic storage allocation).

```
n = Integer.parseInt(args[0]);
int[] nums = new int[n];
```

Array indexing starts with zero, as in the C language. The number of slots in an array can be accessed with .length (an array is an object with a length instance variable; see Section 2.2). Note that System.out.println(···) generates a line feed, whereas System.out.print(···) suppresses the line feed. This is useful for generating prompts.

```
System.out.print("How many years old are you? ");
System.out.flush();
```

Flushing ensures that the prompt appears immediately on the screen.

Program 2.3 shows that Java supports recursion. This program counts the number of ways that N queens can be placed on an N-by-N chessboard such that no queen is attacking any other queen. The fields N and numSolutions are global to the methods place and safe.

Exceptions are Java's way of indicating that some sort of error has occurred. The general construct for detecting and handling exceptions is

```
try {
     block of statements ...
} catch (SomeException e) {
     error, do something ...
} catch (SomeOtherException e) {
     different error, do something else ...
} finally {  // optional
     do this no matter what, error or not ...
}
```

If an error or exceptional condition occurs in the execution of the statements of the try block (including any methods called therein), an exception object is "thrown" that can be "caught" in a catch block that matches the type of exception thrown. The code that catches the exception can do something to handle the error. The finally block is optional. If present, it is executed whether or not an exception is thrown.

Program 2.1 contains a sample run in which the command line argument is omitted; in processing command line arguments, an array index out-of-bounds exception is generated, as shown, since the args array has no components.

```
D:\>java Factorials
java.lang.ArrayIndexOutOfBoundsException: 0
        at Factorials.main(fact.java:11)
```

The exception is not caught with a `try-catch` and therefore aborts the program. A sample run of Program 2.2 shows the exception generated when the user types a command line argument that cannot be parsed as an integer, also uncaught. Program 2.3 checks with a `try-catch` for both the index of `args` being out of bounds and an improperly formatted integer on the command line.

```
try {  // override default from command line argument if any
    N = Integer.parseInt(args[0]);
} catch (ArrayIndexOutOfBoundsException e) {
} catch (NumberFormatException e) {
}
```

If either of these happens, the program does not abort; instead the value of N is left unchanged from its default value (the `catch` blocks are empty).

2.1.2 Multiclass Static Programs

Most Java programs consist of multiple classes. Before using classes in a program to construct objects, we first consider multiclass static programs in which a class accesses a (static) method in another class. By using the `public` modifier, a class makes available to other classes the methods implemented inside it.

```
class Name {
    public static type method(...) {
        ...
    }
}
```

The example in Program 2.4 illustrates this. To make the method `compute` accessible from outside the class `Factorial`, the modifier `public` is used. To access a static method in another class, the dot notation

```
Name.method(arguments);
```

is used. For example, the `main` method in class `SomeFactorials` accesses method `compute` in class `Factorial` with `Factorial.compute(n)`.

Similar to the `exit` of C, `System.exit(0)` is used in Program 2.4 for normal program termination and `System.exit(1)` for abnormal termination, such as an `IOException` indicating a problem reading from `stdin`.

```
try {
    line = in.readLine();
} catch (IOException e) {
    System.err.println("readLine: " + e);
    System.exit(1);
}
```

Note the use of `err` in the error message `System.err.println` statement. On a UNIX platform, these error messages go to the `stderr` output stream instead of `stdout`, which may have been redirected into a file or pipe.

The Java Development Kit comes with several libraries of classes, organized into groups of related classes, each called a *package*. All programs have automatic access to the `java.lang` package, which includes the `System` class we have used for input and output, the `Integer` class with the `parseInt` method, the `Math` class, and many others. If other packages are needed, they must be specifically imported using the `import` reserved word. For example, Program 2.4 needs the `InputStreamReader` and `BufferedReader` classes from the `java.io` package in order to read lines of input from `stdin` with the `readLine` method.

```
import java.io.*;
```

The notation `java.io.*` is used to import all classes in the package. Classes can also be imported individually by name.

```
import java.io.InputStreamReader;
import java.io.BufferedReader;
```

We discuss user-defined packages in Section 2.5.

To execute a Java program that consists of multiple classes, put the name of the class containing the `main` method in the `java` command. For example, the two classes in Program 2.4 could be placed in separate files, say `file1.java` and `file2.java`, and compiled and run with the commands

```
javac file1.java file2.java
java SomeFactorials
```

2.2 Objects

The example Java programs so far have consisted of classes all of whose members are static, and no user-defined objects other than arrays and strings have been constructed. In this section, we discuss classes as templates for object construction. We also distinguish more clearly between a class and an object. Later, we describe how the definition of a class can be based on another class by extending it, inheriting fields and methods from it.

The statement

```
BufferedReader in =
    new BufferedReader(new InputStreamReader(System.in));
```

in Program 2.4 is an example of object construction or instantiation from a class. The variable `in` is declared to be a reference to an object constructed from the `BufferedReader` class in the `java.io` system package imported by the program. The variable is also initialized in the same statement by assigning to it a new object of that type. In general, given a class definition such as

```
class MyClass {
   private int a;
   private double b;
   private boolean c;
   public MyClass(int a, double b, boolean c) {
      this.a = a; this.b = b; this.c = c;
   }
   public void adjust(int x, double y, boolean z) {
      a += x; b *= y; c = c || z;
   }
}
```

we construct an instance of this class, called an object, with declaration and assignment statements such as

```
MyClass mc;
   ...
mc = new MyClass(1, 2.0, false);
```

or, in one statement,

```
MyClass mc = new MyClass(1, 2.0, false);
```

The class MyClass has three private fields, a, b, c, and one public method, adjust. The instance of the class pointed to by mc was constructed with the fields initialized to the given values (1, 2.0, and false). What looks like method MyClass (note the missing return type) is not a method but the object *constructor* code. The reserved word this is used inside the constructor to distinguish object fields from constructor parameters of the same name.

A class can have both static and nonstatic (also called instance) members. Each object constructed from the class has its own storage for the nonstatic members defined in the class. All objects constructed from the class share the static members.

```
class Name {
   static fields ...
   nonstatic fields ...
   constructor code ...
   static methods ...
   nonstatic methods ...
}
```

A class can have additional constructors, used to give data fields in the object default values. For example, the following two constructors could be added to MyClass:

```
public MyClass(int a, double b) {
   this(a, b, true);
}
```

```
public MyClass() {
    this(0, 1.0);
}
```

Note how one constructor invokes another with the keyword `this`.

An object's method is invoked with a statement like

```
mc.adjust(2, 3.0, true);
```

Since the fields of `MyClass` are all private, they can be manipulated only by the method `adjust`. If `MyClass` had a public field `d`, then that field could be both read and written outside the object `mc` with a statement like

```
mc.d = Math.sin(mc.d);
```

One of the important principles of object-oriented programming is data hiding or encapsulation: all of the data fields of an object should be private and accessible only indirectly through the object's public methods. This ensures that the fields are changed only in the specific ways intended by the object's designer and that the fields contain data that stays consistent. Methods in a class may also be private if they are of a utility nature to be called only by other methods in the class.

Since none of the members of `MyClass` is static, this class can be used only as a template to construct objects; the class name `MyClass` cannot be used to access class members.

```
MyClass.adjust(2, 3.0, true);  // illegal since adjust
                               // is not static
```

Even if `MyClass` had a public field `d`, it would be possible to compile something like

```
MyClass.d++; // illegal since there is no public static field d
```

only if `d` were declared static.

A very useful feature of Java is the `toString` method. If a class defines such a method, for example,

```
class MyClass {
    ...
    public String toString() {
        return "MyClass: a=" + a + " b=" + b + " c=" + c;
    }
}
```

then an object instantiated from such a class is easily printed.

```
MyClass x = new MyClass();
    ...
System.out.println("x = " + x);
```

Its toString method is invoked automatically in the print statement. The string constructed for the return value of toString should include the current values of important data fields in the object. Using toString is very effective for program debugging.

Arrays are objects in Java, created from the underlying type with new. Each array has a length field giving the number of components in the array. If the underlying type is a class rather than a base type like int, then each array component must have an object created explicitly for it from that class.

```java
int MAX = 7;
...
int[] p = new int[9];
for (int i = 0; i < p.length; i++) p[i] = 2-i;
...
MyClass[] y = new MyClass[MAX];
for (int i = 0; i < y.length; i++) y[i] = new MyClass();
y[2].adjust(2, 3.0, true);
```

The following single-class programs create objects from Java library classes. Program 2.5 uses a StreamTokenizer object to process keyboard input and determine if a number, a word or string, end of file, or some other unrecognized input was typed.

```java
StreamTokenizer st = new StreamTokenizer(
    new BufferedReader(new InputStreamReader(System.in)));
...
while (st.nextToken() != st.TT_EOF) {
    switch(st.ttype) {
        case st.TT_NUMBER:
            System.out.println("double number=" + st.nval);
            break;
        case st.TT_WORD:
            System.out.println("word=" + st.sval);
            break;
        case st.TT_EOL:
            System.out.println("end of line");
            break;
        default:
            System.out.println("unrecognized character");
            break;
    }
}
```

Program 2.6 shows how to create a binary file containing numbers input to the program on the keyboard. DataOutputStream and DataInputStream objects, dos and dis, are created from the file's FileOutputStream and FileInputStream objects and used to write

```
File f = new File("temp.out");
int numberCount = 0;
...
DataOutputStream dos = new DataOutputStream(
   new BufferedOutputStream(new FileOutputStream(f)));
while (st.nextToken() != st.TT_EOF) {
   if (st.ttype == st.TT_NUMBER) {
      dos.writeDouble(st.nval);
      numberCount++;
   }
}
dos.flush();
dos.close();
```

and then read

```
DataInputStream dis = new DataInputStream(
   new BufferedInputStream(new FileInputStream(f)));
for (int i = 0; i < numberCount; i++) {
   System.out.println("number=" + dis.readDouble());
}
dis.close();
```

the binary numbers to and from the file. Program 2.7 is an example of parsing keyboard input that contains a mixture of numbers and strings. It is based on the "Gift Givers" problem from the 1993 Internet Programming Contest. The program can read the information from a file or the keyboard, depending on the presence of a file name command line argument.

Program 2.8 creates several bank objects from a user-defined class **Bank**.

```
class Bank {
   private static int nextBankID = 0;
   private int bankID = -1;
   private String name = null;
   protected int numCustomers = 0;
   protected Account[] account = null;
   public Bank(String name) { this(name, 10, 1000); }
   public Bank(String name, int numCustomers,
         int initialSavings) {
      this.name = name;
      this.numCustomers = numCustomers;
      bankID = nextBankID++;
      account = new Account[numCustomers];
      for (int i = 0; i < numCustomers; i++)
         account[i] = new Account(initialSavings);
   }
   public static int getNextBankID() { return nextBankID; }
```

```
    public String getBankName() { return name; }
    public final int getBankID() { return bankID; }
    public int getNumCustomers() { return numCustomers; }
    public int getBalance(int customerID) {...}
    public String toString() {
        return name + " Bank (bankID = " + bankID + ") has "
            + numCustomers + " customers";
    }
    public boolean withdraw(int customerID, int amount) {...}
    public boolean deposit(int customerID, int amount) {...}
    public boolean transfer(int fromCustomerID,
            int toCustomerID, int amount) {...}
    public String statement(int customerID) {...}
}
```

It has one static data field, `nextBankID`, and an associated static method, `get-NextBankID`. Since `nextBankID` is private, it can be accessed only outside the class with the `getNextBankID` method. All bank objects share these two static members. Each account is an object with fields for the name of the account's owner and checking and savings balances. The **protected** and **final** modifiers are explained in Section 2.4, where we reuse the `Bank` code to create another type of bank.

2.3   Command Line Argument Parsing

The class `GetOpt`, part of this book's `Utilities` package and defining the `getopt` method, is used in many examples to parse a sequence of command line arguments of the form "$-a$" and "$-ax$" where a is a single letter and x is an integer, a floating-point number, a Boolean value, or a string such as a file name. The `GetOpt` code is listed in Library Class 2.1 in the on-line appendix; the **main** method illustrates its use. Any class can contain a **public static void main** method to test the class and show how it is used. This test processes command line options (in any order) of the form

> -U -a -b *Boolean* -f *string* -h *double* -w *int*

After processing all command line options of this form, the rest of the command line arguments are printed.

```
    public static void main(String[] args) {  // test the class
        GetOpt go = new GetOpt(args, "Uab:f:h:w:");
        go.optErr = true;
        int ch = -1;
        // process options in command line arguments
        boolean usagePrint = false;                 // set
        int aflg = 0;                               // default
        boolean bflg = false;                       // values
```

```
    String filename = "out";                    // of
    int width = 80;                             // options
    double height = 1;                          // here
    while ((ch = go.getopt()) != go.optEOF) {
        if      ((char)ch == 'U') usagePrint = true;
        else if ((char)ch == 'a') aflg++;
        else if ((char)ch == 'b')
           bflg = go.processArg(go.optArgGet(), bflg);
        else if ((char)ch == 'f') filename = go.optArgGet();
        else if ((char)ch == 'h')
           height = go.processArg(go.optArgGet(), height);
        else if ((char)ch == 'w')
           width = go.processArg(go.optArgGet(), width);
        else System.exit(1);            // undefined option
    }                                   // getopt() returns '?'
    if (usagePrint) {
      System.out.println
          ("Usage: -a -b bool -f file -h height -w width");
      System.exit(0);
    }
    System.out.println("These are all the command line " +
        "arguments before processing with GetOpt:");
    for (int i=0; i<args.length; i++)
      System.out.print(" " + args[i]);
    System.out.println();
    System.out.println("-U " + usagePrint);
    System.out.println("-a " + aflg);
    System.out.println("-b " + bflg);
    System.out.println("-f " + filename);
    System.out.println("-h " + height);
    System.out.println("-w " + width);
    // process nonoption command line arguments
    for (int k = go.optIndexGet(); k < args.length; k++) {
      System.out.println
          ("normal argument " + k + " is " + args[k]);
    }
  }
```

The GetOpt class is declared public; it is stored in a file named GetOpt.java that is in a directory, Utilities, of library classes used in many of this book's Java programs. Note that GetOpt.java starts with a matching Utilities package statement.

```
    package Utilities;
```

Suppose that in a Windows 95/NT environment the Utilities directory is a subdirectory of the directory

```
D:\LIB
```

and that the line

```
SET CLASSPATH=C:\TYJAVA\JDK\LIB;.
```

in the system file AUTOEXEC.BAT has been changed to

```
SET CLASSPATH=C:\TYJAVA\JDK\LIB;D:\LIB;.
```

If a program using GetOpt starts with the line

```
import Utilities.*;
```

or

```
import Utilities.GetOpt;
```

the Java compiler is able to find the GetOpt class in the Utilities library directory whenever the program is compiled. The compiler also compiles the GetOpt.java file, if necessary. We discuss the package concept further in Section 2.5.

One field in the GetOpt class, optEOF, is declared static because it will not have different values in different instantiations of the class and thus does not require its own storage in each object. It is declared publicly accessible and serves as the end-of-options flag value for all users of the class. It is accessed as GetOpt.optEOF and declared a constant with the keyword final; once initialized, its value cannot be changed either inside or outside the class. Another field, optErr, is publicly writable so a program using GetOpt can control the printing of error messages.

2.4   Inheritance

As mentioned, one major principle of the object-oriented programming technique is data hiding and encapsulation. The other is *inheritance*: designing a hierarchy of classes where one class definition extends another. This facilitates code reuse and an economy of design effort. A multipurpose general data structure is designed, and then extensions that add functionality and more specific behavior are designed later. For a simple example showing the syntax, class A

```
class A {
   protected double a = 0;
   public A() {}
   public A(double a) { this.a = a; }
   public double a() { return a; }
   public void a(double d) { a = d; }
}
```

is used as the basis for an enhanced class, ScaledA:

```
class ScaledA extends A {
   protected double scale = 1;
   public ScaledA() {}
   public ScaledA(double a) { super(a); }
   public void setScale(double s) { scale = s; }
   public double a() { return a*scale; }
}
```

The **protected** modifier is used in the declaration of field **a** in class **A**, instead of **private**, so that class **ScaledA** inherits **a** and its code can access **a**, but access outside **A**'s package and **A**'s subclasses is not allowed. This code also shows that a method may have the same name as a field. The method **a** in class **A** is defined twice, with different parameter sets, an example of method *overloading*. The parameterless definition of method **a** in class **ScaledA** *overrides*, that is, changes, the definition inherited from the superclass. The single parameter definition of method **a** is inherited and not changed. A constructor of a class can invoke a constructor of its superclass with the keyword **super**; if present, it must be the first statement in a subclass constructor. If not called explicitly, a constructor for a class starts with an implicit call of the no-argument constructor, **super()**, of its superclass.

Any class that does not explicitly extend another class, like **A**, is a subclass of the class **Object**. Thus **Object** is the root of a tree of all Java class definitions, both system defined and user defined.

Program 2.9 is a simple example of extending a previously defined class, **Bank**, to define a particular type of bank, **CommercialBank**, that makes loans. The latter inherits all the fields and methods of the former; however, it has only direct access in its code to the **public** or **protected** ones.

```
final class CommercialBank extends Bank {
   public CommercialBank(String name) { this(name, 10, 1000); }
   public CommercialBank
         (String name, int numCustomers, int initialSavings)
      { super(name, numCustomers, initialSavings); }
   public String toString()
      { return super.toString() + " and is Commercial"; }
   public int getLoanBalance(int customerID) {...}
   public boolean withdraw
         (int customerID, int amount, boolean overdraft) {...}
}
```

Note how **toString** is overridden with the superclass version accessed in the new definition using **super**. The **withdraw** method is also overridden to allow overdraft handling with a loan. The **Account** class is subclassed to add a new field for loan balances.

A class that is extended but not used itself to construct objects is declared **abstract**. It has one or more methods also declared **abstract** that must be implemented in its subclasses. It may contain nonabstract methods that are inherited by its subclasses. A class declared `final` cannot be subclassed; a method declared `final` cannot be overridden.

2.4.1 Interfaces

Java does not have multiple inheritance, that is, only one class name may follow the `extends` keyword in a class definition. Instead, Java offers the `interface`. It has only abstract-like method declarations (keyword `abstract` is optional) and perhaps some `static` `final` constants. An interface's methods are all implicitly public. A class definition declares that it `implements` an interface by providing method bodies or implementations for each interface method. A class may implement any number of interfaces in addition to extending at most one class. An interface is used much like a type in Java: if a variable is declared with an interface as its type, the variable can hold a reference to any object whose class implements the interface.

```
interface Cross {
    public void over(int x, int y);
}
...
class ThisCross implements Cross {...}
class ThatCross implements Cross {...}
...
Cross c1 = new ThisCross(...);
Cross c2 = new ThatCross(...);
```

The example program in Section 2.6 illustrates the use of inheritance, abstract classes, and interfaces.

2.4.2 User-Defined Exceptions

In a procedural language like C, a function that detects an error while processing its arguments often returns a flag value such as -1.

```
count = read(file, buffer, nbytes);
if (count < 0) ...
```

In Java, user-defined exceptions that extend the `Exception` class may be defined and then thrown inside methods that detect errors. For example, the `Factorial` class in Program 2.4 can be modified to throw exceptions for a negative or too large argument.

```
class ArgumentNegativeException extends Exception {}
class ArgumentTooLargeException extends Exception {}
class Factorial {
    public static int compute(int k) throws
            ArgumentNegativeException, ArgumentTooLargeException {
        if (k < 0) throw new ArgumentNegativeException();
        else if (k == 0 || k == 1) return 1;
```

```
        else if (k > 15) throw new ArgumentTooLargeException();
        else return k*compute(k-1);
    }
}
```

The exceptions are caught as follows and the appropriate action taken.

```
try {
    System.out.println
        (n + " factorial is " + Factorial.compute(n));
} catch (ArgumentNegativeException e) {
    System.err.println(e + " (try again)");
    continue;
} catch (ArgumentTooLargeException e) {
    System.err.println(e + " (try again)");
    continue;
}
```

Java requires the programmer to declare in a **throws** clause of a method declaration all exceptions (except subclasses of **RuntimeException**) that may be thrown in the method's body, due either to an explicit **throw new** statement in the body or an exception potentially thrown by some method invoked in the body. This applies to both user-defined exceptions and system exceptions.

```
class MyException extends Exception {}
...
class E {
    public void f(...) throws IOException, MyException {
        BufferedReader in = new BufferedReader(
            new InputStreamReader(System.in));
        ...
        String line = in.readLine();  // not in a try/catch block
        ...
        if (...) throw new MyException();
        ...
    }
}
```

The **IOException** possibly thrown by the call to **readLine** is not caught; thus, the exception must be declared in the **throws** clause of method **f**. Since exceptions derived from **RuntimeException** (**NullPointerException**, etc.) are possible in so many places in a program, their declaration in a **throws** clause is not required by Java, greatly reducing code clutter.

2.5 Packages

A Java program may be written without any **package** statements in its source files. The compiler places all the classes into the default package, which is thought of as having an empty or blank name. Classes that are used in several different programs are placed in a library directory that is added to the user's CLASSPATH variable. Each such class is declared public and stored in a file whose name is the class name followed by the .java extension.

For example, suppose on a Windows 95/NT platform we place the class

```
public class Factorial {
    public static int compute(int k) {
        if (k < 0) return -1;
        else if (k == 0 || k == 1) return 1;
        else return k*compute(k-1);
    }
}
```

in a file named Factorial.java in the library directory

    D:\LIB

If we ensure that the AUTOEXEC.BAT file defines the CLASSPATH variable to include the library directory,

    SET CLASSPATH=C:\TYJAVA\JDK\LIB;D:\LIB;.

then we can use the Factorial library class in any Java program in the "blank" default package. The compiler looks in the library directory for any classes not defined in the program itself. The library classes are compiled automatically, if necessary.

We gain more flexibility by setting up different packages with different names. Into each named package we put a collection of related classes that implement some data structure or computation. Each package has one or more public classes and perhaps other class definitions without the public modifier. The package is stored in one file if it has just one public class, using a file name that matches the public class name. Otherwise one file is needed for each public class. Each file containing source code for package *name* begins with the declaration

    package *name*;

The files are stored in a subdirectory of the library directory, with the subdirectory name matching the package name. For example, Library Class 2.1 is stored in file GetOpt.java in the Utilities subdirectory of the library directory D:\LIB. It starts with a package Utilities declaration. Note how the name in the package declaration matches the subdirectory name. If the programmer puts the line

    import Utilities.*;

or

    import Utilities.GetOpt;

at the beginning of all files containing programs that use `GetOpt`, the compiler will find (and compile if necessary) the `GetOpt` class, just as the compiler found the `Factorial` class in the example above.

With respect to packages, the public and private specifications for class members work as described earlier: public members are accessible from anywhere inside or outside the class, inside or outside the package the class is in; private members are accessible only from code in their class. If neither public nor private is specified, the member is accessible from anywhere in the same package, that is, from inside its class or from any class in the same package. To allow access by a subclass outside the package of the class, the **protected** keyword must be used. Thus no modifier being present, sometimes called "package" access, specifies more strict access permission than **protected**. A public class in a package may be subclassed outside the package if the class is not declared **final**. Nonpublic classes in a package cannot be instantiated by code outside the package.

2.5.1 Mathematical Functions

Java has many mathematical functions in the class `Math` of the `java.lang` package, some of which follow.

`int abs(int x)`	absolute value of x (`long`, `float`, and `double` versions also available)
`int min(int x, int y)`	minimum of x and y (`long`, `float`, and `double` versions also available)
`int max(int x, int y)`	maximum of x and y (`long`, `float`, and `double` versions also available)
`double sqrt(double x)`	square root of x
`double log(double x)`	log of x
`double pow(double a, double b)`	a to the b power
`double sin(double x)`	`cos(x)` and `tan(x)` also available
`double ceil(double x)`	smallest integer not less than x
`double floor(double x)`	largest integer not greater than x
`int round(float x)`	nearest integer to x
`long round(double x)`	nearest integer to x
`double rint(double x)`	nearest integer to x
`double random()`	pseudorandom number between 0.0 and 1.0 (including 0.0, excluding 1.0)

2.6   Genetic Algorithms

Classes, objects, interfaces, abstract classes, packages, and inheritance are illustrated in this section with a program that implements a simple *genetic algorithm*, Program 2.10. Genetic algorithms are used in search and optimization, such as finding the maximum of a function over some domain space. In contrast to deterministic methods like hill climbing, genetic algorithms use randomization. Points in the domain space of the search, usually real numbers over some range, are encoded as bit strings, called chromosomes. Each bit position in the string is called a gene. Chromosomes may also be composed over some other alphabet than {0,1}, such as integers or real numbers, particularly if the search domain is multidimensional.

An initial population of random bit strings is generated. The members of this initial population are each evaluated for their fitness or goodness in solving the problem. If the problem is to maximize a function $f(x)$ over some range [a,b] of real numbers and if $f(x)$ is nonnegative over the range, then $f(x)$ can be used as the fitness of the bit string encoding the value x.

From the initial population of chromosomes, a new population is generated using three genetic operators: reproduction, crossover, and mutation. These are modeled on their biological counterparts. With probabilities proportional to their fitness, members of the population are selected for the new population. Pairs of chromosomes in the new population are chosen at random to exchange genetic material, their bits, in a mating operation called crossover. This produces two new chromosomes that replace the parents. Randomly chosen bits in the offspring are flipped, called mutation.

The new population generated with these operators replaces the old population. The algorithm has performed one generation and then repeats for some specified number of additional generations. The population evolves, containing more and more highly fit chromosomes. When the convergence criterion is reached, such as no significant further increase in the average fitness of the population, the best chromosome produced is decoded into the search space point it represents.

To illustrate the manipulation of chromosomes by the genetic operators reproduction, crossover, and mutation, we will look at some sample program output for a very simple problem: maximize the number of ones in a bit chromosome of length 10. The chromosome class is a modification of **BitCountChromosome** with **chromosomeLength** set to 10. The population consists of four chromosomes. One-point crossover is applied with a probability of 0.7, each gene mutates with a probability of 0.1, the population is printed every generation, and the genetic algorithm runs for three generations. We first see the randomly generated initial population, in which the best fitness is 5.

```
The GA parameters are:
    populationSize      = 4        numXoverPoints    = 1
    crossoverRate       = 0.7      mutationRate      = 0.1
    doElitism           = false    printPerGens      = 1
    maxGenerations      = 3        Debug.flag        = true
    logFileName         = bit.out
```

```
BitCountChromosome: chromosome length is 10
GA: chromosome length = 10
GA: mainLoop
Known solution fitness is 10.0
p0: 0000110100 this chromosome has 3 bits set fitness= 3.0
p1: 1100010110 this chromosome has 5 bits set fitness= 5.0
p2: 1111001000 this chromosome has 5 bits set fitness= 5.0
p3: 0101011001 this chromosome has 5 bits set fitness= 5.0
currentBest (generation=0):
    1100010110 this chromosome has 5 bits set fitness= 5.0
Initial population:
    generation=0 best value=5.0 avg=4.5 stddev=1.0
```

A proportional selection algorithm called the roulette wheel method is used for reproduction. The cumulative fitness values of the chromosomes are computed, then four random numbers between 0 and 1 are generated to select the new population members. The cumulative fitness values that bracket each random number determine which chromosome gets selected; it is possible for a chromosome to be selected multiple times.

```
mem=0, cfitness=0.16666666666666666
mem=1, cfitness=0.4444444444444444
mem=2, cfitness=0.7222222222222222
mem=3, cfitness=1.0
p=0.07431843256287485, selected 0
p=0.25792751503513034, selected 1
p=0.6502614780006086, selected 2
p=0.3749322338318496, selected 1
p0: 0000110100 this chromosome has 3 bits set fitness= 3.0
p1: 1100010110 this chromosome has 5 bits set fitness= 5.0
p2: 1111001000 this chromosome has 5 bits set fitness= 5.0
p3: 1100010110 this chromosome has 5 bits set fitness= 5.0
```

Now that we have the new population, it is time to apply crossover and then mutation. For each chromosome, a random number between 0 and 1 is generated. If the random number is less than the crossover probability input parameter, the chromosome is picked for crossover. Each time two chromosomes have been picked, one-point crossover is applied and the two resulting chromosomes replace the original ones in the new population. Only one crossover occurs in the first generation: chromosomes 2 and 3 exchange their genes to the left of bit position 3.

```
111 | 1001000               110 | 1001000
              are replaced by
110 | 0010110               111 | 0010110
```

After the one crossover, the new population is listed.

```
crossing 2 and 3
OnePointCrossover: just crossed at 3
p0: 0000110100 this chromosome has 3 bits set fitness= 3.0
p1: 1100010110 this chromosome has 5 bits set fitness= 5.0
p2: 1101001000 this chromosome has 4 bits set fitness= 4.0
p3: 1110010110 this chromosome has 6 bits set fitness= 6.0
```

Each chromosome is now given the chance to mutate by generating a random number between 0 and 1 for each of its genes. If the random number is less than the mutation probability input parameter, the value of the gene is changed from 0 to 1 or 1 to 0.

```
mutation, i=0, gene=3: 0001110100
    this chromosome has 4 bits set fitness= 4.0
mutation, i=0, gene=6: 0001111100
    this chromosome has 5 bits set fitness= 5.0
mutation, i=1, gene=9: 1100010111
    this chromosome has 6 bits set fitness= 6.0
mutation, i=2, gene=5: 1101011000
    this chromosome has 5 bits set fitness= 5.0
mutation, i=2, gene=7: 1101011100
    this chromosome has 6 bits set fitness= 6.0
mutation, i=3, gene=3: 1111010110
    this chromosome has 7 bits set fitness= 7.0
mutation, i=3, gene=6: 1111011110
    this chromosome has 8 bits set fitness= 8.0
```

After the seven gene mutations, the new population is listed.

```
Report: generation=1 best value=8.0 avg=6.25 stddev=1.258...
most fit (previous generation=1):
    1111011110 this chromosome has 8 bits set fitness= 8.0
number of crossovers and mutations: 1 and 7
p0: 0001111100 this chromosome has 5 bits set fitness= 5.0
p1: 1100010111 this chromosome has 6 bits set fitness= 6.0
p2: 1101011100 this chromosome has 6 bits set fitness= 6.0
p3: 1111011110 this chromosome has 8 bits set fitness= 8.0
```

This completes the first generation. Notice that both the average fitness of the population and the best fitness in the population have increased.

After two more generations, the population is again listed.

```
Report: generation=3 best value=7.0 avg=6.75 stddev=0.5
most fit (previous generation=1):
    1111011110 this chromosome has 8 bits set fitness= 8.0
number of crossovers and mutations: 3 and 12
p0: 1111001100 this chromosome has 6 bits set fitness= 6.0
```

```
p1: 1111001110 this chromosome has 7 bits set fitness= 7.0
p2: 1101011110 this chromosome has 7 bits set fitness= 7.0
p3: 1111001110 this chromosome has 7 bits set fitness= 7.0
```

The average fitness has increased, but the most fit chromosome generated so far has disappeared from the population.

Genetic algorithms have been very successful at solving many types of problems, such as maximizing discontinuous, multimodal, multidimensional functions. They have also been used on discrete problems, including the traveling salesperson, bin packing, and job-shop scheduling. Two excellent introductory articles are [3, 4]; one of the first textbooks is [19].

Here are two example problems, one discrete and one continuous, that are more realistic. For an arbitrary expression in n Boolean variables, find an assignment of true and false values to the Boolean variables in the expression that make the expression true, if such an assignment exists. This is called the *Boolean satisfiability problem*. Each assignment of true and false values to the variables can be encoded in a bit string of length n, 0 for false and 1 for true. The fitness of such a chromosome is how "close" to being true the assignment makes the Boolean expression, such as how many clauses in the expression are individually made true by the assignment.

Maximize the function

$$f(x_1, x_2, x_3) = 21.5 + x_1 \sin(4\pi x_1) + x_2 \sin(20\pi x_2) + x_3$$

for x_1 in [-3.0,12.1], x_2 in [4.1,5.8], and x_3 in [0.0,1.0]. This function is highly multimodal. A chromosome can be encoded in three real numbers, one for each of x_1, x_2, and x_3, over their respective ranges. The fitness of a chromosome is the value of $f(x_1, x_2, x_3)$ for the x_1, x_2, and x_3 encoded in the chromosome.

Program 2.10 is a simple genetic algorithm organized into four packages: GAutilities, Chromosomes, Crossovers, and Selections. The chromosome class hierarchy is fundamental to the program's design.

```
package Chromosomes;
abstract class Chromosome {
    // designed for genes that are class Number
```

It defines the fields that all chromosome objects have and implements those methods common to all chromosomes; abstract methods are implemented in the subclasses. It has two subclasses,

```
abstract class BitChromosome extends Chromosome {
    // genes are 0/1 (boolean)
```

and

```
abstract class DoubleChromosome extends Chromosome {
    // genes are doubles
```

that fill out some of the specifics for bit genes and floating-point genes. A chromosome with integer genes is easily added to the hierarchy. Three chromosome classes for specific problems with bit genes are in the program.

```
class BitCountChromosome extends BitChromosome {
    // problem-specific class
class ByteCountChromosome extends BitChromosome {
    // problem-specific class
class XtoTenthChromosome extends BitChromosome {
    // problem-specific class
```

Others, such as one for the Boolean satisfiability problem, could be added. Also in the program is a chromosome for one floating-point problem, the continuous function of three variables described above.

```
class SinesChromosome extends DoubleChromosome {
    // problem-specific class
```

Sample output of the genetic algorithm working on these four problems is included in Program 2.10.

The initialization part of the program

```
import java.io.*;
import Utilities.*;
import GAutilities.*;
import Chromosomes.*;
import Selections.*;
import Crossovers.*;
...
private Selection theSelection;
private Crossover theCrossover;
private Chromosome[] population    =
    new Chromosome[populationSize];
private Chromosome[] newPopulation =
    new Chromosome[populationSize];
...
private void mainLoop() {
    initialize();
    findTheBest();
    report("Initial population");
    ...
}
private void initialize() {
    generationNum = 0;
    numCrossovers = 0;
    numMutations = 0;
    theSelection = new ProportionalSelection();
    if (numXoverPoints == 0)
        theCrossover = new UniformCrossover();
    else if (numXoverPoints == 1)
        theCrossover = new OnePointCrossover();
```

```
        else
            theCrossover = new NPointCrossover(numXoverPoints);
        for (int j = 0; j < populationSize; j++) {
            population[j] = new MyChromosome();
            population[j].initializeChromosomeRandom();
            newPopulation[j] = new MyChromosome();
        }
    }
```

constructs the initial population of chromosomes using the class `MyChromosome` that extends the specific problem chromosome class.

```
    final class MyChromosome extends
    // Put your Chromosome class name here (comment out the others):
        SinesChromosome
    // BitCountChromosome
    // XtoTenthChromosome
    // ByteCountChromosome
    { public MyChromosome() {super(); }
    }
```

Note that the `Selection` and `Crossover` interfaces and the `Chromosome` root class are used as the types of the selection and crossover operator objects and the chromosome objects in this part of the code. The rest of the program executes the generational loop.

```
    private void mainLoop() {
        ...
        while (!terminated()) {
            generationNum++;
            theSelection.select
                (population, newPopulation, populationSize);
            swapPopulationArrays();
            crossover();
            mutate();
            if (doElitism) elitism();
            else justUpdateTheBest();
            if (generationNum % printPerGens == 0) report("Report");
        }
        printChromosome("Best member (generation="
            + theBestGeneration + ")", theBest);
    }
```

The crossover genetic operator exchanges genes between two chromosomes. Three versions are supported by the program: uniform, one-point, and n-point. The classes for these implement one interface.

```
interface Crossover {
   public void xOver(Chromosome x, Chromosome y);
}
...
class UniformCrossover implements Crossover {...
class OnePointCrossover implements Crossover {...
class NPointCrossover implements Crossover {...
```

To modify this program to solve a new problem, it is necessary only to design and implement a new chromosome class, say YourChromosome, extending either class BitChromosome or DoubleChromosome, as appropriate (Boolean or floating-point genes). Then modify the class MyChromosome in package Chromosomes so that it extends the new chromosome. Because of the power of object-oriented design, those are the only changes.

Exercise 7.9 describes two approaches to parallelize Program 2.10 with multiple threads.

2.7   Animating Programs with Java's AWT

Many algorithms are difficult to understand when presented in the form of programs or as pseudocode. For example, the *bubble sort* algorithm (similar to the exchange sort in Program 2.2) looks simple enough:

```
void bubbleSort(int[] a) {
   for (int i = a.length - 1; i > 0; i--) {
      for (int j = 0; j < i; j++) {
         if (a[j] > a[j+1]) {
            int temp = a[j+1]; a[j+1] = a[j]; a[j] = temp;
         }
      }
   }
}
```

But there exist much faster sorting algorithms, such as the *shell sort*:

```
void shellSort(int[] a) {
   int n = a.length, incr = n/2;
   while (incr >= 1) {
      for (int i = incr; i < n; i++) {
         int temp = a[i], j = i;
         while (j >= incr && temp < a[j-incr]) {
            a[j] = a[j-incr]; j -= incr;
         }
         a[j] = temp;
      }
      incr /= 2;
```

```
        }
    }
```

We see that the bubble sort is done in two nested for loops and has running time proportional to $n^2/2$ for an array of length n. The outer loop of the shell sort is a while loop that executes roughly $\log n$ times since it halves its limit each iteration. So, yes, the algorithm looks faster. But exactly how does it work? Can we present a visual explanation as an alternative to the conventional verbal one?

Another example is comparing first-fit and best-fit dynamic memory allocation, a topic in operating systems. Algorithm animation provides a way to show graphically the amount of memory fragmentation as a simulation of one of the algorithms runs. An operating systems student could see that first fit results in less memory fragmentation over time, perhaps in contrast to the student's intuition.

If there were some way we could draw moving images in a window on the computer terminal screen showing the algorithm in action, then we could more easily understand how the algorithm works and gain insight, for example, into why shell sort is much faster than exchange or bubble sort. John Stasko and Doug Hayes have written a package called XTANGO [37, 38] that can be used on UNIX workstations with bit-mapped color displays running the X11 windowing system. This package provides a platform for constructing algorithm animations. The package includes many sample animation programs, such as matrix multiplication and searching for substrings in a string.

There are two approaches to using the package. Data structures for and library calls to the animation package are embedded in a C language program that implements a sorting algorithm, such as exchange sort, or that simulates an operating system algorithm, such as first-fit memory allocation. The C program is then compiled with the XTANGO library and with the X11 windowing library. Alternatively, a text file of commands to an animation interpreter included in the XTANGO distribution is constructed. Then the interpreter is executed with the text file of commands as input. The text file of commands can be constructed with an editor or can be the result of print statements in a program written in any high-level programming language.

A Java program can be animated using XTANGO by adding print statements to the program in the appropriate places, saving the output of executing the program in a file, and using the file as input to XTANGO's animation interpreter. However, this technique works only in an X11 windowing environment. In order to retain the platform-independent advantages of Java, an animation class named XtangoAnimator that accepts XTANGO's animation interpreter commands was written using Java's windowing tool kit (AWT). The class is in this book's XtangoAnimation package. Instead of reading animation commands from a file, this class handles method calls that correspond to XTANGO's animation commands. We will study the implementation of this class in Section 5.9.

For example, suppose the file sim.java contains a simulation program, in class Simulation, of some operating system algorithm, such as first-fit memory allocation, in which the programmer has added method calls for animation. The commands

```
javac sim.java
java Simulation
```

runs the animation. The simulation text output appears in the original window on
the screen. A new window is created on the screen in which the animation of the
simulation takes place. The window has a row of buttons along the top. A click
with the left mouse button on "Start" starts the animation; when the simulation is
finished or when enough has been seen, a similar click on "Quit" closes the animation
window. There are two buttons, "Faster" and "Slower," that are used to control the
speed of the animation. The buttons "Single Step On/Off" and "Step" are used to
single-step the animation.

Program 2.11 draws the string "Hello, world!" in the middle of the animation
window. See the animator method descriptions below.

```
XtangoAnimator xa = new XtangoAnimator();
xa.begin();
xa.coords(1.0f, 1.0f, 3.0f, 3.0f);
xa.bg(Color.cyan);
xa.bigText("hw", 2.0f, 2.0f, true, Color.red, "Hello, world!");
xa.delay(100);
xa.delete("hw");
xa.end();
```

Program 2.12 animates the bubble sort discussed above. The comments in the
program listing describe the animation commands used.

```
for (int i = a.length - 1; i >= 0; i--) {
    for (int j = 0; j < i; j++) {
        xa.color("C"+j, Color.blue);    // make candidate to
        xa.fill("C"+j, xa.SOLID);       // bubble solid blue
        xa.delay(1);
        // momentarily connect the two icons compared with a line
        xa.pointLine("temp", scaleX(j), scaleY(a[j]), scaleX(j+1),
            scaleY(a[j+1]), Color.green, xa.THICK);
        xa.delay(1);
        if (a[j] > a[j+1]) {            // swap the icon locations
            xa.color("temp", Color.red);
            xa.delay(1);
            xa.moveAsync("C"+j, scaleX(j+1), scaleY(a[j]));
            xa.move("C"+(j+1), scaleX(j), scaleY(a[j+1]));
            xa.swapIds("C"+j, "C"+(j+1)); // swap ids of the icons
            int temp = a[j+1]; a[j+1] = a[j]; a[j] = temp;
        } else {
            xa.fill("C"+j, xa.OUTLINE); // make the smaller icon
            xa.color("C"+j, Color.red);    // ... outline red ...
            xa.delay(1);
            xa.color("C"+(j+1), Color.blue); // ... and the larger
```

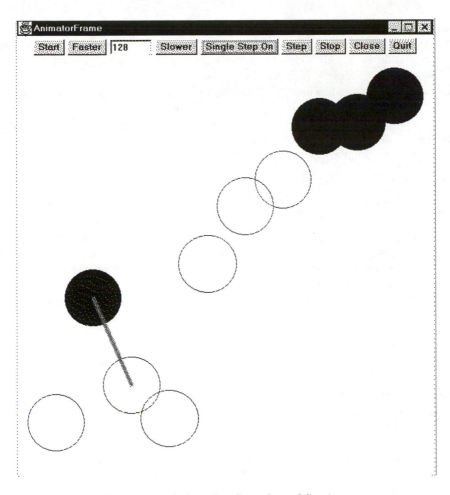

Figure 2.1: Animation Snapshot of Sorting.

```
        xa.fill("C"+(j+1), xa.SOLID);  // ... solid blue
        xa.delay(1);
    }
    xa.delete("temp");
}
// color the icon black to indicate it is in final position
xa.color("C"+i, Color.black);
xa.delay(1);
}
xa.fill("C0", xa.SOLID);
xa.delay(1);
```

A snapshot of the animation window during the sorting is shown in Figure 2.1. Note
the call to xa.begin() in the main method; this blocks the sorting algorithm from

executing and generating animation commands until the user clicks "Start" in the animation window on the screen. Also note the calls to `xa.delay(1)` throughout the animation code. All animation commands are executed immediately although the animation window is redrawn only periodically (controlled with the "Faster" and "Slower" buttons). Therefore the results of many animation commands appear each time the window is redrawn unless the commands are separated by delays. This gives the animation designer the flexibility to execute a group of animation commands together followed by a delay.

A list of the animation commands and their description follows. This material is based on the documentation for the **animator** interpreter contained in the XTANGO software distribution. Animations developed with this system are carried out in a real-valued coordinate system that originally runs from 0.0 to 1.0 from left to right and from 0.0 to 1.0 from bottom to top (Java's AWT goes from top to bottom). Note, however, that the coordinate system is infinite in all directions. One can create and place graphical objects within the coordinate system and then move them, change their color, visibility, fill, and so forth, in order to depict the operations and actions of a computer algorithm. The animator method calls should be placed in the program at the appropriate positions to provide a trace or display of what the program is doing.

Each animation command is associated with a method of the same name in the **XtangoAnimator** class. Each graphical object created is designated by a unique string identifier. That string identifier is used in subsequent commands that move, color, alter, and so forth, the object. In essence, the string identifier is a handle to the object. Most of the commands and their parameters should be self-explanatory. Arguments named **steps** are of integer type; arguments named **centered** are of Boolean type. Arguments named **xpos**, **ypos**, **xsize**, **ysize**, **radius**, **lx**, **by**, **rx**, **ty** are floating-point numbers (Java's **float**). The argument **fillval** should be one of the following defined integer constants: **XtangoAnimator.OUTLINE**, **XtangoAnimator.HALF** or **XtangoAnimator.SOLID**. The argument **widthval** should be one of the following defined integer constants: **XtangoAnimator.THIN**, **XtangoAnimator.MEDTHICK**, or **XtangoAnimator.THICK**.

The parameter **colorval** can be any color defined with the Java AWT **Color** class. Predefined color constants are **white**, **black**, **lightGray**, **gray**, **darkGray**, **red**, **green**, **blue**, **yellow**, **magenta**, **cyan**, **pink**, and **orange**; for example **Color. orange**. Other colors are created with

```
Color c = new Color(red, green, blue);
```

where each of the three parameters is an integer in the range 0 to 255, inclusive.

The format for the individual commands is described below.

```
begin()
```

Begin the animation. This should be called at the beginning of the algorithm being animated, so that the algorithm is blocked until the user clicks the "Start" button.

```
bg(Color colorval)
```

Change the background to the given color. The default background color is white.

```
coords(int lx, int by, int rx, int ty)
```

Change the displayed coordinates to the given values. The bottom left and top right corners of the animation window are set to coordinates (lx,by) and (rx,ty), respectively. Repeated applications of this command pan or zoom the animation view. It is required that rx-lx == ty-by.

```
delay(int steps)
```

Delay or block the caller while the given number of animation frames is generated.

```
line(String id, float xpos, float ypos, float xsize,
     float ysize, Color colorval, int widthval)
```

Create a line with one endpoint at the given position and of the given size.

```
pointLine(String id, float xpos1, float ypos1, float xpos2,
          float ypos2, Color colorval, int widthval)
```

Create a line with its two endpoints at the given positions.

```
rectangle(String id, float xpos, float ypos, float xsize,
          float ysize, Color colorval, int fillval)
```

Create a rectangle with lower left corner at the given position and of the given size (the size must be positive).

```
circle(String id, float xpos, float ypos, float radius,
       Color colorval, int fillval)
```

Create a circle with the given radius centered at the given position.

```
triangle(String id, float v1x, float v1y, float v2x, float v2y,
         float v3x, float v3y, Color colorval, int fillval)
```

Create a triangle whose three vertices are located at the given three coordinates. Note that triangles are moved (for move, jump, and exchange commands) relative to the center of their bounding box.

```
text(String id, float xpos, float ypos, boolean centered,
     Color colorval, String string)
```

Create text with lower left corner at the given position if centered is false. If centered is true, the position arguments denote the place where the center of the text is put. The text string is allowed to have blank spaces included in it but should include at least one nonblank character.

```
bigText(String id, float xpos, float ypos, boolean centered,
        Color colorval, String string)
```

This works just like the text command except that this text is in a much larger font.

```
smallText(String id, float xpos, float ypos, boolean centered,
          Color colorval, String string)
```

This works just like the text command except that this text is in a much smaller font.

```
move(String id, float xpos, float ypos)
```

Smoothly move, via a sequence of intermediate steps, the object with the given identifier to the specified position.

```
moveRelative(String id, float xdelta, float ydelta)
```

Smoothly move, via a sequence of intermediate steps, the object with the given identifier by the given relative distance.

```
moveTo(String id1, String id2)
```

Smoothly move, via a sequence of intermediate steps, the object with the first identifier to the current position of the object with the second identifier.

```
jump(String id, float xpos, float ypos)
```

Move the object with the given identifier to the designated position in a one-frame jump.

```
jumpRelative(String id, float xdelta, float ydelta)
```

Move the object with the given identifier by the provided relative distance in one jump.

```
jumpTo(String id1, String id2)
```

Move the object with the given identifier to the current position of the object with the second identifier in a one-frame jump.

```
color(String id, Color colorval)
```

Change the color of the object with the given identifier to the specified color value.

```
delete(String id)
```

Permanently remove the object with the given identifier from the display, and remove any association of this identifier string with the object.

```
fill(String id, int fillval)
```

Change the object with the given identifier to the designated fill value. This has no effect on lines and text.

```
vis(String id)
```

Toggle the visibility of the object with the given identifier.

```
lower(String id)
```

Push the object with the given identifier backward to the viewing plane farthest from the viewer.

```
raise(String id)
```

Pop the object with the given identifier forward to the viewing plane closest to the viewer.

```
exchangePos(String id1, String id2)
```

Make the two objects specified by the given identifiers smoothly exchange positions.

```
switchPos(String id1, String id2)
```

Make the two objects specified by the given identifiers exchange positions in one instantaneous jump.

```
swapIds(String id1, String id2)
```

Exchange the identifiers used to designate the two given objects.

```
moveAsync(String id, float xpos, float ypos)
```

Smoothly move asynchronously, via a sequence of intermediate steps, the object with the given identifier to the specified position. While this command is being performed, subsequent animation commands are executed and displayed.

```
moveRelativeAsync(String id, float xdelta, float ydelta)
```

Smoothly move asynchronously, via a sequence of intermediate steps, the object with the given identifier by the given relative distance.

```
moveToAsync(String id1, String id2)
```

Smoothly move asynchronously, via a sequence of intermediate steps, the object with the first identifier to the current position of the object with the second identifier.

```
exchangePosAsync(String id1, String id2)
```

Make the two objects specified by the given identifiers smoothly exchange positions asynchronously.

```
end()
```

Terminate the animation.

Summary

Java is a modern object-oriented language with many advantages and features of particular interest to instructors of programming and novice users of the language. We examined the sequential aspects of Java in this chapter. Simple programs are written as one or more classes having only static members. Exceptions are generated by the Java virtual machine when an error occurs in a program, such as an out-of-bounds array subscript. Most Java programs create objects from system and user-defined classes. One of the most important concepts in an object-oriented language is inheritance. Another is data hiding and encapsulation. Java provides the interface as an alternative to multiple inheritance. Packages are used to organize collections of classes so they can be used as libraries. We saw how to parse command line arguments with `GetOpt`. A program implementing a genetic algorithm was used to illustrate all of these Java features. Java includes a graphics library, used to implement an algorithm animation package called `XtangoAnimation`. The animation methods available to the programmer were described and a sorting example shown.

2.8   Exercises

1. **Generating Prime Numbers.** Write a single-class Java program that reads a number from the command line and then prints all prime numbers that are less than or equal to the number read.

Rewrite your prime generating program so that it consists of two or more classes.

2. **Neighborhood Banking.** Add methods to Program 2.8 so that a customer can move funds between checking and savings in an account.

3. **Used-Car Dealership.** Write a multiple class program using inheritance and multiple objects that represents the collection of automobiles for sale at a used-car dealership and the transactions that occur between the customers and dealership staff.

4. **The "Game of Life."** Write a multiclass sequential Java program that simulates the "Game of Life." The simulation occurs on an M-by-N rectangular array of cells. Each cell has only two values: 0 and 1. Each cell has eight neighbors: up, down, left, right, and four diagonally. Cells on the four edges of the grid have fewer than eight neighbors, of course. If the grid is declared as

```
int[][] grid = new int[M][N];
```

then the neighbors of an interior cell `grid[i][j]` are `grid[i-1][j]`, `grid[i+1][j]`, `grid[i][j-1]`, `grid[i][j+1]`, `grid[i-1][j-1]`, `grid[i-1][j+1]`, `grid[i+1][j-1]`, and `grid[i+1][j+1]`.

The game works like this. Fill the grid with the initial values. Then for each cell in the grid, compute the new value that the cell becomes in the next generation of the game. All changes occur simultaneously, called a generation.

- A 1 cell value stays 1 if exactly two or three neighbors are 1 valued.
- A 1 cell value becomes 0 if less than two or greater than three neighbors are 1 valued.
- A 0 cell value becomes 1 if exactly three neighbors are 1 valued.
- A 0 cell value stays 0 if less than three or greater than three neighbors are 1 valued.

The input data to the simulation consist of M and N, the size of the rectangular grid; maxGenerations, the number of generations to simulate; and the initial values of the cells, which can be either user-specified or random. Remember to check for illegal input values, like negative numbers or cell initial values that are not 0 or 1.

Here are some sample input data sets to try. This initial population dies out.

```
0 0 0 0 0
0 1 0 0 0
0 0 1 0 0
0 0 0 1 0
0 0 0 0 0
```

This initial population dies more slowly.

```
0 0 0 0 0
0 1 0 0 0
0 1 0 0 0
0 0 1 0 0
0 0 0 0 0
```

This initial population reaches a stable state.

```
0 0 0 0 0
0 1 1 0 0
0 1 0 0 0
0 0 0 0 0
0 0 0 0 0
```

And this initial population oscillates.

```
0 0 0 0 0
0 0 1 0 0
0 0 1 0 0
0 0 1 0 0
0 0 0 0 0
```

5. **Exceptions.** Enhance Program 2.8 so that the Bank methods throw exceptions like NoSuchCustomerException and InsufficientFundsException rather than return error values like false and −1. See Section 2.4.2. Enhance Program 2.9 in a similar way.

6. **Genetic Algorithms.** Write a chromosome class for use in Program 2.10 to solve some problem of interest to you.

Lengthen the `BitCountChromosome` from 32 to 100 bits. Can you get the genetic algorithm to converge? If not, how close can you get in 100 generations? In 1000 generations? What crossover and mutation rates work best? Does it help to change the fitness function from the bit count to the bit count squared? Why or why not?

Write a new abstract class `IntChromosome` to be extended by chromosome classes having integer genes. Find an interesting problem to solve using this class.

Find out what *conjunctive normal form* is for Boolean expressions. Write a chromosome class for Program 2.10 to search for solutions to the Boolean satisfiability problem where the Boolean expression is in conjunctive normal form.

7. **Algorithm Animation.** Remove the `xa.begin()` statement from Program 2.12 and execute the program. What happens? Why is it a good idea to call `xa.begin()` at the beginning of the animation?

Remove all `xa.delay(1)` statements from Program 2.12 and execute the program. Why were the delay statements put into the animation?

Animate the shell sort algorithm shown on page 38. Explain in your own words how it works and why it is faster than the bubble sort algorithm shown on page 38. Use the technique employed in Program 2.12 that draws lines connecting elements of the array being moved or swapped.

Three problems usually examined in the study of operating systems are (a) memory allocation using first fit, best fit, or next fit; (b) virtual memory paging using LRU, FIFO, MIN, or working set; and (c) disk seek scheduling using FCFS, SSTF, SCAN, or C-SCAN ([15], Chapters 7–9 and 12), ([34], Chapters 8–9 and 12), ([36], Chapters 6–7 and 11), ([41], Chapters 3 and 5), ([43], Chapters 4 and 5). Add `XtangoAnimator` method calls to a program simulating one of these algorithms so that an animation of the algorithm is seen.

Animate the *N*-queens search algorithm, Program 2.3, to show it in action.

Animate the "Game of Life" simulation you did in Exercise 4.

Animate the simple genetic algorithm shown in Program 2.10.

Chapter 3

Concurrent Programming

The focus of this book is the discipline of concurrent programming in the Java language. This chapter shows how to write Java programs that contain multiple concurrently executing threads. It also discusses the fundamental problems that must be dealt with in multithreaded programs: race conditions, starvation, and deadlock. After reading this chapter, you will know how to create additional threads of control in a Java program. You will have a good intuitive understanding of race conditions, lost updates, deadlock, and starvation; how they occur; and how to prevent them.

The following terms and concepts, also covered in standard operating systems books such as ([15], Chapters 4 and 5), ([34], Chapter 6), ([36], Chapter 4), ([41], Sections 2.2 and 2.3), ([43], Sections 2.2 and 2.3), are defined and discussed. If the threads in a program share data, we will see that race conditions are possible while updating the shared data. Several Java programs containing different kinds of race conditions are shown. Preventing race conditions is an instance of the critical section and mutual exclusion problem. We will see several software and hardware solutions to the mutual exclusion problem. However, they use busy waiting, which consumes CPU cycles and is wasteful particularly on a uniprocessor. The next chapter examines a blocking solution, the semaphore, usually implemented in the operating system. The mutual exclusion problem is one circumstance where concurrently executing threads need to be synchronized. Later chapters examine other cases and introduce additional techniques for synchronizing threads. Starvation and deadlock are terms for undesirable situations in which one or more threads are not getting the resources they need to continue.

If a multithreaded program is running on a uniprocessor computer and if the CPU is switched frequently among the threads, as previously described in Section 1.1.4, the threads appear to run concurrently. If the program is running on a shared-memory multiprocessor, one or more threads execute, again concurrently, on each CPU allocated to the program by the operating system. The Java language is suitable, as we will see later, for the kind of coarse-grained parallel computing, sometimes called workstation cluster programming, in which the threads of a concurrent program are distributed across several workstations connected by a LAN, one or more threads per workstation. The threads use message passing over the network to synchronize and communicate, covered in Chapters 6 and 7.

Many of the concepts discussed in the rest of this book apply to both (a) the threads in a process that share an address space and therefore all data and (b) a collection of processes that share some data. Instead of repeatedly using "thread or process" and "processes and threads," the concepts are described in terms of threads only. The reader may assume that "process" can be used interchangeably with "thread" unless stated otherwise.

3.1   Java Threads

There are two ways to spawn off additional threads in a Java program. One way is to extend the class Thread and override the public run method with the code for the new thread, then create an instance of the Thread subclass and call its start method. The JVM starts a new thread executing the run method.

```
class A extends Thread {
    public A(String name) {super(name);}
    public void run() {
        System.out.println("My name is " + getName());
    }
}
class B {
    public static void main(String[] args) {
        A a = new A("mud");
        a.start();
    }
}
```

The second way is to implement the Runnable interface in a class with a public run method, create an instance of the class, and pass a reference to that object to the Thread constructor.

```
class A extends ... implements Runnable {
    public void run() {
        System.out.println("My name is "
            + Thread.currentThread().getName());
    }
}
class B {
    public static void main(String[] args) {
        A a = new A();
        Thread t = new Thread(a, "mud, too");
        t.start();
    }
}
```

The advantage of the second approach is that class **A** is allowed to extend some other system or user-defined class. Java's restriction to single inheritance prevents this in the first approach.

When a Java class *Name* with a **main** method is executed with the command

```
java Name
```

the JVM spawns a new thread to execute the code of the **main** method, much like the **run** method is executed in a new thread above.

Four very useful methods for multithreaded simulation programs of the kind we write are **nap**(*ms*), **age()**, **random**(*ub*), and **seed**(*number*). The first suspends a thread for *ms* milliseconds. It is used in many example programs to simulate a thread performing some computation or activity. The second returns the number of milliseconds elapsed since the program was invoked or started. It is used to tag print statements in threads to get some idea of when during a simulation the print statement was executed. The random number generator returns a **double** value in the range 0 to *ub* (including 0 but not *ub*). It is often used to generate a random time that some simulated activity will take.

```
napping = ((int) random(napTime)) + 1;
nap(napping);
```

The random number generator can be seeded with a specific number so that the same sequence of pseudorandom numbers is generated each time the program runs. This is useful for debugging. By default, the random number generator is seeded with a value derived from the system clock.

These four methods are defined as **static** in class **MyObject**, part of this book's **Utilities** package and shown in Library Class 3.1. This class is designed to be extended so these methods will be inherited by all subclasses. It also contains an instance method, **getName**, that returns a string name for an object created from a subclass; the string name is set by calling **super** in the subclass constructor, passing the name as the argument.

```
class A extends MyObject {
    int id;
    public A(int id) {
        super("A" + id);
        this.id = id;
        System.out.println(getName() + " exists");
    }
    ...
}
```

This class also contains several methods for later use with semaphores, condition variables, and message passing. Most of our thread objects extend **MyObject** and implement **Runnable**.

Program 3.1 shows how to create multiple, identically coded, concurrently executing threads, using the **Runnable** approach shown above:

```
class Helper extends MyObject implements Runnable {...}
```

where each thread simulates some computation that takes a random amount of time.
When Program 3.1 is run, the main method sets up a running time and a napping
time, with default values overridable from the command line. The GetOpt class,
shown in Library Class 2.1, is used for this.

```
// parse command line arguments, if any, to override defaults
GetOpt go = new GetOpt(args, "Uh:n:R:");
go.optErr = true;
String usage = "Usage: -h numHelpers -n napTime -R runTime";
int ch = -1;
int numHelpers = 4;
int napTime = 3;      // defaults
int runTime = 60;     // in seconds
while ((ch = go.getopt()) != go.optEOF) {
    if       ((char)ch == 'U') {
       System.out.println(usage);   System.exit(0);
    }
    else if ((char)ch == 'h')
       numHelpers = go.processArg(go.optArgGet(), numHelpers);
    else if ((char)ch == 'n')
        napTime = go.processArg(go.optArgGet(), napTime);
    else if ((char)ch == 'R')
       runTime = go.processArg(go.optArgGet(), runTime);
    else {
       System.err.println(usage);   System.exit(1);
    }
}
System.out.println("HelperThreads: numHelpers=" + numHelpers
    + ", napTime=" + napTime + ", runTime=" + runTime);
```

Then, multiple threads are started up,

```
// start the Helper threads
Thread[] helper = new Thread[numHelpers];
for (int i = 0; i < numHelpers; i++)
  helper[i] = new Thread(new Helper("Helper", i, napTime*1000));
for (int i = 0; i < numHelpers; i++) helper[i].start();
System.out.println("All Helper threads started");
```

each doing the same thing in its run method: a "do forever" loop that prints a
message and naps for a random amount of time.

```
public void run() {
    int napping;
    while (true) {
```

```
        napping = ((int) random(napTime)) + 1;
        System.out.println("age()=" + age() + ", " + getName()
            + " napping for " + napping + " ms");
        nap(napping);
    }
}
```

The value of the variable `napTime` is passed to all threads when constructed.

```
    public Helper(String name, int id, int napTime) {
        super(name + " " + id);
        this.id = id;
        this.napTime = napTime;
        System.out.println
            (getName() + " is alive, napTime=" + napTime);
    }
```

We write one class containing the code for the thread, then construct the class multiple times. Note how the class constructor is parameterized. Each time an object is constructed from the `Helper` class in the `main` method loop, we pass its identity `i` and the value of `napTime`. Each time the `start` method in a `Helper`-derived thread object is called, the JVM starts a new thread to execute the `Helper` method `run`.

You will see the intermixed output of all the threads on the screen. After the `main` method naps for a while, it terminates all threads with `stop` method calls.

```
    // let the Helpers run for a while
    nap(runTime*1000);
    System.out.println
        ("age()="+age()+", time to stop the threads and exit");
    for (int i = 0; i < numHelpers; i++) helper[i].stop();
    System.exit(0);
```

Normally a Java program with multiple threads terminates when all of its threads terminate. Since the threads in Program 3.1 never terminate, an explicit call of the `stop` method for each thread is used. If this program did not have the statements `nap(runTime*1000)` and `System.exit(0)` at the end of the `main` method, the user could type control-C on the Windows 95/NT and Solaris 2.x platforms to abort the program. Control-C is also used on these platforms to abort a program before normal termination when enough output has been seen.

Notice that the threads in this program do not interfere with each other and need not be synchronized because they do not update any shared data and are not cooperating in the solution of a problem. Thus, there cannot be any race conditions (see Section 3.4).

3.1.1 Thread States and Scheduling

A thread in a Java program is in one of seven states: new, runnable, running, suspended, blocked, suspended-blocked, or dead. Threads make transitions from one state to another when various events occur.

new When a new thread object is created, for example with

> `Thread t = new Thread(a);`

its thread enters the *new* state.

runnable When the `start` method of a new thread is called, for example,

> `t.start();`

the thread enters the *runnable* state. All runnable threads in a Java program are organized by the JVM into a data structure called the runnable set, also sometimes called the round robin queue or the ready queue. A thread entering the runnable state is placed into this set. The code in the `run` method of the thread will be executed by the CPU.

running Whenever the thread is actually executing — that is, allocated CPU cycles by the computer's operating system scheduler — the thread is in the *running* state. If a thread in the running state calls its `yield` method, it gives up the CPU and is put back in the runnable set in the runnable state.

suspended A runnable or running thread enters the *suspended* state when its `suspend` method is called, for example,

> `t.suspend();`

A thread can suspend itself or be suspended by some other thread. From the suspended state, a thread reenters the runnable state and is placed in the runnable set when its `resume` method is called by some other thread.

> `t.resume();`

blocked A thread enters the *blocked* state when it calls its `sleep` method, when it calls `wait()` inside a `synchronized` method of some object, when it calls the `join` method on another thread object whose thread has not yet terminated, or when it performs some blocking input-output operation (like reading from the keyboard). From the blocked state, a thread reenters the runnable state and is put back in the runnable set. Depending on how it blocked, this happens when its `sleep` method call completes, when it joins with a terminated thread, when its blocking input-output request is fulfilled by the operating system, or when some other thread calls `notify()` or `notifyAll()` in a `synchronized` method of the object in which the blocked thread earlier called `wait()`.

suspended-blocked If a blocked thread is suspended by another thread, it enters the *suspended-blocked* state. If the blocking operation subsequently completes, it enters the suspended state. If, on the other hand, the thread is resumed by another thread before the blocking operation completes, it reenters the blocked state.

Current State	New State					
	runnable	running	suspended	blocked	suspended-blocked	dead
new	start					
runnable		scheduled	suspend			stop
running	time slice ends, yield		suspend	blocking IO, sleep, wait, join		stop, run ends
suspended	resume					stop
blocked	IO completes, sleep expires, notify, notifyAll, join completes				suspend	stop
suspended-blocked			IO completes	resume		stop

Table 3.1: Thread State Transitions.

dead A thread terminates and enters the *dead* state when its `run` method completes execution or when its `stop` method is called, usually in some other thread.

```
t.stop();
```

We will learn much more about `synchronized` methods and the `wait`, `notify`, and `notifyAll` methods in Chapter 5, specifically Section 5.3.1. Table 3.1 summarizes the states a thread is in and the events that cause a transition from one state to another.

Java threads have a priority that affects their scheduling to run on the CPU. A thread inherits the priority of the thread that created it. Priorities range from `MIN_PRIORITY` to `MAX_PRIORITY`, constants defined in the class `Thread`; the default priority is `NORM_PRIORITY`. A thread's priority is changed with the `setPriority` method and queried with the `getPriority` method.

The Java thread scheduler ensures that the highest priority runnable thread (or one of them if there are several) is running on the CPU. If a thread of a higher priority enters the runnable set, the Java thread scheduler places back in the runnable set the currently running thread so the higher priority thread executes. Thus the currently running thread is *preempted* by the higher priority thread. If the currently running thread yields, suspends itself, or enters the blocked state, the Java scheduler chooses to run next the highest priority thread (or one of them if there are several) from the runnable set.

Another component of thread scheduling is time slicing: switching the CPU among the highest priority, runnable threads rather than waiting for one to block, suspend, or yield before assigning the CPU to another runnable thread. Time slicing is also called *round robin* scheduling. The time slice or time quantum is usually on the order of 100 milliseconds. Under time slicing, if the currently running thread has not stopped, finished, blocked, suspended itself, or yielded before its time slice expires, and if there are other equally high priority threads in the runnable set, the CPU is reallocated to another one. The thread whose time slice just expired is placed back in the runnable set.

The Solaris 2.x version of JDK 1.1 does not time slice threads: a thread runs until it terminates, stops, blocks, suspends itself, yields, or a higher priority thread becomes runnable. The JDK 1.1 for Windows 95/NT does implement time slicing of threads. Program 3.2 tests for the time slicing of Java threads by starting up several threads that execute CPU-intensive infinite loops. Each loop periodically prints something. We examine the program's output to see if the thread print statements are interleaved, evidence of time slicing.

```java
class Beeper extends MyObject implements Runnable {
    private int beep = 0;
    public Beeper(String name, int beep) {
        super(name);
        this.beep = beep;
        System.out.println(getName() + " is alive, beep=" + beep);
        Thread t = new Thread(this);
        t.setPriority(t.getPriority()-1); // so main() thread has
                // priority and surely gets CPU later to stop() us
        t.start();
    }
    public void run() {
        long value = 1;
        System.out.println
            ("age()="+age()+", "+getName()+" running");
        while (true) {
            if (value++ % beep == 0)
                System.out.println("age()=" + age()
                    + ", " + getName() + " beeps, value=" + value);
        }
    }
}
```

The constructor for class **Beeper** starts a thread to execute the **run** method of the class. The first two sample runs show the results for Windows 95/NT and Solaris 2.x, respectively. We see that the former time slices threads but the latter does not.

```
D:\>java Beeping -R7
...
age()=550, Beeper0 beeps, value=100001
age()=610, Beeper1 beeps, value=100001
age()=610, Beeper2 beeps, value=100001
age()=720, Beeper3 beeps, value=100001
age()=1100, Beeper0 beeps, value=200001

% java Beeping -R7
...
age()=327, Beeper0 beeps, value=100001
age()=679, Beeper0 beeps, value=200001
age()=1030, Beeper0 beeps, value=300001
age()=1381, Beeper0 beeps, value=400001
age()=1732, Beeper0 beeps, value=500001
```

The beeping threads run at a lower priority than the thread executing the main method so that the latter is guaranteed the CPU to terminate the beepers when its nap call expires. Without this, the program never terminates on Solaris 2.x.

To implement pseudo time slicing of threads for Solaris 2.x, use the Scheduler class, part of the Utilities package.

```
public class Scheduler extends MyObject implements Runnable {
    private int timeSlice = 0; // milliseconds
    private Thread t = null;
    public Scheduler(int timeSlice) {
        super("Scheduler");
        this.timeSlice = timeSlice;
        t = new Thread(this);
        t.setPriority(Thread.MAX_PRIORITY);
        t.setDaemon(true);
        t.start();
    }
    public void run() {
        int napping = timeSlice;
        while (true) {
            nap(napping);
        }
    }
}
```

The complete code is shown in Library Class 3.2. The scheduler thread's priority is set to the highest possible value with a call to the setPriority method. The thread is also made into a daemon thread with a call to the setDaemon method, described below in Section 3.1.2. Each time the scheduler's nap ends, it preempts whatever thread is running because the scheduler thread has the highest priority.

The preempted thread is placed back in the runnable set. This class is also used to decrease the time slice below the default value in Windows 95/NT. Before calling the **start** method of the threads, execute

```
new Scheduler(time slice);
```

to activate time slicing of the given value.

For convenience, the class **MyObject** has a method **ensureTimeSlicing** that is used to introduce pseudo time slicing of threads on Solaris 2.x. It has no effect when called on the Windows 95/NT platform.

```
/*
 * Windows 95 time-slices threads but Solaris does not as
 * of JDK 1.1.  To enable time slicing on Solaris, set the
 * Boolean variable timeSlicingEnsured to true or call
 * ensureTimeSlicing().
 */
    private static final String OSname =
        System.getProperty("os.name");
    private static int timeSlice = 100;
    private static boolean timeSlicingEnsured = false;
    private static Scheduler scheduler =
        timeSlicingEnsured && OSname.equals("Solaris") ?
        new Scheduler(timeSlice) : null;
    protected static final void ensureTimeSlicing() {
        if (scheduler == null && OSname.equals("Solaris"))
            new Scheduler(timeSlice);
    }
```

The third sample run of Program 3.2 shows what happens on Solaris when this method is invoked.

```
// enable time slicing Solaris; noop on Windows 95
if (timeSlice > 0)
    ensureTimeSlicing(timeSlice); // so threads share CPU
```

To reduce the time slice size on Windows 95/NT, create a **Scheduler** object explicitly instead of calling **ensureTimeSlicing**.

One thread waits for another to terminate with the **join** method. Note that the **yield** and **sleep** methods are static in class **Thread** and therefore apply only to the calling thread when invoked. Since **join**, **resume**, **stop**, and **suspend** are instance methods, they can be invoked by any thread on any thread object. In any method, a reference to the calling thread is obtained with the **currentThread** method, for example,

```
System.out.println(Thread.currentThread().getName());
```

Also note that wait(), notify(), and notifyAll() must be called from inside a synchronized block or method of some object (Chapter 5).

A thread interrupts another thread by calling the latter's interrupt instance method. If the thread being interrupted is blocked in a call to sleep, join, or wait, then these methods throw an InterruptedException object instead of returning normally. If the thread is not blocked, an internal Boolean flag of the thread is set. This flag is checked with the Boolean isInterrupted instance method. For convenience, the Thread class has a Boolean static method interrupted that calls currentThread().isInterrupted(). It also clears the Boolean interrupted flag, which the isInterrupted method does not do. The interrupt functionality allows one thread to send a signal to another thread to suspend or stop itself, or return allocated resources, but only if it is not in the middle of some critical operation. The interrupted thread checks its flag outside of such operations and then takes appropriate action. This feature was only partially implemented in JDK 1.0.2 and is fully functional in JDK 1.1. It is not used in any of this book's programs.

At some time in the future, the JDKs for shared-memory multiprocessors will support symmetric multiprocessing: scheduling to run on all available CPUs the Java threads in the runnable state. Sun Microsystems has announced that its Solaris 2.6 platform includes this feature for Java.

3.1.2   Other Thread Methods

Normally, a Java application that has several threads executing in it terminates only when the last thread terminates. However, if one or more of the threads is a *daemon* thread, then the program terminates when all nondaemon threads terminate. Daemon threads are usually created to perform services for nondaemon threads. When all nondaemon threads have terminated, there is no longer any need for the daemon threads. An example is the scheduler thread described above, Library Class 3.2. A thread is made into a daemon by calling setDaemon(true), as shown in the constructor of the scheduler thread. The isDaemon method is used to determine if a thread is a daemon; it returns true or false. The isAlive method is used to determine if a thread has terminated; it also returns true or false. For more information, see [31].

The Thread class has a constructor with two arguments, an object implementing Runnable and a string, used above in an example illustrating the second way to spawn a thread. The string argument gives a name to the thread object created. That name is the string return value of an instance method, getName, in the Thread class.

```
Thread t = new Thread(a, "mud, too");
...
System.out.println(... + t.getName() + ...);
```

3.2   Why Use Threads?

As mentioned in Section 1.1.2, many situations are more easily handled with a multithreaded program. Program 3.3 is a simple (contrived) example of event-driven programming in Java. It creates two windows, a TextArea in each window for printing, and then starts two threads. Each thread prints a sequence of numbers in its window using the Fibonacci algorithm, $x_i = x_{i-1} + x_{i-2}$, $i = 3,\ldots$. Instead of starting with x_1 and x_2 equal to 1, the algorithm starts with two random numbers between 1 and 99.

```
class ComputeFibonacci extends MyObject implements Runnable {
    private TextArea textArea = null;
    private int napping = 256;
    public ComputeFibonacci(TextArea textArea) {
        super("ComputeFibonacci");
        this.textArea = textArea;
    }
    public void run() {
        while (true) {
            long x = (long)random(1,100);
            long y = (long)random(1,100);
            long z;
            do {
                z = x + y;
                textArea.append("x=" + x + ", y=" + y
                    + ", z=" + z + "\n");
                nap(napping);
                x = y;  y = z;
            } while (z > 0);
        }
    }
}
```

There are eight buttons along the top of each window to control the behavior of the program: "Start," "Suspend," "Resume," "Faster," "Slower," "Stop," "Close," and "Quit." When one of the buttons in a window is activated (clicked with the mouse), a thread in the Java virtual machine executes the actionPerformed method of the Frame object associated with the window containing the button.

```
class FibonacciFrame extends Frame implements ActionListener {
    private static final String[] buttonLabel =
        {"Start", "Suspend", "Resume", "Faster", "Slower",
        "Stop", "Close", "Quit"};
    public FibonacciFrame(int id) {
        super();
        setTitle("FibonacciFrame " + id);
        setLayout(new BorderLayout());
```

```
    Panel p = new Panel();
    p.setLayout(new FlowLayout());
    for (int i = 0; i < buttonLabel.length; i++) {
        Button b = new Button(buttonLabel[i]);
        b.addActionListener(this);
        p.add(b);
    }
    add("North", p);
    textArea = new TextArea(12, 40);
    textArea.setEditable(false);
    textArea.setFont(new Font("Helvetica", Font.PLAIN, 16));
    add("Center", textArea);
    fibonacci = new ComputeFibonacci(textArea);
  }
  public void actionPerformed(ActionEvent evt) {
    Object o = evt.getSource();
    if (o instanceof Button) {
        String label = ((Button) o).getLabel();
        if (buttonLabel[0].equals(label))
            thread = new Thread(fibonacci);
        ...
    }
  }
}
```

The threads in each of the two `Fibonacci` objects, one per window, calculate and display the numbers, appending each line to the `TextArea` objects passed to them. Each thread sleeps a short time between each append to give the viewer time to analyze the results. The "Start" button initiates a new thread displaying numbers generated from two new random numbers. Each thread's priority is set to the minimum so that the method `actionPerformed` will be invoked with a higher priority, ensuring speedy response to button clicks. "Suspend" and "Resume" invoke the `suspend` and `resume` methods on the window's `Fibonacci` thread. The next two buttons decrease and increase the napping time in the window's thread. "Stop" stops the window's thread, "Close" closes and disposes of the window, and "Quit" terminates the program. A snapshot of the program's two windows is shown in Figure 3.1. Multiple threads simplify the design and implementation of this program (Exercise 1).

3.3 Debugging Techniques

The best way to debug a Java program is with the `System.out.println` statement, as is the case with any high-level programming language. During design and coding, think about what you would like to see printed as the program executes to determine if it is working correctly. In particular, think about variables whose values you

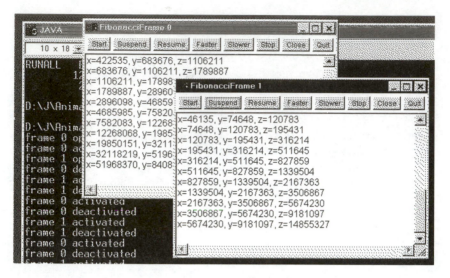

Figure 3.1: Snapshot of Fibonacci Frames.

would like to track and the places in the program to print those values. Recall
from Section 2.2 that a `toString` method in an object is invoked automatically by
compiler-generated code in print statements. Think about where to insert marker
statements, such as

```
if (debug) System.out.println
    ("DEBUG: entering delete method to unlink first node")
```

A Boolean variable is a good way to control debugging output during program
execution.

Most of the Java programs we write contain multiple threads. The output of all
`println` statements in all threads is intermixed on the screen, or in a file if `stdout`
has been redirected. On the Windows 95/NT and Solaris 2.x platforms, `stdout` is
redirected as follows.

```
java Name command line arguments >file
```

Tagging write statements with a thread identifier and the elapsed time since the
program began with the `age` method helps cope with interleaved output. Here is an
example.

```
if (debug) System.out.println
    ("At time " + age() + ", helper " + id + " is sleeping")
```

It is possible to send the output of each thread to a different file. Program 3.4
shows how to do this.

```
String outFileName = "helper";
Thread[] helper = new Thread[numHelpers];
```

```
PrintWriter[] outFile = new PrintWriter[numHelpers];
for (int i = 0; i < numHelpers; i++) {
    String fileName = outFileName + i + ".out";
    boolean autoFlush = true;
    outFile[i] = new PrintWriter(new BufferedWriter(
        new FileWriter(new File(fileName))), autoFlush);
    helper[i] = new Thread(
        new Helper("Helper", i, napTime*1000, outFile[i]));
}
for (int i = 0; i < numHelpers; i++) helper[i].start();
```

Each `Helper` thread uses `outFile[i]` for printing instead of `System.out`. The output of thread i goes to file `helperi.out` instead of the screen. On a UNIX workstation that supports multiple windows on the screen, it is possible to see the output of each thread in a separate window as the output is generated. Open up as many shell or command windows as there are output files and execute the command

```
tail -f helperi.out
```

in each window (replace i with the appropriate number).

The Java run-time system generates error messages before aborting a program due to an exception. Many more error conditions are detected than in most C and C++ run-time systems. For example, using a subscript value outside the bounds of an array generates an exception and a message like the following before the program is terminated (assuming the exception is not caught).

```
java.lang.ArrayIndexOutOfBoundsException
        at Z.z(test.java:21)
        at Q.main(test.java:30)
```

Some Java platforms have a debugging version of the command starting the JVM, called `java_g`. It has two command line options, `-t` and `-tm`. These turn on an instruction execution trace and a method call trace, respectively. Try them to see if they are useful.

The print statement is one of the most useful and powerful debugging techniques. Although using animation as described in Section 2.7 to animate programs will itself involve debugging, it also helps determine if an algorithm is working correctly.

3.4 Race Conditions and Thread Synchronization

A major concern in concurrent programming is the "lost update" problem that potentially occurs when two or more threads share data. If two threads share a variable n, if they both update n at about the same time on an architecture with CPU registers and load/store register instructions, and if the register loads and stores are interleaved, one of the updates may be lost and overwritten by the other. For example, suppose n currently has the value of 1:

one thread:
```
    n = n + 1;
```
another thread:
```
    n = n + 2;
```

If the two threads execute their statements at about the same time, n might end up as 2 or 3 instead of the correct value, 4.

On a computer with a load/store register instruction set, the assignment statement n = n+1 compiles into machine language instructions like this.

load the value at address n into a register R
add 1 to R
store R to address n

On a shared-memory multiprocessor or a uniprocessor with context switching, the machine language instructions of two threads A and B executing n = n+1 at about the same time using a shared variable n might interleave as follows.

A: load n into R
B: load n into R
A: R = R + 1
B: R = R + 1
A: store R to n
B: store R to n

Recall that on a multiprocessor each CPU has its own register set. If the threads are sharing the one CPU on a uniprocessor, then the values of the registers are saved and restored each time there is a context switch.

The above interleaving would occur on a uniprocessor if there were a context switch after each instruction. This is highly unlikely. However, on a multiprocessor this interleaving could actually occur. A more likely scenario on a uniprocessor is this interleaving.

A: load n into R
A: R = R + 1
... context switch from thread A to B
B: load n into R
B: R = R + 1
B: store R to n
... later context switch back to thread A
A: store R to n

In both cases, the final value of n reflects just one of the increments, leading to the term "lost update."

This is an example of a *race condition*. Race conditions occur when two or more threads share data, they are reading and writing the shared data concurrently, and the final result, which may be erroneous, depends on which thread does what when, that is, depends on the specific interleaving of the machine language instructions executed by the threads.

As another example, consider a room that has `numChairs` chairs in it for waiting customers. A customer needing service comes to the waiting room door to see if there is a free chair; it compares the current number of waiting customers, `waiting`, to the total number of chairs, `numChairs`:

```
if (waiting < numChairs) waiting++;
```

If there is room, the customer takes a seat. If there is just one free chair left and two customers A and B approach the door at about the same time, it is possible for them both to take the last seat (`R1` and `R2` are CPU registers).

A: load `waiting` into `R1`
A: load `numChairs` into `R2`
A: compare `R1` and `R2`
A: `R1 = R1 + 1`
... context switch from thread A to B
B: load `waiting` into `R1`
B: load `numChairs` into `R2`
B: compare `R1` and `R2`
B: `R1 = R1 + 1`
B: store `R1` to `waiting`
... later context switch back to thread A
A: store `R1` to `waiting`

Concurrently executing threads that share data need to synchronize their operations and processing in order to avoid race conditions on shared data. Only one customer thread at a time should be allowed to examine and update the `waiting` variable.

Race conditions are also possible in an operating system. If the ready queue is implemented as a linked list and if the ready queue is being manipulated during the handling of an interrupt, then interrupts must be disabled to prevent another interrupt of the same type being handled before the first one completes. If interrupts are not disabled then the linked list could become corrupted.

Another example of a race condition is in an algorithm animation program with a loop that draws objects in a window, using the current (x, y) position of each object. Suppose a thread processing animation commands moves an object from one location to another just as the drawing loop is about to draw the object in the window. The object may be drawn at a position corresponding to the old position, the new position, or at an erroneous position given by the new value of x and the old value of y. The thread moving the object needs to synchronize with the drawing thread so that the former moves the object either before or after it has been drawn.

We can create a race condition in a Java program, but not easily at such a low level as incrementing a variable, `n = n+1`, since the Java interpreter may not always interleave threads at that fine a granularity. Instead we interleave the execution of two loops in two threads that share data, as is done in Program 3.5.

```
class Racer extends MyObject implements Runnable {
    private int M = 0;
    private volatile long sum = 0;
    public Racer(String name, int M) {
        super(name);   this.M = M;
    }
    private long fn(long j, int k) {
        long total = j;
        for (int i = 1;   i <= k; i++) total += i;
        return total;
    }
    public void run() {
        for (int m = 1; m <= M; m++) sum = fn(sum, m);
    }
}
```

Note that only one Racer object is created; two threads are then created in that object and the two threads share the sum variable. With a loop, each thread repeatedly calls a method fn that updates the shared variable sum. The statement sum = fn(sum,m) is subject to race conditions and lost updates if a context switch occurs during a call to fn, just as in the statement n = n+1. If two calls to the method fn by the two threads are interleaved, then the variable sum will not be updated the way the programmer desires because the value of sum is passed to the method and stored in the method's local variable total. Updates to sum are lost during the concurrent execution of sum = fn(sum,m) if the statements of the method are interleaved, just as can happen with the concurrent execution of a statement like n = n+1 if its compiled machine language instructions are interleaved.

Notice that sum is declared with the volatile attribute. This tells the compiler that the variable is accessed by more than one thread at a time and inhibits inappropriate code optimizations by the compiler ([21], page 147), such as caching the value of sum in a CPU register instead of updating main memory with each assignment to sum. We discuss volatile further in Section 3.4.1.

On a Windows 95/NT platform, Java may not interleave the method calls if they are short in duration, such as happens with a small value of M. On a Solaris 2.x platform, there is no time slicing and therefore no interleaving. We force interleaving on Windows 95/NT by decreasing the time slice or increasing M. On Solaris, we introduce time slicing. In an exercise, you are asked to store this program in a file named race.java, add code to start the Scheduler thread described in Library Class 3.2 with a time slice of 10 milliseconds, and then compile and run the program with the following sequence of commands.

```
javac race.java
java RaceTwoThreads -M 200
```

The thread in the Scheduler object runs at a priority higher than the other two threads. It sleeps 10 milliseconds, then becomes runnable. Since it has the highest priority, it preempts the currently running thread, which is placed back in the runnable set. The effect is a time slice of 10 milliseconds. You are asked to observe and explain the output.

If we increase M, the number of times each thread executes sum = fn(sum,m), from 10 to 2000, then context switches will more likely occur during the calls to fn, leading to a race condition. This is shown on Windows 95/NT in the second sample run of Program 3.5.

A more subtle race condition is illustrated in Program 3.6, based on ([1], Figure 2.4). Suppose we have a town with a single bank. The bank has 10,000 accounts and at the present time each account has exactly $1,000. Therefore the town's bank has assets of exactly ten million dollars. We simulate activity in the bank with a Java program that has two threads.

```
class ATM extends Bank implements Runnable {
                        // inherits numAccounts, savingsAccount
    public void run() {
        int fromAccount, toAccount, amount;
        while (true) {
            fromAccount = (int) random(numAccounts);
            toAccount = (int) random(numAccounts);
            amount = 1 +
                (int) random(savingsAccount[fromAccount].balance);
            savingsAccount[fromAccount].balance -= amount;
            savingsAccount[toAccount].balance += amount;
        }
    }
}
class Auditor extends Bank implements Runnable {
                        // inherits numAccounts, savingsAccount
    public void run() {
        int total;
        while (true) {
            nap(1000);
            total = 0;
            for (int i = 0; i < numAccounts; i++)
                total += savingsAccount[i].balance;
            System.out.println
                ("age()=" + age() + ", total is $" + total);
        }
    }
}
```

The automatic teller machine (ATM) thread picks two accounts at random and moves a random amount of money from one account to the other. The auditor thread periodically wakes up and adds up the money in all the accounts to check for the embezzlement of funds from the bank. The sample output shows that sometimes the bank has more and sometimes less money than it should.

```
age()=1100, total is $10000000
age()=2250, total is $10001948
age()=3300, total is $9994887
```

The race condition is not the auditor summing the accounts during the add or
subtract statement of the ATM thread (the auditor summing after the ATM has
loaded an account balance into a CPU register but before the updated balance has
been stored back into memory). An ATM transaction sometimes occurs between
two accounts while the auditor is summing accounts. The auditor may have already
added one account's balance into the sum but not the other when the ATM transfer
occurs. To fix this, it is not enough to make each of the two ATM statements that
add/subtract the accounts into one uninterruptible, atomic action; all accounts must
be frozen while the auditor loop sums.

Figure 3.2 shows a race condition that sometimes occurs when two threads each
add a node at about the same time to the end of a linked list queue. The steps to
add a new node are

```
addNewNode(Queue queue, Node newNode) {
    Node oldTail; // oldTail is a local variable
    newNode.nextEntry = null;
    oldTail = queue.tail;
    queue.tail = newNode;
    oldTail.nextEntry = newNode;
}
```

Suppose thread B starts to add a new node (number 6)

```
addNewNode(queue, node6);
```

and before it completes all the necessary steps, a context switch occurs. Now suppose
thread A executes and adds a new node (number 4)

```
addNewNode(queue, node4);
```

to the end of the queue, completing all the above steps. When thread B later resumes
execution and completes the steps, the node (number 4) that thread A added is no
longer in the queue, even though thread A executed all the necessary steps.

The output of the second sample run in Program 3.7 shows this race condition
happening, although the timings are contrived with calls to nap. A context switch
is forced in the middle of the code of the enQueue method with a nap(1500) while
the node with value item6 is added to the end of the queue by the Benq thread.
When this code later resumes, the node with value item4, added by thread Aenq in
the meantime, is lost. Program 3.7 shows how to do linked lists in Java; however,
this kind of code is not often used due to the versatile java.util.Vector class.

This linked list race condition potentially occurs in an operating system if there
are queues manipulated in response to interrupts. If two interrupts occur that
require manipulation of the same queue, then the operating system must make sure

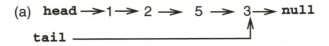

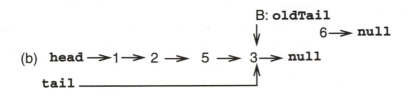

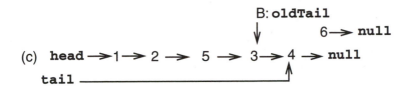

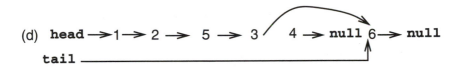

(a) Initial condition of the queue.
(b) Process B gets as far as saving a local copy of the tail pointer before a context switch occurs.
(c) Process A adds a new node to the end of the queue.
(d) Process B completes its code to add a new node. Note that the node A added is now "lost."

Figure 3.2: A Queue Race Condition.

that the handling of the interrupts is not nested. This is done by masking (disabling) or prioritizing interrupts.

For a concurrent program to be correct, it must be written so that it is not dependent in any way on when context switches occur, on how long time slices (times between context switches) are, or on the relative speeds of the CPUs in a multiprocessor system. To make concurrent programs work correctly on a multiprocessor, or on a uniprocessor in the presence of arbitrary context switches and with any time slice size, we need to coordinate or synchronize the execution of the threads so they will not try to read-update-write a shared variable or data structure simultaneously. In the ATM/auditor and queue examples, we need to make sure that no other thread accesses a data structure, the array of accounts or linked list, while it is being manipulated by a thread and while the data structure may not be in a consistent state. In other words, there must be no interleaving of two or more threads' instructions that manipulate a shared data structure. Actions on shared variables and data structures, like n = n+1 and addNewNode(queue, node), must be done in an uninterruptible, indivisible, atomic action.

Eliminating these undesirable interleavings is called the *mutual exclusion problem*. To avoid race conditions and erroneous results, we must identify in each thread those *critical sections* of code that

1. Reference one or more variables in a read-update-write fashion while any of those variables is possibly being altered by another thread, or

2. Alter one or more variables that are possibly being referenced in a read-update-write fashion by another thread, or

3. Use a data structure such as a linked list while any part of it is possibly being altered by another thread, or

4. Alter any part of a data structure such as a linked list while it is possibly in use by another thread.

The following sections and chapters describe various ways to solve this problem using software, hardware, and system calls to the operating system. Sections 3.5.1 and 3.5.2 look at software solutions and Section 3.5.3 looks at hardware solutions. Chapter 4 examines semaphores, usually implemented with system calls to the operating system. Chapter 5 describes monitors, in which synchronization is part of the programming language. But first we need to discuss the behavior of the shared memory system on which our concurrent Java threads are running.

3.4.1   Memory System Behavior

Threads represent independently executing flows of control in the address space of one process and use variables in the shared address space to communicate. We assume that the uniprocessor or shared-memory multiprocessor on which the threads are executing has a load/store instruction set: instructions use the memory bus to load data from memory into CPU registers or store data from CPU registers into memory. As each thread executes, it generates a sequence of read and write operations to shared variables in memory.

Updates to any one shared variable by a particular thread are seen by other threads in the order performed by the particular thread. However, the Java language specification ([21], Chapter 17) does not require other threads to see updates to different shared variables in the order performed by the updating thread unless the variables are declared volatile.

For example, consider the following class.

```
class C {
    static int w = 0;
    static void d() { w = 3;   w = 4; }
```

```
        static int e() { int z = w;   z += 2*w;   return z; }
    }
```

If one thread calls method **d** and another thread calls method **e**, the possible values returned by **e()** are 0, 6, 8, 9, 11, and 12 (Exercise 3). However, it is impossible for **e()** to return 10 because this would require the thread calling **e()** to see **w** updated to 4 before 3.

Next, consider this class.

```
    class D {
        static int x = 0, y = 0;
        static void a() { x = 3;  y = 4; }
        static int b() { int z = y;   z += x;   return z; }
    }
```

If one thread calls method **a** and another thread calls method **b**, the possible values returned by **b()** are 0, 3, 4, and 7. If **b()** completes before **a()** starts, then the return value is 0; if **a()** completes before **b()** starts, the return value is 7; if **b()** assigns 0 to **z** and then **a()** is called and completes before **b()** loads **x** from memory, the return value is 3. The value 4 is returned by a call to **b()** if the store of 4 into **y** by the call to **a()** is visible to the thread calling **b()** before the store of 3 to **x** is visible. However, if both the variables **x** and **y** are declared **volatile**,

```
        static volatile int x = 0, y = 0;
```

then a return value of 4 is not possible. To quote from the Java language specification ([21], page 147), "... operations on ... one or more volatile variables [by] a thread are performed by the main memory in exactly the order that the thread requested."

For another illustration, consider two threads, a producer and a consumer, executing on two CPUs of a shared-memory multiprocessor. The threads share a bounded buffer, implemented as a circular array, in which the producer deposits items and from which the consumer fetches items, calling the **deposit** and **fetch** methods, respectively. They need to coordinate or synchronize their activities so that the producer does not deposit an item into a full buffer, overwriting the item already there, and the consumer does not fetch an item from an empty buffer, perhaps retrieving the same item twice. We will see this bounded buffer producer and consumer problem again in Section 4.3. Class 3.8 (used with Program 3.9), shows a solution that involves *busy waiting*. If the buffer is full, the producer "spins" in a loop until the consumer empties the buffer; if the buffer is empty, the consumer busy waits until the producer fills the buffer.

```
    public void deposit(double value) {
        while (buffer[putIn].occupied)            // busy wait
            Thread.currentThread().yield();
        buffer[putIn].value = value;              // A
        buffer[putIn].occupied = true;            // B
        putIn = (putIn + 1) % numSlots;
```

```
//   count++;                               // race condition!!!
}
public double fetch() {
   double value;
   while (!buffer[takeOut].occupied)     // busy wait
      Thread.currentThread().yield();
   value = buffer[takeOut].value;        // C
   buffer[takeOut].occupied = false;     // D
   takeOut = (takeOut + 1) % numSlots;
//   count--;                              // race condition!!!
   return value;
}
```

In Java, a ";" by itself is used to mean *noop* or "do nothing" so

```
while(condition) /* do nothing */ ;
```

is a busy waiting loop. However, yielding the CPU is more efficient if *condition* is true, so the busy waiting loops are coded instead as

```
while(condition) /* busy wait */ Thread.currentThread().yield();
```

This program does not work correctly if the consumer thread "sees" the memory updates of the producer's two statements labeled A and B in the program in the reverse order, that is, if the occupied field is seen by the consumer to be updated by the producer before the value field is seen by the consumer to be updated by the producer. Likewise, the producer has to see the two memory updates labeled C and D in the same order they are performed by the consumer. The variables value and occupied must be declared volatile to force this behavior by the Java memory system shared by the threads.

```
class BufferItem {
      // multiple threads access these so make them 'volatile'
   public volatile double value = 0;
   public volatile boolean occupied = false;
}
 ...
private BufferItem[] buffer = new BufferItem[numSlots];
for (int i = 0; i < numSlots; i++) buffer[i] = new BufferItem();
```

Class 3.8 uses busy waiting to synchronize the producer and consumer threads. Besides wasting CPU cycles, this program has two other disadvantages compared to the versions we will see later. Because of race conditions on the variables putIn and takeOut, there cannot be either multiple producer threads or multiple consumer threads. Also, even with only one producer and consumer thread, there would be race conditions on a variable count used to maintain the current number of full buffer slots. Therefore count was commented out.

3.4.2 Thread Priorities and Starvation

Another feature Class 3.8 needs for correct operation is equal priorities for all threads so that a high-priority thread, one that is scheduled before lower priority threads, cannot spin in a busy waiting loop waiting for an event to occur and keep a low-priority thread from being scheduled so it can generate the event. For example, if the consumer thread has a higher priority than the producer and the bounded buffer is empty, then it is possible for the consumer thread to busy wait and prevent the producer thread from being scheduled to run. This is a form of starvation. Neither thread is getting what it needs to continue: the consumer a buffer item and the producer the CPU. In general, starvation occurs when a thread has requested a resource or needs a resource to continue but the amount of time until the resource is granted is not bounded, that is, cannot be predicted or guaranteed.

In general, we assume that all threads have equal priorities, particularly when those threads share a CPU. The only exception is the thread in Library Class 3.2, used to change the time slice size (or, in the case of Java running under Sun's Solaris 2.x, to introduce time slicing). This assumption prevents a high-priority busy waiting thread from starving a lower priority thread that wants to release the resource on which the high-priority thread is waiting. See ([1], pages 84–86) for more information.

3.5 The Mutual Exclusion Problem

Recall from Section 3.4 that a critical section is a sequence or block of code in a thread that

1. References one or more variables in a read-update-write fashion while any of those variables is possibly being altered by another thread, or

2. Alters one or more variables that are possibly being referenced in a read-update-write fashion by another thread, or

3. Uses a data structure such as a linked list while any part of it is possibly being altered by another thread, or

4. Alters any part of a data structure such as a linked list while it is possibly in use by another thread.

To prevent race conditions and lost updates, there should be *mutual exclusion*: only one thread at a time should be allowed to execute a critical section of code. The mutual exclusion problem is to devise a *preprotocol* or *entry protocol* and a *postprotocol* or *exit protocol*, used as shown in Figure 3.3, to keep two or more threads from being in their critical sections at the same time.

When stated as an abstract problem, we make no assumptions about the number of CPUs or their relative speeds. There are desirable properties that any solution to mutual exclusion problem should have ([1], Section 3.1), whether it uses only load/store instructions, uses special hardware instructions like test-and-set (Section 3.5.3) or uses system calls to the operating system (Section 3.5.4).

thread T_i , $i = 0, 1, 2, \ldots$

```
while (true) {
      ...
      noncritical section code;
      ...
      wantToEnterCS(i); /* preprotocol */
      ...
      critical section code;
      ...
      finishedInCS(i); /* postprotocol */
}
```

Figure 3.3: Pre- and Postprotocol for Mutual Exclusion.

- There should be no *deadlock*, called a "safety" property (something "bad" does not happen: never enter the deadlock state). Deadlock would occur if two threads tried to enter their critical sections at about the same time, and neither succeeded (both entered the blocked state or got stuck in busy waiting loops) even though no other threads were in their critical sections. In general, deadlock occurs when each thread in a set of threads is blocked, waiting for an event to occur that can only be triggered by another thread in the set. There should be no *livelock*, a form of deadlock in which the threads are not in the blocked state or stuck in busy waiting loops but continue to execute code in their preprotocol without end.

- No thread outside its critical section should block other threads outside their critical sections from entering. This is another "safety" property (absence of unnecessary delay).

- No thread should wait forever to enter its critical section; it should not busy wait or be blocked forever when trying to enter. In other words, there should be no *starvation*, also called a "liveness" property (something "good" does happen: eventual entry).

We identify two kinds of starvation.

1. Starvation in the absence of contention: this would occur if a thread tried to enter its critical section and even though no other threads were in their critical sections, it could not enter.

2. Starvation in the presence of contention: this would occur if two or more threads were trying to enter their critical sections, but one never gets in while the other(s) get in over and over again.

In a computer architecture, an *atomic instruction* is a machine language instruction that is executed completely without interruption, that is, with no interleaving of other instructions from another thread, no context switching, no hardware interrupts. For example, a register load from memory and a register store to memory are each atomic instructions. Some architectures have an instruction that increments a memory location atomically. Some architectures let a processor lock the system bus for a sequence of instructions so they are done atomically as a group.

In general, an *atomic action* makes an indivisible state transition: "any intermediate state that might exist in the implementation of the action must not be visible to other [threads]" ([1], page 60). This means no instructions from another thread can interleave in the implementation of the action for it to be atomic. Critical sections need to be done as if they were one atomic action to avoid race conditions.

In summary, the mutual exclusion problem is to devise a preprotocol and postprotocol, used as shown in Figure 3.3 and based on either hardware or software, that prevent two threads from being in their critical sections at the same time and that have the desirable absence of deadlock and starvation properties described above. In this problem, we have

- a load/store register architecture,

- multiple concurrently executing threads that share data,

- single or multiple CPUs where we make no relative speed assumptions, and

- accesses to shared variables that are interleaved if two threads get into their critical sections at the same time.

We assume

- that threads do not halt or crash in their pre- or postprotocols,

- that threads do not halt or crash in their critical sections,

- that threads may halt or crash outside their critical sections.

There are several approaches to solving the mutual exclusion problem: busy waiting versus blocking (with a call to the operating system), and pure user-level software versus hardware versus operating system assistance.

3.5.1 Software Solutions for Two Threads

To see more examples of race conditions and to get a better understanding of the mutual exclusion problem, we look at a sequence of attempts to solve the mutual exclusion problem with software using busy waiting. Special hardware instructions such as test-and-set are also used to solve the mutual exclusion problem (Section 3.5.3). The next chapter looks at how the operating system assists in a solution. See ([15], Chapter 4), ([34], Chapter 6), ([36], Chapters 4–5), ([41], Chapter 2), ([43], Chapter 2).

The following attempts to solve the mutual exclusion problem in software with busy waiting are based on ([6], page 28) and are coded in Java. The preprotocol wantToEnterCS and postprotocol finishedInCS methods are shown. These code

fragments are tested with the Java driver code, Program 3.10. Each of the two
threads brackets its critical section with the pre- and postprotocols implemented in
the Arbitrator.

```
class Node implements Runnable {...
   private Arbitrator arb = // from driver
   private void outsideCS() {...}
   private void insideCS() {...}
   public void run() {                 // thread
      while (true) {
         outsideCS();
         arb.wantToEnterCS(id);        // preprotocol
         insideCS();
         arb.finishedInCS(id);         // postprotocol
      }
   }
}
```

A more specific example of using the entry and exit protocols to prevent race
conditions is the following modification of Program 3.5.

```
class Racer implements Runnable {...
...
   public void run() {                 // thread
      for (int m = 1; m <= M; m++) {
         arb.wantToEnterCS(i);         // entry protocol
         sum = fn(sum, m);
         arb.finishedInCS(i);          // exit protocol
      }
   }
}
```

It should be clear that something as simple as

```
boolean lockFlag = false;       // shared by the threads
wantToEnterCS(int i) {          // preprotocol
   while (lockFlag) /* busy wait */ ;
   lockFlag = true;
}
finishedInCS(int i) {           // postprotocol
   lockFlag = false;
}
```

does not work. We still have a race condition if two threads call wantToEnterCS at
about the same time (R is a CPU register):

Thread A: load lockFlag into R
... context switch from thread A to B

Thread B: load `lockFlag` into R
Thread B: compare R and `false`
Thread B: store `true` to `lockFlag`
Thread B: enter critical section
... later context switch back to thread A
Thread A: compare R and `false`
Thread A: store `true` to `lockFlag`
Thread A: enter critical section

It is possible for both threads to retrieve a false `lockFlag` at the same time, so mutual exclusion is not enforced.

The first attempt, Class 3.11, is strict alternation using a "turn" variable. The two threads take turns executing their critical sections.

```
public void wantToEnterCS(int i) {        // preprotocol
    while (turn != i)   // busy wait
        Thread.currentThread().yield();
}
public void finishedInCS(int i) {         // postprotocol
    turn = other(i);
}
```

Alternation works but suffers from starvation in the absence of contention. The sample output shows that between times 5380 and 7190, the critical sections are free, node 0 wants to enter its critical section, but it must wait because it is the turn of node 1 to enter.

The second attempt, Class 3.12, uses a "flag" variable to indicate a thread's desire to enter its critical section.

```
class Flag { public volatile boolean value = false; }
...
private Flag[] desiresCS = new Flag[2];
for (int i = 0; i < 2; i++) desiresCS[i] = new Flag();
...
public void wantToEnterCS(int i) {        // preprotocol
    while (desiresCS[other(i)].value)   // busy wait
        Thread.currentThread().yield();
    desiresCS[i].value = true;
}
public void finishedInCS(int i) {         // postprotocol
    desiresCS[i].value = false;
}
```

However, it does not work. Two threads enter their critical sections at the same time if they both execute their busy waiting loops, checking the other's flag, at the same time. Each will observe the other's flag is false and then enter.

The third attempt, Class 3.13, tries to fix the second attempt by reversing the order of checking the other thread's flag and signaling its own desire to enter its critical section.

```
public void wantToEnterCS(int i) {        // preprotocol
    desiresCS[i].value = true;
    while (desiresCS[other(i)].value)   // busy wait
        Thread.currentThread().yield();
}
public void finishedInCS(int i) {         // postprotocol
    desiresCS[i].value = false;
}
```

Reversing the order fixes the mutual exclusion problem but introduces the possibility of deadlock (both threads getting stuck in their busy waiting loops) if both threads try to enter at about the same time. Each will observe that the other's flag is true and will then busy wait forever. Note that our use of volatile, described in Section 3.4.1, is important in how this algorithm enforces mutual exclusion. It is not possible for the threads to set their flags at about the same time and then both see that the other's flag is not yet set in their busy waiting loops.

The fourth attempt, Class 3.14, tries to fix the third attempt by having the threads back off entering their critical sections if they detect they are both trying to enter at about the same time.

```
public void wantToEnterCS(int i) {        // preprotocol
    desiresCS[i].value = true;
    while (desiresCS[other(i)].value) {
        desiresCS[i].value = false;       // back off
        Thread.currentThread().yield();
        desiresCS[i].value = true;
    }
}
public void finishedInCS(int i) {         // postprotocol
    desiresCS[i].value = false;
}
```

Unfortunately, this only changes the deadlock problem to a related problem called livelock, in which the threads continually back off and try again in lockstep. This livelock could last an arbitrarily long time but will eventually end because the clock chips controlling the instruction issue rates on two CPUs cannot stay synchronized forever, called *clock skew*. Clock skew will not get two threads out of busy waiting deadlock but it will get them out of livelock. On a uniprocessor, time slicing is not precise enough to prolong the livelock indefinitely.

The next attempt, Class 3.15, is the first working software solution, developed by Dekker in the early 1960s. It fixes the fourth attempt's livelock flaw by having the threads take turns backing off.

```
public void wantToEnterCS(int i) {          // preprotocol
    desiresCS[i].value = true;
    while (desiresCS[other(i)].value) {
        if (turn != i) {
            desiresCS[i].value = false;     // back off
            while (turn != i)   // busy wait
                Thread.currentThread().yield();
            desiresCS[i].value = true;
        }
    }
}
public void finishedInCS(int i) {           // postprotocol
    desiresCS[i].value = false;
    turn = other(i);
}
```

It enforces mutual exclusion, does not deadlock (both threads stuck in their busy waiting loops), and does not permit starvation in the absence of contention. But it does allow starvation in the presence of contention (Exercise 6).

Many years later in 1981, Peterson discovered a complete working solution, Class 3.16, that is also shorter and simpler than Dekker's ([15], Section 4.9), ([34], Section 6.2.1.3), ([36], Section 4.2), ([41], Section 2.2.3), ([43], Section 2.2.3). The shared variable last records which thread last tried to enter its critical section. This thread is delayed if both try to enter at about the same time. In contrast to Dekker's solution, starvation in the presence of contention is prevented (Exercise 6).

```
public void wantToEnterCS(int i) {          // preprotocol
    desiresCS[i].value = true;
    last = i;
    while (desiresCS[other(i)].value && last == i) // busy wait
        Thread.currentThread().yield();
}
public void finishedInCS(int i) {           // postprotocol
    desiresCS[i].value = false;
}
```

3.5.2   Software Solution for More than Two Threads

If there are more than two threads, none of the above algorithms works without extensive and complicated modifications. Lamport's bakery algorithm ([6], page 39) is designed for the multiple thread situation. A thread wishing to enter its critical section computes the next ticket number and waits its turn, analogous to customers entering a bakery shop, drawing a number from the ticket dispenser on the counter, and waiting for their number to be called by the next available sales associate. Since our computer architecture has only memory load and store instructions, it does not have a special instruction to compute the next higher ticket number and hand it to the thread in one atomic action. Instead, each thread uses the maximum of all outstanding ticket numbers plus one. Two or more threads might compute the same number with this scheme, so a unique, constant, numeric identifier associated with each thread is used to break ties. This is analogous to a bakery shop with no ticket dispenser requiring each entering customer to look at all outstanding tickets to compute its own number (ties are broken by customer age, say).

For two threads, the bakery algorithm is shown in Class 3.17. It is a complete working solution, as Peterson's is.

```
class Ticket { public volatile int value = 0; }
...
private Ticket[] ticket = new Ticket[2];
for (int i = 0; i < 2; i++) ticket[i] = new Ticket();
...
public void wantToEnterCS(int i) {        // preprotocol
   ticket[i].value = 1;
   ticket[i].value =
      ticket[other(i)].value + 1;  // compute next ticket
   while (!(ticket[other(i)].value == 0
         || ticket[i].value < ticket[other(i)].value
         || (ticket[i].value == ticket[other(i)].value
        && i == 0)  // use i to break a tie
      )) /* busy wait */ Thread.currentThread().yield();
}
public void finishedInCS(int i) {        // postprotocol
   ticket[i].value = 0;
}
```

It has the property, though, that no variable is updated by more than one thread. Exercise 7 discusses the reason for the ticket[i].value = 1 assignment statement.

For an arbitrary number of threads, the bakery algorithm is shown in Class 3.18.

```
public void wantToEnterCS(int i) {        // preprotocol
   ticket[i].value = 1;
   ticket[i].value = 1 + maxx(ticket);    // compute next ticket
   for (int j = 0; j < numNodes; j++) if (j != i)
      while (!(ticket[j].value == 0
            || ticket[i].value < ticket[j].value
            || (ticket[i].value == ticket[j].value
           && i < j)  // compare i and j to break a tie
         )) /* busy wait */ Thread.currentThread().yield();
}
public void finishedInCS(int i) {        // postprotocol
   ticket[i].value = 0;
}
```

Table 3.2 summarizes the properties of the above attempts at a busy waiting software solution to the mutual exclusion problem.

| | Enforces Mutual | Does Not | Does Not | Starvation Prevention | |
Attempt	Exclusion	Deadlock	Livelock	Absence of Contention	Presence of Contention
first	yes	yes	yes	no	yes
second	no				
third	yes	no			
fourth	yes	yes	no	yes	no
Dekker's	yes	yes	yes	yes	no
Peterson's	yes	yes	yes	yes	yes
Lamport's	yes	yes	yes	yes	yes

Table 3.2: Properties of the Mutual Exclusion Software Solution Attempts.

3.5.3 Hardware Solutions

Two possible hardware solutions to the mutual exclusion problem are

```
wantToEnterCS(int i) {    // preprotocol
    disable interrupts;
}
finishedInCS(int i) {     // postprotocol
    enable interrupts;
}
```

and

```
wantToEnterCS(int i) {    // preprotocol
    lock the bus;
}
finishedInCS(int i) {     // postprotocol
    unlock the bus;
}
```

These work and do not busy wait, but it is not a good idea to allow disabling of interrupts or locking of the memory bus in user mode of the CPU. No other process or thread can execute until interrupts are reenabled or the memory bus unlocked. It is acceptable for the operating system, running in CPU kernel mode, to use these hardware techniques for mutual exclusion, for example when manipulating the ready queue in response to a clock interrupt. Interrupts are disabled or the bus locked by the operating system for only a short period of time.

Note that disabling interrupts does not work in a symmetric shared-memory multiprocessor architecture, one in which any available CPU handles interrupts. Many such shared-memory multiprocessors have a test-and-set instruction used instead. It is a single, uninterruptible, atomic, machine-language instruction

TS(*CPU-register*, *memory-address*, *value*)

that (a) retrieves the contents of the given memory address into the designated
CPU register and then (b) stores the specified value into the memory address. This
instruction is usually implemented by locking the system bus for the duration of the
two memory operations so no other CPU or thread accesses memory. We write a
Boolean function testAndSet that uses TS

```
boolean testAndSet(boolean flag) {
    register R;
    TS(R, flag, true);
    return R;
}
```

and then implement the preprotocol and postprotocol with busy waiting.

```
boolean lockFlag = false;              // shared by the threads
wantToEnterCS(int i) {                  // preprotocol
    while testAndSet(lockFlag) /* busy wait */ ;
}
finishedInCS(int i) {                   // postprotocol
    lockFlag = false;
}
```

This test-and-set solution works for any number of threads, does not deadlock,
and does not suffer from starvation in the absence of contention. However, if several
threads are concurrently executing test-and-set instructions on the same flag variable, one particular thread could repeatedly test the flag in its while loop and find
it true for an arbitrarily long period of time, starving in the presence of contention.
Note that busy waiting, in either the hardware or software solutions, consumes CPU
cycles. This is certainly wasteful on a uniprocessor; blocking the thread would be
more efficient. On a multiprocessor, busy waiting is more acceptable, particularly if
the busy waiting is expected to take less time than performing a context switch.

3.5.4   Blocking Solutions

To avoid busy waiting and wasting CPU cycles in a solution to the mutual exclusion
problem, we could try adding two system calls (see Section 1.1.3) to the operating
system, delay() and wakeup(). A thread calling delay() is removed from the ready
queue and placed at the end of a queue of delayed threads; its state is changed from
running to blocked. When a thread calls wakeup(), the thread at the head of the
delay queue, if any, is moved back to the ready queue and its state is changed to
runnable. If the delay queue is empty, a wakeup() has no effect. Note that there
is no busy waiting and no wasting of CPU cycles by threads waiting for a wakeup
signal.

Unfortunately, this scheme is still subject to race conditions. Suppose one thread
contains code like this,

```
while (condition) delay();
```

and another thread contains a `wakeup()`. Consider the machine language instructions into which the `while` loop is compiled. Suppose the first thread loads *condition* into its accumulator, finds that it is true, then a context switch occurs before it calls `delay()`. The second thread executes and sends a wakeup signal. Because the context switch occurred too early, the first thread misses the wakeup signal intended for it. The wakeup signal is lost. Therefore, we cannot use delay/wakeup in a solution to the mutual exclusion problem. The following modification to Peterson's algorithm does not work.

```
public void wantToEnterCS(int i) {          // preprotocol
    desiresCS[i].value = true;
    last = i;
    while (desiresCS[other(i)].value && last == i) delay();
}
public void finishedInCS(int i) {           // postprotocol
    desiresCS[i].value = false;
    wakeup();
}
```

For another specific example, consider the bounded buffer producer and consumer problem, introduced in Section 3.4.1, in which the buffer has room for at most N items ([41], Section 2.2.4), ([43], Section 2.2.4). Suppose we attempt to use `delay()` and `wakeup()` to avoid busy waiting in synchronizing the two thread. In pseudocode, the producer and consumer algorithms follow.

```
int N, count = 0; // shared by the producer and consumer threads
producer() {
    while (true) {
        produceItem();
        if (count == N) delay();
        enterItem();
        count++;
        if (count == 1) wakeup();
    }
}
consumer() {
    while (true) {
        if (count == 0) delay();
        removeItem();
        count--;
        if (count == N-1) wakeup();
        consumeItem();
    }
}
```

Like the previous example, this code has a race condition and is therefore incorrect. One thread may decide to delay but miss the other thread's wakeup because of an unfortunate context switch.

As described in Section 3.1.1, Java thread objects have **suspend**, **resume**, and
yield methods. Class 3.19 is a modification of Class 3.8 that replaces busy waiting
with the delay/wakeup idea to synchronize the producer and the consumer.

```
public void deposit(double value) {
    if (buffer[putIn].occupied) {
        Thread producer = Thread.currentThread();
        buffer[putIn].thread = producer;
//              producer.yield(); // force "bad" context switch
        producer.suspend();
        buffer[putIn].thread = null;
    }
    buffer[putIn].value = value;
    buffer[putIn].occupied = true;
    Thread consumer = buffer[putIn].thread;
    putIn = (putIn + 1) % numSlots;
    if (consumer != null)
        consumer.resume();   // a consumer is waiting
}
public double fetch() {
    double value;
    if (!buffer[takeOut].occupied) {
        Thread consumer = Thread.currentThread();
        buffer[takeOut].thread = consumer;
//              consumer.yield(); // force "bad" context switch
        consumer.suspend();
        buffer[takeOut].thread = null;
    }
    value = buffer[takeOut].value;
    buffer[takeOut].occupied = false;
    Thread producer = buffer[takeOut].thread;
    takeOut = (takeOut + 1) % numSlots;
    if (producer != null)
        producer.resume();   // a producer is waiting
    return value;
}
```

If the consumer thread finds the bounded buffer empty, it saves a reference to itself
in the next buffer slot to be filled and suspends itself. When the producer thread fills
the slot, it resumes the consumer thread. If the producer finds the bounded buffer
full, it suspends itself in a similar manner for later resumption by the consumer. If
a context switch occurs at the "right" place, shown by the commented-out call to
yield() in the **fetch** method, it is possible for the consumer to find the bounded
buffer empty, but before suspending itself, the producer tries to resume it. Deadlock
occurs later when the producer fills the bounded buffer. We need to store these
wakeup signals so they are not lost. This is the subject of the next chapter.

Summary

Many terms and concepts related to concurrent programming are covered in this chapter. Race conditions and lost updates are possible when threads interleave the actions they perform on shared data. Deadlock and starvation are also of concern. The programmer must identify the critical sections of code in each thread and bracket those critical sections with calls to an entry and exit protocol to enforce mutual exclusion. We examined several implementations of an entry/exit protocol. The busy waiting algorithms of Peterson, Dekker, and Lamport use no special or privileged instructions. Hardware implementations disable interrupts, lock the bus, or use the test-and-set instruction in a busy waiting loop. An attempt at a blocking implementation with delay and wakeup did not work. Executing critical sections with mutual exclusion is not the only situation in which threads need to synchronize or coordinate their activities. We looked at the bounded buffer producer and consumer problem and saw a busy waiting solution. However, our blocking implementation did not work.

We learned how to start additional threads in a Java program. Each thread is in one of several states, such as running, runnable, blocked, or suspended. Various events cause a transition from one state to another. Java threads are time sliced on Windows 95/NT but not on Solaris 2.x. Each Java thread has a priority; the scheduler ensures that the highest priority thread is always running on the CPU. The `volatile` modifier in a variable declaration tells the compiler the variable is shared by several threads and inhibits code optimizations such as register caching of the variable. The advantages of multiple threads in the design and implementation of a program were illustrated with a Java example. The program's computational output is displayed in two windows, and its execution is controlled with buttons in each window.

3.6 Exercises

1. **Why Use Threads?** Rewrite Program 3.3 so that is has only one thread, in other words, as a purely sequential program. Is your program more or less complicated than the original multithreaded version?

2. **Race Conditions.** Identify the race condition in Program 3.5. Draw a diagram showing side-by-side the step-by-step interleaved execution of the two threads when the race condition occurs and one of the updates gets lost.

Store Program 3.5 in a file named `race.java`. Compile and run the program with the usual two commands:

```
javac race.java
java RaceTwoThreads
java RaceTwoThreads -M 2000
```

The first run produces the correct output on a Windows 95/NT platform because the normal context switch interval (time between context switches, also called the time quantum) in the Java run-time system (JVM) is long enough so that the first thread finishes before the second thread starts and the statements of the two threads are not interleaved. In the second run, the method **fn** is called 2000 times rather than 10. Explain what happens on Windows 95/NT. Try some other values between 10 and 2000, and see if you can figure out approximately what the default Java thread time slice is under Windows 95/NT.

On a Solaris 2.x platform, the output of both runs is correct because there is no time slicing.

Create a **Scheduler** object (Library Class 3.2) that introduces 10 millisecond time slicing by removing the line

```
if (timeSlicingEnsured)
    ensureTimeSlicing(50); // so threads share CPU
```

and inserting the line

```
new Scheduler(10); // start the Scheduler thread
```

before creating the racing threads. Now compile and run with these commands instead:

```
javac race.java
java RaceTwoThreads -M 200
java RaceTwoThreads -M 1000
```

The 10 argument to **Scheduler** causes a thread context switch every 10 milliseconds (both Solaris 2.x and Windows 95/NT). What is the output of the program this time? Explain exactly how this output happens and compare this run of the program to the previous one for your platform. When **fn** is called 1000 times, why do you think **RaceTwoThreads** takes longer to run with a 10 millisecond time quantum than with the default time quantum on Windows 95/NT or no time slicing on Solaris?

On a Solaris platform, experimentally determine the largest time slice value passed to the **Scheduler** constructor that consistently causes incorrect output as a result of a race condition for M equal to 1000. On either platform, use a time slice of 10 milliseconds and experimentally determine the smallest value of M that consistently causes incorrect output due to a race condition.

3. **Thread Interleavings.** One thread calls method **d** and another thread calls method **e**. Consider all possible interleavings and determine all possible return values of **e()**.

```
class C {
    static int w = 0;
    static void d() { w = 3;  w = 4; }
    static int e() { int z = w;  z += 2*w;  return z; }
}
```

4. **Thread Interleavings.** Two threads call method `swap` at about the same time. Consider all possible interleavings and determine all possible resulting values for the data fields `a` and `b`.

```
class Swap {
   private volatile int a = 17, b = 42;
   public void swap() { int temp = a;  a = b;  b = temp; }
}
```

Does removing the `volatile` modifier change your answer?

5. **Busy Waiting Producers and Consumers.** Identify the race condition(s) that could occur in Class 3.8 if there were more than one producer and/or consumer thread.

6. **The Software Attempts at Mutual Exclusion.** Show how one thread might starve in the absence of contention in the first attempt. Show how livelock is possible in the fourth attempt. Show how starvation in the presence of contention might occur in Dekker's solution. Hint ([25], page 25): Suppose thread T_0 executes on a fast CPU and thread T_1 on a slow CPU. T_0 is in its critical section and T_1 is busy waiting in its `while (turn != i)` loop. What happens if T_0 leaves its critical section, sets `turn` to one, and then tries to enter its critical section again before T_1 can set its `desiresCS` flag to true?

Show how Peterson's code is a complete solution in that it enforces mutual exclusion, does not let the threads get stuck in their busy waiting loops, does not allow livelock, and does not allow either kind of starvation.

Explain why the `volatile` modifier (see Section 3.4.1) is necessary for the third attempt, Class 3.13, to enforce mutual exclusion.

Suppose we switch the order of the first two statements of Class 3.16, Peterson's software busy waiting solution to the mutual exclusion problem for two threads:

```
last = i;
desiresCS[i].value = true;
while (desiresCS[other(i)].value && last == i) /* busy wait */ ;
```

Is mutual exclusion still enforced or is there a possible sequence of events in which the two threads are simultaneously in their critical sections? Recall that context switches occur at arbitrary times if the two threads are sharing the CPU. If the two threads have dedicated CPUs, the relative speeds of the CPUs may be different.

7. **Lamport's Bakery Algorithm.** Identify the race condition in Class 3.17 if the assignment statement `ticket[i].value = 1` is deleted. Draw a diagram showing side-by-side the step-by-step interleaved execution of the two threads when the race condition occurs. Identify the race condition in Class 3.18 if the same assignment statement is deleted. Draw a similar diagram.

Show how the two-thread version enforces mutual exclusion, does not let either
thread get stuck in its busy waiting loop, does not livelock, and does not allow
either kind of starvation. Do the same thing for the N-thread version.

8. **Suspend/Resume Producer and Consumer.** Uncomment the yield() calls
in Class 3.19 and test it with Program 3.9 (invoke ensureTimeSlicing() in the
main method). No race conditions occur; the producer and consumer threads do
not deadlock. Why?

Now replace the nap(napping) statements in the producer and consumer run methods of Program 3.9 with

```
long total = 0;
for (int i = 0; i < 500*napping; i++) total += i;
```

and retest Class 3.19. Deadlock now occurs in at least some of the runs. Why?

Chapter 4

Semaphores

The study of *semaphores* is important in concurrent programming and operating systems because semaphores are used to protect and control access to critical sections and provide a mechanism for thread synchronization. In this chapter, we define binary and counting semaphores and look at how they are implemented at the user level and the operating systems level. We will see that Java synchronized blocks are used as binary semaphores in certain situations. For more general use, binary and counting semaphores are implemented with two classes. Semaphore solutions to four classic synchronization problems, the bounded buffer, the dining philosophers, the sleeping barber, and the readers and writers, are shown. The chapter concludes with an animation example of the dining philosophers, using the `XtangoAnimator` class from Section 2.7. After reading this chapter, you will be able to write multithreaded Java programs that use binary and counting semaphores for mutual exclusion and event synchronization.

4.1   Definitions and Implementation

A general or *counting* semaphore ([15], Section 4.12), ([34], Section 6.4), ([36], Section 4.4), ([41], Section 2.2.5), ([43], Section 2.2.5) is created from an abstract data type that has only two access operations: P and V. Dijkstra [16] designed semaphores in the 1960s as a tool to solve synchronization problems in multithreaded programs. He chose the names P and V from the Dutch words *passeren* (to pass) and *vrygeven* (to release). Tanenbaum calls them *down* and *up*, respectively, in [41, 43]. A semaphore is usually thought of more informally as a special kind of integer variable that is accessed with only these two operations. In object-oriented terms, a semaphore is an object S created from a class that has a private integer data field and two public access methods: P and V. If the integer value of a semaphore S is positive, a thread invoking $P(S)$ decrements S in an atomic action; otherwise the thread waits. If a thread invokes $V(S)$ and no thread is waiting at a $P(S)$, then the value of S is incremented atomically; otherwise one waiting thread is released and allowed to continue past its $P(S)$. The released thread is not necessarily the one that waited the longest. A (strict) *binary* semaphore is limited to the values 0 and 1. In particular, a *V* operation applied to a binary semaphore whose value is 1 has no effect.

The *P* and *V* operations must be done atomically to avoid race conditions. Suppose we have a semaphore *S* whose current value is 1. We must prevent two threads from checking the value of *S* at about the same time and decrementing it to 0. One of the threads should decrement to 0 and the other wait. Similarly, we must prevent lost updates; that is, two threads incrementing a semaphore from 1 to 2 at about the same time. The resulting value should be 3.

Semaphores are synchronization tools that allow threads to wait for an event to occur. A binary semaphore whose initial value is 1 solves the critical section mutual exclusion problem described in Chapter 3.

```
shared binary semaphore mutex with initial value 1
in each thread:
    P(mutex);                              // preprotocol
        critical section;
    V(mutex);                              // postprotocol
```

A binary semaphore also saves a wakeup signal so it is not lost if the delay queue is empty (Section 3.5.4).

```
int N, count = 0;               // shared by producer and consumer
semaphore S = 0, mutex = 1;    // shared binary semaphores
producer() {
    while (true) {
        produceItem();
        if (count == N) P(S);          // delay
        enterItem();
        P(mutex); count++; V(mutex);
        if (count == 1) V(S);          // wakeup
    }
}
consumer() {
    while (true) {
        if (count == 0) P(S);          // delay
        removeItem();
        P(mutex); count--; V(mutex);
        if (count == N-1) V(S);        // wakeup
        consumeItem();
    }
}
```

A counting semaphore can represent the number of resource units currently available for allocation. A thread invokes P(S) to request a resource unit and V(S) to return the unit to the allocation pool.

```
shared counting semaphore S
```

initialized to the total number of resource units

in each thread:

```
P(S);                                    // request a resource unit
     use the resource unit;
V(S);                                    // release the resource unit
```

Resource units are allocated until exhausted; additional threads requesting a unit must wait until one is released. Dijkstra and his research group used semaphores in the implementation of an operating system to synchronize device drivers and interrupts. A device driver sends a command to a device, then uses P to block until the device signals completion of the command with an interrupt. The interrupt handler for the device uses V to awaken the driver when the device generates the interrupt.

Semaphores can be implemented at the user level — that is, outside the operating system — with busy waiting. To make the semaphore operations atomic, one of the software busy waiting solutions to the mutual exclusion problem, say the bakery algorithm from Section 3.5.2, is used.

```
class Semaphore {         // counting semaphore
    private int value;
    public Semaphore() { value = 0; }
    public Semaphore(int initial) { value = initial; }
    public void P() {
        wantToEnterCS();
        while (value == 0) { finishedInCS(); wantToEnterCS(); }
        value--;
        finishedInCS();
    }
    public void V() {
        wantToEnterCS();
        value++;
        finishedInCS();
    }
}
```

However, busy waiting consumes CPU cycles. If we remove a thread waiting inside $P(S)$ from the ready queue and change its state from runnable to blocked, we avoid wasting CPU cycles. This requires operating system assistance, or in the case of Java, assistance from the JVM. If semaphores are implemented in the operating system, P and V are system calls.

counting semaphore S

$P(S)$: trap to the kernel

　　　　disable interrupts (so semaphore access is atomic)

　　　　if $S > 0$ then $S = S - 1$

　　　　else { queue the thread on S, change its state to blocked,

　　　　　　　and schedule another thread }

enable interrupts

return

$V(S)$: trap to the kernel

disable interrupts

if $S == 0$ and queue on S is not empty then

{ pick a thread from the queue on S

and change its state from blocked to ready }

else $S = S + 1$

enable interrupts

return

Note the similarities and differences between this implementation of semaphores and the delay/wakeup system calls of Section 3.5.4. Both are blocking (no busy waiting) and involve operating system assistance. However, a counting semaphore saves all wakeup signals ("up" or V) sent to it when its queue of waiting threads is empty. Even a (strict) binary semaphore saves one wakeup signal sent to it when its queue is empty.

If we have a shared-memory multiprocessor instead of a uniprocessor, disabling interrupts to access a semaphore atomically is not sufficient since disabling interrupts on one processor has no effect on another processor. It is necessary to lock the memory bus or use a busy waiting loop inside the operating system implemented with a test-and-set or similar instruction.

An alternate implementation of the semaphore P and V system calls is as follows. Here the internal value of the counting semaphore S is allowed to be negative; when this happens, the absolute value of S is equal to the number of threads blocked on S. This implementation also uses a lock variable and the test-and-set instruction TS (Section 3.5.3) on a shared-memory multiprocessor machine.

counting semaphore S

$P(S)$: trap to the kernel

while $TS(S.lock)$ noop, i.e., busy wait

$S.value = S.value - 1$

if $S.value < 0$ then { queue the thread on S,

change its state to blocked,

and schedule another thread }

$S.lock = false$

return

$V(S)$: trap to the kernel

while $TS(S.lock)$ noop, i.e., busy wait

$S.value = S.value + 1$

if $S.value <= 0$ then { pick a thread from the queue on S

and change its state from blocked to ready }

$S.lock = false$

return

4.2 Java Semaphores

Explicit binary and counting semaphores are not present in Java; however, classes for them are very easily implemented with the synchronization tools Java does have, described in Chapter 5 on monitors. The classes `BinarySemaphore` and `CountingSemaphore` are instantiated for each binary and counting semaphore needed in a program. They are part of this book's `Synchronization` package. We use these classes in the example programs in the sections that follow but defer examining their implementations until Chapter 5. Most books on operating systems describe semaphores first, followed by monitors, reflecting the historical order of development of these tools. We follow this order. Java provides monitors as the built-in primitive, requiring the examples in this book to use semaphores derived from Java monitors.

We look first at (strict) binary semaphores, those that only ever take on the values 0 and 1 and act like locks. Then we look at (general) counting semaphores. Java supports object locking with the synchronized block construct. A Java object lock is equivalent to a binary semaphore with initial value 1 that must be unlocked by the locking thread. We call a synchronized block an implicit binary semaphore.

4.2.1 Binary Semaphores

Semaphores used for mutual exclusion are initialized to 1 and take on only two values: 1 when the critical section is free, and 0 when the critical section is in use. A (strict) binary semaphore is limited to these two values in the sense that a V operation on a binary semaphore with the value 1 has no effect. Counting semaphores can be used as binary semaphores as long as the programmer is careful to avoid a V on a semaphore whose value is 1 (giving the semaphore a nonbinary value of 2).

Binary semaphores are also called mutual exclusion ("mutex") locks. There are two operations on these locks: lock (corresponds to P) and unlock (corresponds to V). Unlocking an unlocked lock has no effect. The concept of a lock is sometimes refined to include the idea that only the holder of a lock is allowed to release it. A lock is often used to access a particular resource exclusively, so naturally only the lock holder should release the resource. On the other hand, a binary semaphore is sometimes used to block a thread until some event caused by another thread has occurred.

```
shared binary semaphore S
in one thread:
    P(S);
in another thread:
    V(S);
```

Consequently, binary semaphores do not have the restriction that only the thread that did the "down" on the binary semaphore may do the "up."

Each Java object has a lock. This lock can be used as an implicit binary semaphore in a block of code **synchronized** on the object. To enter the block, a thread must acquire the object's lock; the thread waits or blocks if the object's lock is held by some other thread. When the thread exits the block, it releases the object's lock. Only one thread at a time is allowed to hold an object's lock. These locks are implemented in the JVM. If `obj` is a reference to some object, then `obj` is used as an implicit binary semaphore in the following way.

```
synchronized (obj) {
    block of code, e.g., critical section;
}
```

Any object can be used in a synchronized block as an implicit binary semaphore.

If all the critical sections of code needing mutual exclusion synchronization are in the methods of a single object, then the synchronized blocks use `this`, a reference to that object, for locking.

```
synchronized (this) {...}
```

Furthermore, if the entire body of a method is a synchronized block on `this`,

```
type method(...) {
    synchronized (this) {
        critical section;
    }
}
```

the Java compiler allows the programmer to use the abbreviation

```
synchronized type method(...) {
    critical section;
}
```

If the critical sections requiring mutual exclusion synchronization are spread over several different classes or several different objects created from one class, then a common object for the synchronized blocks must be created outside the classes and passed to their constructors.

We eliminate the race condition in Program 3.5 very easily with synchronized blocks acting as binary semaphores, as shown in Program 4.1.

```
private Object mutex = null;
...
mutex = this; // in the constructor
...
public void run() {
    for (int m = 1; m <= M; m++)
        synchronized (mutex) {
            sum = fn(sum, m);
        }
}
```

The object `mutex` is used as an implicit binary semaphore to prevent any interleaving of the `fn` method calls. Since both threads are executing in one `Racer` object, it is used as the object the implicit binary semaphore locks. Hence `this` is assigned to `mutex` in the `Racer` constructor instead of creating another object. In an exercise, you are asked to do the same things (compile and run several different ways) with this example program that you were asked to do with Program 3.5. An implicit binary semaphore also prevents the race condition in Program 3.6, as shown in Program 4.2.

```
class ATM {...
    synchronized (mutex) {
        savingsAccount[fromAccount] -= amount;
        savingsAccount[toAccount] += amount;
    }
}
class Auditor {...
    synchronized (mutex) {
        for (int i = 0; i < numAccounts; i++)
            total += savingsAccount[i];
    }
}
```

Notice that no variables are declared `volatile` in Programs 4.1 and 4.2. Compiler optimizations, such as register caching, need not be inhibited since only one thread at a time can read-update-write the shared variables. Also, the values of shared variables are guaranteed to be written back to shared memory when a synchronized block is exited and the lock on the object released ([21], Chapter 17).

Binary semaphores are used for *mutual exclusion synchronization* and for *condition synchronization*. Program 4.1 is an example of the former: using semaphores to enforce mutual exclusion and control access to critical sections. Program 4.3 in the next section is an example of the latter: using binary semaphores to block threads until some condition becomes true or some event occurs.

```
shared binary semaphore S
in one thread:
    if (!condition) P(S);
in another thread:
    V(S);
```

In the following sections we will see more examples of both these uses of semaphores.

A Java synchronized block on an object acts as a binary semaphore with initial value 1; only the thread that obtains the object's lock ever releases it. This is adequate for mutual exclusion synchronization but makes condition synchronization difficult. For this, a binary semaphore needs an initial value of 0 and/or needs to be released by a thread other than the acquiring one. To handle condition synchronization, a `BinarySemaphore` class was designed with Java's built-in monitors and placed in the `Synchronization` package. The class allows initialization to either

1 or 0. Its implementation and the implementation of counting semaphores are
described in Chapter 5.

4.2.2   Counting Semaphores

As mentioned, counting semaphores are implemented in this book's Synchronization package with the class CountingSemaphore, from which the counting semaphores in a program are constructed and initialized. Binary semaphores are also
implemented in the class BinarySemaphore, from which explicit binary semaphores
are constructed and initialized to 0 or 1. The class MyObject, shown in Library
Class 3.1, contains some methods that allow the use of P(S) and V(S), instead of
S.P() and S.V(), in the methods of classes that extend MyObject.

Program 4.3 starts three threads, Pa, Pb, and Pc. Thread Pa repeatedly prints the
letter "A," Pb the letter "B," and Pc the letter "C." Utilizing two binary semaphores
and one counting semaphore, the threads are synchronized so their output satisfies
the following three conditions.

1. A "B" must be output before any "C's" are output.

2. "B's" and "C's" must alternate in the output string, that is, after the first
   "B" is output, another "B" cannot be output until a "C" is output. Similarly
   once a "C" is output, another "C" cannot be output until a "B" is output.

3. The total number of "B's" and "C's" that have been output at any given point
   in the output string cannot exceed the number of "A's" that have been output
   up to that point.

Instead of using synchronized blocks as implicit binary semaphores, explicit binary
semaphores are constructed since one of them needs to be initialized to 0. The three
threads are blocked from further execution until the required conditions for each are
met, an example of condition synchronization.

```
class ABCs extends MyObject {
        // since these semaphores are static,
        // subclasses Pa, Pb, and Pc share them
    protected static final BinarySemaphore B
        = new BinarySemaphore(0);
    protected static final BinarySemaphore C
        = new BinarySemaphore(1);
    protected static final CountingSemaphore sum
        = new CountingSemaphore(0);
    ...
}
class Pa extends ABCs implements Runnable {
    public void run () {
        while (true) { nap(1+(int)(random(500)));
            System.out.print("A"); System.out.flush();
```

```
                V(sum);
            }
        }
    }
    class Pb extends ABCs implements Runnable {
        public void run () {
            while (true) { nap(1+(int)(random(800)));
                P(C); P(sum);
                System.out.print("B"); System.out.flush();
                V(B);
            }
        }
    }
    class Pc extends ABCs implements Runnable {
        public void run () {
            while (true) { nap(1+(int)(random(800)));
                P(B); P(sum);
                System.out.print("C"); System.out.flush();
                V(C);
            }
        }
    }
}
```

The B and C binary semaphores are used to force the Pb and Pc threads to alternate their character printing. The sum counting semaphore tracks the number of characters printed by the Pa thread. Since Pb and Pc must perform P(sum) before printing, the total number of characters they print cannot exceed the number printed by Pa.

4.3 Classical Operating Systems Problems

Most operating systems textbooks ([15], Chapters 4 and 5), ([34], Section 6.5), ([36], Sections 4.4 and 5.5), ([41], Sections 2.2 and 2.3), ([43], Sections 2.2 and 2.3) discuss the following so-called classical synchronization problems: the *bounded buffer producer and consumer*, the *sleeping barber*, the *dining philosophers*, and the database *readers and writers*.

In the bounded buffer problem, a buffer with a finite number of slots holds items made by the producer thread. The buffer is usually implemented with a circular array (the first and last array components are conceptually contiguous) or circular linked list. See Figure 4.1. The consumer thread uses the items by accessing a slot and removing its item. The synchronization problems are to suspend the producer when the buffer is full, to suspend the consumer when the buffer is empty, and to make sure that only one thread at a time manipulates a buffer slot so there are no race conditions, lost updates, or meaningless bits read from a partially written buffer slot.

The sleeping barber problem is to synchronize the barber and customers in a

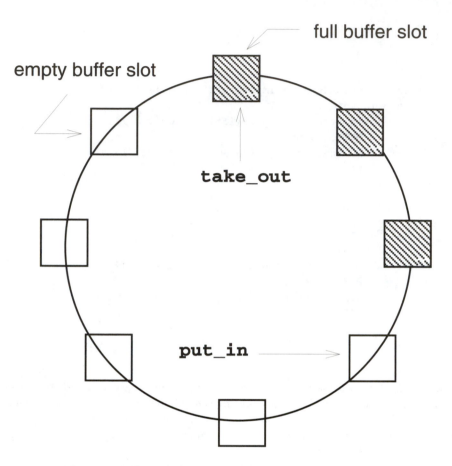

Figure 4.1: Bounded Buffer Producers and Consumers.

barber shop. The shop has a barber, a barber chair, and a waiting room with several chairs, as shown in Figure 4.2. When the barber finishes cutting a customer's hair, the barber fetches another customer from the waiting room if there is a customer or stands by the barber chair and daydreams if the waiting room is empty. Customers who need a haircut enter the waiting room. If the waiting room is full, the customer comes back later. If the barber is busy but there is a waiting room chair available, the customer takes a seat. If the waiting room is empty and the barber is daydreaming, the customer sits in the barber chair and wakes the barber.

The dining philosophers problem involves five philosophers sitting at a round table with five forks interleaved between them. A bowl of spaghetti sits in the center of the table, as shown in Figure 4.3. Philosophers think for a while, become hungry, and try to eat. After eating for a while, a philosopher is ready to think again and the cycle repeats. A philosopher needs both forks to eat, the one on its right and the one on its left. Sometimes the problem is presented with chop sticks

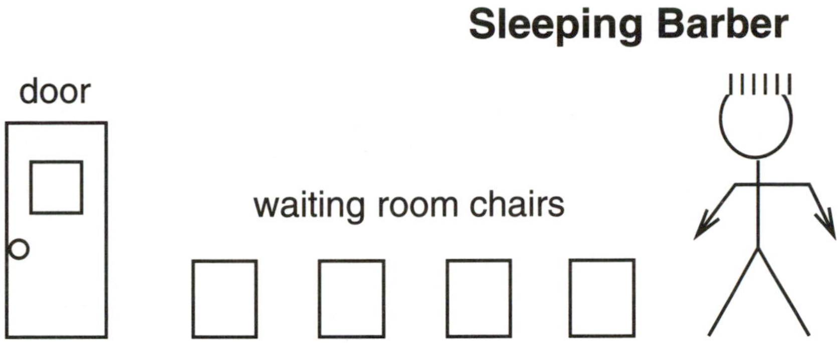

Sleeping Barber

door

waiting room chairs

Figure 4.2: Sleeping Barber.

instead of forks to emphasize that a philosopher needs both at the same time to eat. Only one philosopher at a time can use a fork. The synchronization problem is to coordinate the use of the forks so that only one philosopher at a time uses a fork, there is no deadlock (each philosopher holding a fork and refusing to relinquish it), there is *maximal parallelism* (a hungry philosopher eats if its forks are not being used by other philosophers to eat), and no philosopher starves (as a result of its neighbors collaborating).

In the readers and writers problem, readers may read a database simultaneously as long as no writer writes, but only one writer at a time may write (if there are no active readers). See Figure 4.4. The synchronization problem is to coordinate the threads so that readers may read simultaneously if no writer is writing and writers write one at a time if no readers are reading. Another synchronization issue is to prevent starvation: a continual stream of incoming readers preventing writer access and vice versa.

4.4 Semaphore Solutions

This section presents solutions to the classical operating systems synchronization problems using the binary and counting semaphore classes, `BinarySemaphore` and `CountingSemaphore`.

4.4.1 The Bounded Buffer Producer and Consumer

Class 4.4, used with Program 3.9, solves the bounded buffer producer and consumer problem with semaphores.

```
public void deposit(double value) {
   P(spaces);
   buffer[putIn] = value;
   putIn = (putIn + 1) % numSlots;
   P(mutex);
```

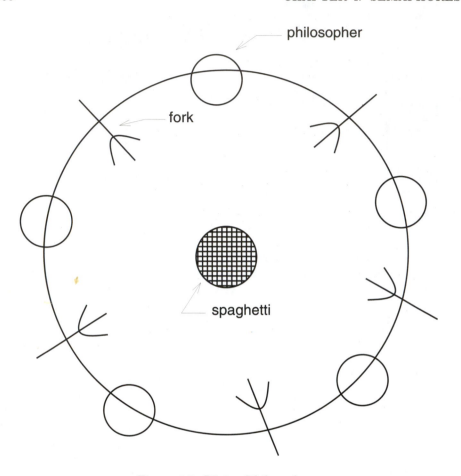

Figure 4.3: Dining Philosophers.

```
    count++;
    V(mutex);
    V(elements);
}
public double fetch() {
    double value;
    P(elements);
    value = buffer[takeOut];
    takeOut = (takeOut + 1) % numSlots;
    P(mutex);
    count--;
    V(mutex);
    V(spaces);
    return value;
```

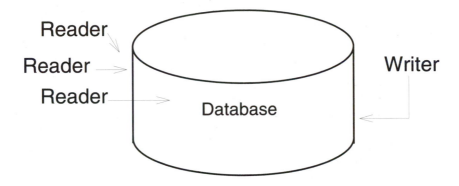

Figure 4.4: Database Readers and Writers.

```
}
```

The bounded buffer code is a direct translation into Java of the classical semaphore solution presented in many operating systems textbooks, such as ([43], page 67). There is one producer thread and one consumer thread. Each one sleeps for a random amount of time, then tries to access the buffer. Program 3.1 shows how to change Program 3.9 to have multiple producer and consumer threads (see Exercise 2).

In this program, the binary semaphore `mutex` is used to synchronize access to the shared variable `count` in critical section code where `count` is updated. This semaphore is used for mutual exclusion synchronization. The other two semaphores, `elements` and `spaces`, are used to synchronize the producer and consumer threads so the producer does not put something into a full buffer and the consumer does not take something from an empty buffer; the former semaphore is initialized to 0 and the latter to `numSlots`, the capacity of the bounded buffer. These counting semaphores are used for condition synchronization, also called *event synchronization*. There are two sample runs included in Class 4.4. In the first the producer gets ahead of the consumer, fills up the buffer, and blocks until the consumer frees a slot. In the second the consumer gets ahead of the producer and blocks.

To illustrate the use of a Java linked list, we change the program somewhat and implement an unbounded buffer, shown in Class 4.5, used with Program 4.6.

```
class QueueItem { double value; QueueItem nextItem;
    QueueItem(double value) { this.value = value; }
}
...
public void deposit(double value)
        throws CorruptedQueueException {
    P(mutex);
    QueueItem oldTail = null;
    QueueItem newOne = new QueueItem(value);
    if (tail == null) { // add to an empty queue
        if (head != null) throw new CorruptedQueueException();
```

```
      else {
          head = newOne; tail = newOne;
      }
   } else {                  // add to end of queue
      oldTail = tail; tail = newOne;
      oldTail.nextItem = newOne;
   }
   count++;
   V(mutex);
   V(elements);
}
public double fetch() throws CorruptedQueueException {
   double value;
   QueueItem oldOne = null;
   P(elements);
   P(mutex);
   if (head == null && tail == null)
          // elements semaphore should prevent this
      throw new CorruptedQueueException();
   else if (head != null && tail != null) {
      if (head == tail) { // dequeue from a singleton queue
          oldOne = head;
          head = null; tail = null;
      } else {                  // dequeue from beginning of queue
          oldOne = head;
          head = oldOne.nextItem;
      }
      count--;
   } else throw new CorruptedQueueException();
   value = oldOne.value;
   V(mutex);
   return value;
}
```

Storage for a new buffer element is allocated with new. The semaphore elements is used to block a consumer thread if the buffer is empty. This program has multiple producer and multiple consumer threads. The single binary semaphore mutex is used to prevent race conditions on the linked list (see Program 3.7): two producers trying to add an element at the same time, two consumers trying to remove an element at the same time, or a producer and a consumer trying to manipulate a single element list at the same time. Class 4.5 shows how to do thread-safe linked lists in Java; however, the linked list code is not often needed because of the versatile java.util.Vector class.

4.4.2 Using Bounded Buffers

Bounded buffers are useful for many things, such as connecting a collection of threads in a pipeline. If a sequence of computations can each be broken into several parts, each part taking about the same amount of time, then the sequence of computations can be performed in an assembly line, conveyor belt, or pipeline fashion. Each part is handled by its own thread. If a CPU is dedicated to each thread, then the computation is performed in parallel.

The same basic idea is used in the vector or pipeline units of the Cray architecture. Adding two floating-point vectors is a sequence of computations,

```
for (int i = 0; i < C.length; i++) C[i] = A[i] + B[i];
```

one floating-point addition operation for each value of i. Each addition operation is broken into several parts or suboperations, such as compare the exponents, align the mantissas, add the mantissas, and normalize the result. A vector unit is built from hardware circuits for each suboperation, connected together in a pipeline. Each suboperation is performed on the pairs of vector components in an assembly line fashion as the pairs stream through the vector unit.

Bounded buffers are used to implement pipelining at the software level. Each thread in the pipeline inputs an item, performs some work on the item, and outputs its result. Each thread (except the first) reads from a bounded buffer and each thread (except the last) writes to another bounded buffer. The bounded buffers even out the flow of items through the pipeline if some threads take more or less time to perform their work than the others.

Program 4.7 is a software pipeline example. Three (contrived) operations or steps are performed by three threads on a sequence of random floating-point numbers: take the square root, compute the trigonometric sine, and square the result. The three threads, A, B, and C, use two bounded buffers to implement the communication of intermediate results from A to B and from B to C.

```
public void run() {    // thread A
    double work;
    for (int i = 0; i < limit; i++) {
        work = random();
        System.out.println("A: work " + i + " =" + work);
        work = Math.sqrt(work);        nap(1+(int)random(2000));
        ABbb.deposit(work);
    }
}
public void run() {    // thread B
    double work;
    for (int i = 0; i < limit; i++) {
        work = ABbb.fetch();
        work = Math.sin(work);        nap(1+(int)random(2000));
        System.out.println("      B: work " + i + " =" + work);
        BCbb.deposit(work);
```

```
      }
  }
  public void run() {    // thread C
     double work;
     for (int i = 0; i < limit; i++) {
        work = BCbb.fetch();
        work = work * work;        nap(1+(int)random(2000));
        System.out.println
           ("                C: work " + i + " =" + work);
     }
  }
```

Two bounded buffer objects are created from Class 4.4. The first thread creates the next number in the sequence, takes its square root, and sends the result to the second thread. The second and third threads perform the other two steps. Each thread uses a random **nap** in its computational step to simulate a variable processing time. A bounded buffer holds intermediate results if its depositing thread gets ahead of its fetching thread.

4.4.3   The Sleeping Barber

Program 4.8 solves the sleeping barber problem. It is a direct translation into Java of the C-like solution that appears in ([43], page 82). The following pseudocode shows the algorithm contained in the complete Java program.

```
binary semaphore mutex = 1;
counting semaphore customers = 0, cutting = 0, barber = 0;
int waiting = 0;
...
wantToCut() {                       // barber
   while (true) {
      P(customers);        // wait for or get next customer
      P(mutex);
      waiting--;
      V(barber);          // allow customer to continue
      V(mutex);
      P(cutting);          // cut hair
   }
}
wantHairCut(int i) {        // customer
   while (true) {
      P(mutex);                     // check waiting room
      if (waiting < numChairs) {
         waiting++;
         V(customers);      // take a seat
         V(mutex);
```

```
            P(barber);        // wait for barber
            V(cutting);       // get hair cut
        } else V(mutex);
    }
}
```

The barber waits for the next customer on the counting semaphore `customers`, then decrements the count of waiting customers using the mutual exclusion binary semaphore `mutex`. The barber then signals the counting semaphore `barber`, allowing the next customer into the barber chair for a haircut. A customer who needs a haircut accesses the count of waiting customers and increments the count if there is a free waiting room chair. After entering the waiting room, a customer signals the semaphore `customers`, which wakes a daydreaming barber, and then waits for the barber on the semaphore `barber`. The customer determines how long the hair cut lasts and releases the barber with the `cutting` semaphore.

This example nicely illustrates the use of semaphores for both mutual exclusion and condition synchronization of threads. The customers and barber use semaphores to control each other's flow through the barber shop. This interaction of the customers and barber is a good example of a *client-server* relationship. The customer and the barber *rendezvous* to interact: each waits at a certain point in its code for the other to arrive. We return to these concepts in Chapter 6. Despite its contrived appearance, this problem succinctly characterizes some of the synchronization problems that occur in many real-world multithreaded applications. You are asked to extend the sleeping barber algorithm for multiple barbers in Exercise 4.

4.4.4   The Dining Philosophers

Class 4.9 (used with Program 4.10) solves the dining philosophers problem with semaphores and a *central server* object encapsulating the states of the philosophers.

```
state = new int[numPhils];
for (int i = 0; i < numPhils; i++) state[i] = THINKING;
self = new BinarySemaphore[numPhils];
for (int i = 0; i < numPhils; i++)
    self[i] = new BinarySemaphore(0);
mutex = new BinarySemaphore(1);
...
public void takeForks(int i) {
    P(mutex);
    state[i] = HUNGRY;
    test(i);
    V(mutex);
    P(self[i]);
}
public void putForks(int i) {
    P(mutex);
```

```
        state[i] = THINKING;
        test(left(i));
        test(right(i));
        V(mutex);
    }
    private void test(int k) {
        if (state[left(k)] != EATING && state[right(k)] != EATING
                && state[k] == HUNGRY) {
            state[k] = EATING;
            V(self[k]);
        }
    }
```

Again, the program is a direct translation into Java of the classical semaphore solution presented in many operating systems textbooks, such as ([43], page 78). A philosopher thinks for a random amount of time, gets hungry, then asks the DiningServer central server object for its forks. The central server checks the availability of the forks by examining the states of the hungry philosopher's two neighbors. If neither neighbor is eating, the hungry philosopher eats. Otherwise it must wait, which it does with P(self[i]). Once the philosopher obtains its two forks, it eats for a random amount of time, puts down the forks, and then repeats the cycle. Whenever a philosopher puts down its two forks, the central server checks the philosopher's two neighbors with two calls to the test method to see if either of those neighbors is hungry. If either is hungry and its two forks are available, the neighbor is unblocked with V(self[k]). Even though the dining philosophers problem looks contrived and of academic interest only, it exemplifies an important kind of synchronization problem, that of overlapping sets of resources whose use must be coordinated.

The issue of starvation is not addressed. Starvation occurs if this program is run with the following command line arguments.

```
    javac dphi.java
    java DiningPhilosophers -n5 -R300 1 100 10 1 1 100 100 1 100 1
```

You are asked to fix the starvation problem in an exercise. Stallings ([36], Problem 5.4) criticizes the solution in Class 4.9 because it allows starvation and suggests Class 4.11 as an alternative.

```
    state = new int[numPhils];
    for (int i = 0; i < numPhils; i++) state[i] = THINKING;
    fork = new BinarySemaphore[numPhils];
    for (int i = 0; i < numPhils; i++)
        fork[i] = new BinarySemaphore(1);
    room = new CountingSemaphore(numPhils-1);
    ...
    public void takeForks(int i) {
        state[i] = HUNGRY;
```

```
      P(room); P(fork[i]); P(fork[right(i)]);
      state[i] = EATING;
   }
   public void putForks(int i) {
      V(fork[i]); V(fork[right(i)]); V(room);
      state[i] = THINKING;
   }
```

Here, each fork is represented by a binary semaphore and a hungry philosopher first tries to pick up its left fork, blocking if it is in use. After obtaining its left fork, it tries to pick up its right fork. If not available, the philosopher blocks, retaining the left fork. Without the **room** counting semaphore, this version deadlocks if all philosophers get hungry at the same time and pick up their left fork. The **room** semaphore allows at most all but one of the philosophers into the room at the same time to eat, preventing deadlock. This version also does not allow two philosophers to starve the one between them by alternating their eating cycles. The hungry philosopher between them will grab its left fork as soon as it is put down.

As you will do in an exercise, it is fairly easy to prevent starvation in Class 4.9. However, Stallings' alternative, Class 4.11, has a serious flaw that is not easy to fix: it does not allow maximal parallelism. As shown in its second example run, it is possible for the philosophers (assuming they have assigned seats) to enter the room to eat in a "bad" order.

```
% java DiningPhilosophers -p8 \
     1 10000 263 10 131 10 65 10 31 10 15 10 7 10 3 10
DiningPhilosophers: numPhilosophers=8, runTime=60
Dining room limited to 7
Philosopher 0 is alive, napThink=1000, napEat=10000000
Philosopher 1 is alive, napThink=263000, napEat=10000
Philosopher 2 is alive, napThink=131000, napEat=10000
Philosopher 3 is alive, napThink=65000, napEat=10000
Philosopher 4 is alive, napThink=31000, napEat=10000
Philosopher 5 is alive, napThink=15000, napEat=10000
Philosopher 6 is alive, napThink=7000, napEat=10000
Philosopher 7 is alive, napThink=3000, napEat=10000
All Philosopher threads started
age()=110, Philosopher 0 is thinking for 910 ms
age()=110, Philosopher 1 is thinking for 246148 ms
age()=170, Philosopher 2 is thinking for 63677 ms
age()=170, Philosopher 3 is thinking for 47525 ms
age()=220, Philosopher 4 is thinking for 20629 ms
age()=220, Philosopher 5 is thinking for 7549 ms
age()=220, Philosopher 6 is thinking for 5058 ms
age()=220, Philosopher 7 is thinking for 2274 ms
age()=1040, Philosopher 0 wants to eat
age()=1040, Philosopher 0 is eating for 7382505 ms
```

```
age()=2640, Philosopher 7 wants to eat
age()=5380, Philosopher 6 wants to eat
age()=7850, Philosopher 5 wants to eat
age()=20930, Philosopher 4 wants to eat
age()=47790, Philosopher 3 wants to eat
age()=60090, time to stop the Philosophers and exit
```

The first philosopher eats, but the rest enter and pick up their left fork and block, waiting for their right fork to become available. Every other one could eat, but only one actually does. Class 4.9 does not have this flaw; that is, it allows maximal parallelism. The starvation fix suggested in Exercise 5 does not have the flaw either.

Class 4.12 shows that the room semaphore is not the only way to prevent deadlock in Class 4.11. If one philosopher is designated as "odd" and picks up the forks in reverse order from the others, then deadlock cannot occur.

```
state = new int[numPhils];
for (int i = 0; i < numPhils; i++) state[i] = THINKING;
fork = new BinarySemaphore[numPhils];
for (int i = 0; i < numPhils; i++)
    fork[i] = new BinarySemaphore(1);
...
public void takeForks(int i) {
    state[i] = HUNGRY;
    if (i > 0) { P(fork[i]); P(fork[right(i)]); }
    else       { P(fork[right(i)]); P(fork[i]); }
    state[i] = EATING;
}
public void putForks(int i) {
    V(fork[i]); V(fork[right(i)]);
    state[i] = THINKING;
}
```

This version also does not allow maximal parallelism, as shown by its second example run.

4.4.5   The Readers and Writers

Class 4.13 (used with Program 4.14) solves the readers and writers problem with semaphores, without addressing starvation.

```
private int numReaders = 0;
private BinarySemaphore mutex = new BinarySemaphore(1);
private BinarySemaphore ok = new BinarySemaphore(1);
...
public void startRead(int i) {
    P(mutex);
    numReaders++;
```

```
        if (numReaders == 1) P(ok);
        V(mutex);
    }
    public void endRead(int i) {
        P(mutex);
        numReaders--;
        if (numReaders == 0) V(ok);
        V(mutex);
    }
    public void startWrite(int i) {
        P(ok);
    }
    public void endWrite(int i) {
        V(ok);
    }
```

The program is a direct translation into Java of the classical semaphore solution presented in many operating systems textbooks, e.g., ([43], page 79). Several reader and writer threads are created, each one sleeping for a random amount of time and then trying to read or write the database by calling the `startRead` or `startWrite` method in the `Database` server object. Reader threads are allowed to read the database concurrently as long as no writer thread is writing, but writer threads must have exclusive access to the database. After reading or writing for a random amount of time, each calls `endRead` or `endWrite`. The server uses a semaphore ok to allow only reading or writing. If the database is currently being written, only the first reader to call `startRead` waits at `P(ok)`. Other readers that come along wait at `P(mutex)`. When the writer finishes, the reader blocked at `P(ok)` enters the database. Subsequent readers bypass the `P(ok)` and do not block. The readers and writers problem is of more than academic interest because it exemplifies a problem frequently encountered in the real world. Many resources, such as reservation system databases, can be accessed concurrently in a read-only fashion but must be accessed exclusively to be updated, at least on the record or file level. Sometimes the terms *shared lock* and *exclusive lock* are used to describe reader and writer access.

Starting at millisecond 1700, the sample output shows it is possible for readers to "starve" a waiting writer if enough readers continue to come along to keep the database in the concurrent read state. A reader thread is given permission to access the database if it is in the concurrent read state even though there is a waiting writer.

```
    ...
        age=1480 reader 1 has begun reading, numReaders=2
    age=1480, Reader1 reading for 963 ms
    age=1700, WRITER0 wants to write
    age=1860, Reader3 wants to read                         reader 3
        age=1860 reader 3 has begun reading, numReaders=3   starts reading
    age=1860, Reader3 reading for 1631 ms                   after writer 0
```

```
age=2190, Reader2 wants to read                    started waiting
   age=2190 reader 2 has begun reading, numReaders=4
age=2190, Reader2 reading for 1247 ms
   age=2190 reader 0 finished reading, numReaders=3
age=2190, Reader0 finished reading
age=2190, Reader0 napping for 1213 ms
   age=2470 reader 1 finished reading, numReaders=2
age=2470, Reader1 finished reading
age=2470, Reader1 napping for 1097 ms
age=2630, WRITER1 wants to write
age=3400, Reader0 wants to read
   age=3400 reader 0 has begun reading, numReaders=3
age=3400, Reader0 reading for 1920 ms
...
```

We will see in Section 5.3.4 how to prevent starvation of waiting writers.

4.5 Deadlock

Care must be taken when programming with semaphores. The following easy typing mistake leads to deadlock.

> P(S); *critical section*; P(S);

One thread is blocked forever in its critical section, and all other threads wanting to enter their critical sections are also blocked forever.

More subtle is deadlock resulting from nested critical sections or multiple resource acquisition. Suppose thread A executes the code

```
P(S);
   ...
   P(T); ... V(T);
   ...
V(S);
```

and at about the same time, thread B executes the code

```
P(T);
   ...
   P(S); ... V(S);
   ...
V(T);
```

in a program that has only two threads. Here S and T are binary semaphores (for critical sections) or counting semaphores (for resource allocation) with current values one and shared by the two threads. If the following sequence of events occurs,

A: P(S) succeeds
B: P(T) succeeds
A: blocks on P(T)
B: blocks on P(S)

the two threads are deadlocked. See standard operating systems books, such as ([15], Chapter 6), ([34], Chapter 7), ([36], Chapter 5), ([41], Chapter 6), ([43], Section 3.3), for more information about avoiding and preventing deadlock.

One scheme to guarantee that deadlock does not occur is to assign a global order to all semaphores in a program and require that all threads decrement semaphores according to this global order. In programs in which this is feasible, it is impossible for a set of threads to develop in which each thread is blocked waiting for a semaphore to be released (incremented) while holding another semaphore.

4.6 Counting Semaphores from Binary

A common example or exercise in operating systems textbooks is to implement general counting semaphores using only binary ones ([15], Exercise 4.32), ([34], Section 6.4.4), ([36], Problem 4.14), ([43], Exercise 11 of chapter 2).

To implement a general counting semaphore S and the two operations down and up on it using only binary semaphores, we define two integers, value and waiting, where value represents the integer value of the semaphore S and waiting is the number of threads blocked on S in a down operation. We also need a binary semaphore mutex for mutual exclusion and a binary semaphore blocked to simulate threads blocking on S. The operations P and V in the following code are those defined for (strict) binary semaphores.

```
import Utilities.*;
import Synchronization.*;

class CountingSemaphoreFromBinary extends MyObject {
    private int value = 0;
    private int waiting = 0;
    private BinarySemaphore mutex = new BinarySemaphore(1);
    private BinarySemaphore blocked = new BinarySemaphore(0);

    public CountingSemaphoreFromBinary(int n) {
        value = n;
    }

    public void down() {
        P(mutex);
        if (value == 0) {
            waiting++;
            V(mutex);
            // ...            // This is "point A" mentioned in the text.
            P(blocked);
        } else {
```

```
            value--;
            V(mutex);
         }
      }

      public void up() {
         P(mutex);
         if (value == 0 && waiting > 0) {
            waiting--;
            V(blocked);      // This is "point B" mentioned in the text.
         } else {
            value++;
         }
         V(mutex);
      }
   }
```

We can combine value and waiting into a single integer variable count as follows. Here count is always equal to the number of up's that have been performed on S minus the number of down's.

```
import Utilities.*;
import Synchronization.*;

class CountingSemaphoreFromBinary extends MyObject {
   private int count = 0;
   private BinarySemaphore mutex = new BinarySemaphore(1);
   private BinarySemaphore blocked = new BinarySemaphore(0);

   public CountingSemaphoreFromBinary(int n) {
      count = n;
   }

   public void down() {
      P(mutex);
      count--;
      if (count < 0) {
         V(mutex);
         // ...            // This is "point A" mentioned in the text.
         P(blocked);
      } else {
         V(mutex);
      }
   }

   public void up() {
      P(mutex);
      count++;
      if (count <= 0) {
         V(blocked);      // This is "point B" mentioned in the text.
      }
```

```
        V(mutex);
    }
}
```

But there is a flaw [23] (see also [36], Problem 4.14) in the above implementations of counting semaphores using only binary semaphores. If a context switch occurs at point A labeled above in the **down** code, and if before the **down** thread resumes several threads do an **up**, then some signals (V's) at point B labeled above are lost because binary semaphores can have only the values 0 and 1. This means subsequent **down**'s on S will not work correctly.

We can prevent these "lost signals" from occurring by moving the **else** from the **down** method to the **up** method, as follows.

```
import Utilities.*;
import Synchronization.*;

class CountingSemaphoreFromBinary extends MyObject {
    private int count = 0;
    private BinarySemaphore mutex = new BinarySemaphore(1);
    private BinarySemaphore blocked = new BinarySemaphore(0);

    public CountingSemaphoreFromBinary(int n) {
        count = n;
    }

    public void down() {
        P(mutex);
        count--;
        if (count < 0) {
            V(mutex);
            P(blocked);
        }
        V(mutex);
    }

    public void up() {
        P(mutex);
        count++;
        if (count <= 0) {
            V(blocked);
        } else {
            V(mutex);
        }
    }
}
```

Since **mutex** is not released in **up** when V(**blocked**) is done, the effect is to force a blocked **down** operation to complete for each **up** done, preventing the V(**blocked**) signal from getting lost.

This solution still has an undesirable feature. If there are several threads blocked inside of **down** on the binary semaphore **blocked**, then a bunch of **up** operations waking up those threads cannot be executed sequentially but must be strictly interleaved with each thread completing its P(blocked) and its down operation. As explained in [26], this has performance penalties because of the extra context switching.

The fix for this is to keep track of the number of V(blocked) operations explicitly as follows.

```
import Utilities.*;
import Synchronization.*;

class CountingSemaphoreFromBinary extends MyObject {
    private int count = 0;
    private BinarySemaphore mutex = new BinarySemaphore(1);
    private BinarySemaphore blocked = new BinarySemaphore(0);
    private int wakeup = 0;   // new variable

    public CountingSemaphoreFromBinary(int n) {
        count = n;
    }

    public void down() {
        P(mutex);
        count--;
        if (count < 0) {
            V(mutex);
            P(blocked);
            P(mutex);
            wakeup--;
            if (wakeup > 0) V(blocked);
        }
        V(mutex);
    }

    public void up() {
        P(mutex);
        count++;
        if (count <= 0) {
            wakeup++;
            V(blocked);
        }
        V(mutex);
    }
}
```

Both of these problems are avoided by adding to the original solution one more binary semaphore serial that serializes execution of the down code ([34], pages 180–181). Therefore, at most one thread is at point A mentioned above, and there is no restriction on the CPU scheduler.

```
import Utilities.*;
import Synchronization.*;
```

```
class CountingSemaphoreFromBinary extends MyObject {
   private int count = 0;
   private BinarySemaphore mutex = new BinarySemaphore(1);
   private BinarySemaphore blocked = new BinarySemaphore(0);
   private BinarySemaphore serial = new BinarySemaphore(1);

   public CountingSemaphoreFromBinary(int n) {
      count = n;
   }

   public void down() {
      P(serial);
      P(mutex);
      count--;
      if (count < 0) {
         V(mutex);
         P(blocked);
      } else {
         V(mutex);
      }
      V(serial);
   }

   public void up() {
      P(mutex);
      count++;
      if (count <= 0) {
         V(blocked);
      }
      V(mutex);
   }
}
```

This example shows how difficult it is to write correct programs in the presence of arbitrary context switches, even when binary semaphores or locks are available as a tool.

4.7   Animating Operating Systems Algorithms

As we saw in Section 4.3, the four classic synchronization problems are the bounded buffer producer and consumer, the database readers and writers, the dining philosophers, and the sleeping barber. A program that simulates the dining philosophers usually generates its output in the form of lines of philosopher state changes (hungry, eating, thinking) perhaps tagged with a time stamp. The lines of output from the different philosophers are intermixed, which makes following the output or debugging the program difficult. An algorithm that constrains the philosophers to eat in a starvation-free fashion would be much easier to understand if the output were presented in a graphical or animated form with dining philosopher icons sitting around a circular table, each labeled or colored with its current state.

Using the technique described in Section 2.7, `XtangoAnimator` method calls can be added to Class 4.9 to animate the program.

```
XtangoAnimator xa = new XtangoAnimator();            // animation...
xa.begin();
xa.coords(-1.5f, -1.5f, 1.5f, 1.5f);
// circular table
xa.circle("C0", 0.0f, 0.0f, 1.0f, Color.black, xa.OUTLINE);
// bowl of spaghetti
xa.circle("Cf", 0.0f, 0.0f, 0.5f, Color.orange, xa.HALF);
// legend
xa.circle("C1", -1.4f, -1.0f, 0.05f, Color.black, xa.OUTLINE);
xa.text("T1", -1.3f, -1.025f, false, Color.black, "THINKING");
xa.circle("C2", -1.4f, -1.2f, 0.05f, Color.green, xa.SOLID);
xa.text("T2", -1.3f, -1.225f, false, Color.black, "HUNGRY");
xa.circle("C3", -1.4f, -1.4f, 0.05f, Color.blue, xa.SOLID);
xa.text("T3", -1.3f, -1.425f, false, Color.black, "EATING");
for (int i = 0; i < numPhilosophers; i++) {
    double radianp = i*gap;
    float sinp = (float) Math.sin(radianp);
    float cosp = (float) Math.cos(radianp);
    double radianf = radianp + 0.5f*gap;
    float sinf = (float) Math.sin(radianf);
    float cosf = (float) Math.cos(radianf);
    xa.circle
        ("phil"+i, sinp, cosp, 0.3f*gap, Color.black, xa.OUTLINE);
    xa.bigText
        ("TP"+i, sinp*0.55f, cosp*0.55f, true, Color.black, ""+i);
    // philosopher 1 is to the left of philosopher 0
    // fork 0 is to the left of philosopher 0
    xa.pointLine("fork"+i, sinf, cosf, 0.4f*sinf, 0.4f*cosf,
        Color.white, xa.THICK);
    xa.lower("fork"+i);                              // ...animation
}
...
private void eat() {
    int napping;
    napping = 1 + (int) random(napEat);
    xa.color("phil"+id, Color.blue);                // animation
    xa.fill("phil"+id, xa.SOLID);                   // animation
    nap(napping);
}
public void run() {
    while (true) {
        think();
        xa.color("phil"+id, Color.green);           // animation
```

```
        xa.fill("phil"+id, xa.SOLID);                    // animation
        ds.takeForks(id);
        eat();
        ds.putForks(id);
        xa.fill("phil"+id, xa.OUTLINE);                  // animation
        xa.color("phil"+id, Color.black);                // animation
    }
}
public void takeForks(int i) {
    P(mutex);  state[i] = HUNGRY;  test(i);  V(mutex);
    P(self[i]);
    xa.color("fork"+i, Color.gray);                      // animation
    xa.color("fork"+right(i), Color.gray);               // animation
}
public void putForks(int i) {
    P(mutex);  state[i] = THINKING;
    xa.color("fork"+i, Color.white);                     // animation
    xa.color("fork"+right(i), Color.white);              // animation
    test(left(i));  test(right(i));  V(mutex);
}
```

The philosophers are represented by circles equally spaced around a larger circle representing the table. A bowl of spaghetti, represented by a half-tone orange circle, sits in the center of the table. The state of each philosopher is represented by a different color: outline black for thinking, solid green for hungry, and solid blue for eating. While a philosopher is eating, the forks or chopsticks it uses are shown as thick lines extending from the philosopher's sides into the spaghetti in the table's center. Program 4.15 shows the complete code, and Figure 4.5 is a snapshot of the animation.

Summary

Although low-level, semaphores are an important synchronization tool. They are subject to easily made errors and must be employed with care. Their use is hard to trace in a program whose matching P's and V's are separated by many pages of code. Semaphores are implemented with procedure calls in the run-time library of a programming language or with system calls to the operating system. A thread that "downs" a semaphore whose value is 0 usually blocks rather than busy waits until it can proceed. Java does not have explicit binary or counting semaphores, that is, system classes with P and V methods. However, such classes are easily written, as we will see in the next chapter. Java has the synchronized block construct. It is equivalent to a binary semaphore with initial value 1 that must be unlocked by the locking thread. We called a synchronized block used in this fashion an implicit binary semaphore.

We looked at many example programs using the **BinarySemaphore** and **Count-**

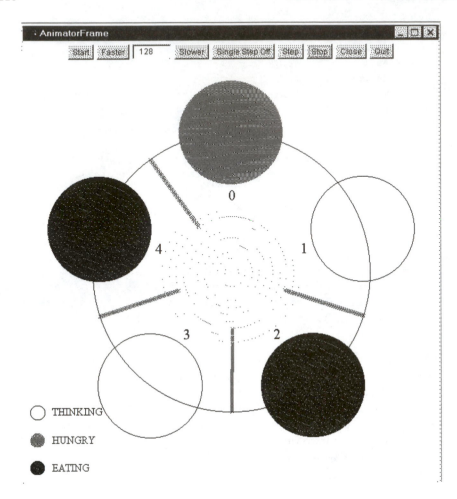

Figure 4.5: Animation Snapshot of the Dining Philosophers.

ingSemaphore classes from the Synchronization package for mutual exclusion synchronization and condition synchronization, including the four classical operating
systems problems (bounded buffer producer and consumer, sleeping barber, dining
philosophers, and readers and writers). These amusing problems represent recurring
real-world situations that require synchronization. Two of these problems, the dining philosophers and the readers/writers, can be solved with or without starvation
prevention. Some of the dining philosophers solutions are subject to deadlock. The
chapter ended with an XtangoAnimator animation of the dining philosophers.

4.8   Exercises

Be sure not to use busy waiting in any program written for these exercises.

1. **Fix the Race Condition.** Compile and run Program 4.1 as is and then again after adding the `Scheduler` class as was done in Exercise 3.2. Explain exactly how the semaphore prevents interleaving regardless of the time slice size.

Remove the semaphore `mutex` from the `auditor` thread in Program 4.2 and run the program. Explain what you see. Is the semaphore `mutex` really necessary in the `auditor`? Why or why not?

Use a semaphore to prevent race conditions in Program 3.7. Run your program with both `true` and `false` as the command line argument. Explain what you see in the program output compared to the two sample runs of the original program.

2. **Multiple Producers and Consumers.** Modify Program 3.9 so that there are multiple producer and consumer threads. The `main` method parses two additional command line options to override the default number of producer threads and consumer threads to create (the defaults are 3 and 5, respectively). Refer to Program 3.1. Then modify Class 4.4 so that a single bounded buffer created from the class works correctly when shared by multiple producer and multiple consumer threads.

All default values should be overridable with command line arguments:

```
javac bbou.java bbpc.java
java BBPC -s slots -p pNap -c cNap -P numP -C numC -R runTime
```

Consider the following while designing your modifications. Are race conditions on the variable `putIn` possible if multiple producers call the `deposit` method at about the same time? Are race conditions on the variable `takeOut` possible if multiple consumers call the `fetch` method at about the same time? If so, how can you prevent these race conditions?

3. **Other Classical Problems.** Write a Java program that solves, using semaphores, another classical operating systems problem, such as the cigarette smokers ([1], Problem 4.25), ([34], Problem 6.8), ([41], Problem 29 on page 73) or the bakery ([41], Problem 30 on page 73). In the former, the agent and each smoker is a thread. In the latter, each of the m customers and n salespersons is a thread.

4. **Multiple Sleeping Barbers.** Study the semaphores and algorithm used for condition synchronization in the sleeping barber program (Program 4.8). Can the algorithm be extended to work with more than one barber ([41], Problems 17, 28 on pages 72–73)? Verify your hypothesis by modifying and generalizing Program 4.8 so that it works with any number of barbers, each with its own room and barber chair. There is still just one common waiting room with n chairs for all the customers. There are m customers, $m > n + k$, where k is the number of barbers.

Have the program take values from the command line to override default values for the number of customers, the number of chairs in the shop, the number of barbers, and the maximum grow (wander around) and cut times for each customer.

```
javac slba.java
java SleepingBarbers -m m -n n -k k -g g -c c -R R
```

where m is the number of customers, n the number of waiting room chairs, k the number of barbers, and g and c the maximum grow and cut times for a customer, respectively. R is the number of seconds to let the simulation execute.

If Program 4.8 is modified to handle multiple barbers, the following consideration is more aesthetic or philosophical. Suppose customer C_1 releases barber B_1 at semaphore **customers**, then customer C_2 releases barber B_2. Then suppose B_2 races ahead of B_1 (faster CPU) so that B_2 releases C_1 at semaphore **barber** and B_1 releases C_2. Effectively B_1 cuts customer C_2 and B_2 cuts customer C_1 rather than the customer who released the barber. Is this incorrect? It is a matter of opinion since the correct number of customers and barbers flow through the semaphores. To get each barber cutting the correct customer, we would have to introduce a bounded buffer into which the barbers put their IDs, and change the **cutting** semaphore into an array.

5. **Dining Philosophers.** Explain exactly what can go wrong if the binary semaphore **mutex** is removed from the methods of the **DiningServer** in Class 4.9. Show a specific sequence of events.

The Java code for the dining philosophers, Class 4.9, is not completely correct because it allows two philosophers to collaborate and starve their common neighbor (starvation in the presence of contention). Instrument the program so that it detects and prints out when a particular philosopher is starving. A philosopher is starving when the following situation occurs repeatedly without the philosopher being able to eat: the philosopher is hungry and one of its neighbors puts down its forks but the hungry philosopher cannot eat because the neighbor on its other side is eating. If starvation is not prevented, then two philosophers could collaborate and coordinate their eating times to prevent the philosopher between them from ever eating.

Modify the dining philosophers program so that it is starvation-free. One way to avoid starvation is to add another state, "starving" say, and not let a hungry philosopher eat if it has a "starving" neighbor. A hungry philosopher enters this new state if its neighbors have put down their forks and the philosopher under consideration has not been able to eat. You can be more elaborate and count the number of times a hungry philosopher has not been able to pick up the forks, and make a philosopher "starving" if this number exceeds some specified maximum. You can be even more elaborate and keep separate counts for not being able to pick up the forks because the left fork is in use or the right fork is in use, and change to the starving state if both of these counts exceed the maximum, and the left and right forks not being usable has been alternating.

It is not correct to change the state of a philosopher from hungry to starving at any time other than when one of its neighbors puts down its forks. If you make the transition when a philosopher gets hungry and first tries to pick up its forks, then a hungry philosopher starves right away if its forks are not available, and you have gained nothing. It is not correct to have two neighboring philosophers starving at the same time because either they will deadlock (if you never allow a philosopher regardless of state to eat if it has a starving neighbor) or your solution will still allow starvation (you should construct such a scenario). Finally, the philosophers have very tight grips and forks cannot be taken away from them until they are finished eating.

You may have your philosopher threads eat and think for random amounts of time, but to check for starvation prevention, you will have to exercise more control over the random numbers generated in your modified version of Class 4.9:

```
javac dphi.java dpdr.java
java DiningPhilosophers -n5 -R300 1 100 10 1 1 100 100 1 100 1
```

Run your program first with starvation prevention disabled, then again with starvation prevention enabled and scrutinize the difference.

6. **Fair Readers and Writers.** Modify the readers and writers, Class 4.13, so that it is fair, i.e., so that a continuous stream of arriving readers cannot starve a writer. There are two ways to implement fairness. One way is strict serialization or FIFO: readers and writers queue up on the database and enter in the order of their arrival with any group of consecutive readers allowed to read at the same time. This can be done with a single binary semaphore to serialize access to the **startRead** and **startWrite** methods. The other way tries to allow more concurrent database access: whenever a writer finishes, it sweeps into the database **all** waiting readers, called a platoon or batch, even those that arrived after any waiting writer.

7. **Baboons Crossing a Canyon.** Write a Java program to coordinate or synchronize baboons crossing a rope over a canyon so they do not deadlock ([41], Problems 15, 16 on page 264), ([43], Problems 35, 36 on pages 151–2). A canyon cuts through the territory of a colony of baboons. The baboons use a rope stretching across the canyon to cross from one side to the other. The rope is strong enough to permit any number of baboons to cross in the same direction at the same time. However, the rope is too thin for the baboons to cross the canyon in both directions at the same time. Consequently, a baboon that wants to cross from west to east must wait until all westward-moving baboons have finished crossing and the rope is free. If the rope is being used by westward-moving baboons, then other baboons may start to cross from east to west no matter how many eastward-moving baboons are waiting on the other side.

Think of multiple baboons crossing in one direction as multiple readers reading a database: many may cross (read) simultaneously. In the readers/writers problem, a reader reads the database for as long or as short a time as it wants. Allow the same for the baboons: baboons take as long a time or as short a time to cross as they want, i.e., a baboon may climb over and pass another baboon while crossing if that baboon is going in the same direction. This problem is also posed as "The Unisex Bathroom" problem ([1], Exercise 4.27) and is equivalent to a variation of the database readers and writers in which multiple writers are allowed to write concurrently, just as multiple readers are allowed to read concurrently, but reading and writing must be done exclusively.

Do this in two steps. First write your program without worrying about a series of eastward-moving baboons holding up the waiting westward-moving baboons indefinitely, or vice versa, that is, do not worry about starvation. However, to see that starvation is possible, run your simulation with parameters that generate enough eastward-moving baboons so that westward-moving baboons wait indefinitely. Save these parameters for the next step.

Then modify your program so that it is fair and there is no starvation. For example, when a baboon that wants to cross to the east arrives at the rope and finds baboons crossing to the west, it waits until the rope is empty, but no more westward-moving baboons are allowed to start crossing until at least one waiting baboon has crossed the other way. Pick either strict serialization or platooning, described in Exercise 6, as your strategy. Run your program with the parameters that led to starvation in the first step.

8. **A Fraternity Party.** A group of M fraternity brothers and sorority sisters is having a party and drinking from a large communal keg that can hold N servings of soda. One unlucky pledge is responsible for replacing the key each time it empties. When a partier wants to drink, he or she fills a cup from the keg, unless it is empty. If the keg is empty, the partier wakes up the pledge and then waits until the pledge has returned with a new keg. The behavior of the partiers and pledge is specified by the following threads.

Partier:

```
while (true)
    { tellPledgeIfKegEmpty(); getServingFromKeg(); drink() }
```

Pledge:

```
while (true)
    { waitForKegToEmpty(); getNewKegOfNservings() }
```

Develop Java code for the actions of the partiers and pledge. Use semaphores for thread synchronization. Your solution should avoid deadlock and awaken the pledge only when the keg is empty (adapted from [1], Exercises 4.31 and 6.18).

9. **Roller Coaster with One Car.** Suppose there are n passenger threads (default value 10) and one car thread. The passengers repeatedly wait to take rides in the car, which holds C passengers (default 4), $C < n$. However, the car can go around the track only when it is full. The car takes the same T seconds (default 6) to go around the track each time it fills up. After getting a ride, each passenger wanders (**nap** method) around the amusement park for a random amount of time between 0 and W seconds (default 5) before returning to the roller coaster for another ride. Develop code for a Java program containing the passenger threads and the car thread (adapted from [1], Exercises 4.32 and 6.23).

Use semaphores for synchronization. Run the simulation for R seconds (default 90). Compute the average time that a passenger must wait to be seated after deciding to take a ride.

All default values should be overridable with command line arguments:

```
javac rollerCoaster.java
java RollerCoaster -C C -T T -n n -W W -R R
```

10. **Roller Coaster with Multiple Cars.** Generalize your program of the previous exercise to contain m car threads, $m > 1$. Since there is only one track, cars cannot pass each other, i.e., they must finish going around the track in the order in which they started. For passenger safety, only one car at a time is permitted to go around the track. As before, a car can go around the track only when it is full. Develop code for a Java program containing the passenger threads and the car threads.

11. **Jurassic Park Safari Ride.** Jurassic Park consists of a dinosaur museum and a park for safari riding. There are n passengers and m single-passenger cars. Passengers wander around the museum for a while, then line up to take a ride in a safari car. When a car is available, it loads the one passenger it can hold and rides around the park for a random amount of time. If the m cars are all out riding passengers around, then a passenger who wants to ride waits; if a car is ready to load but there are no waiting passengers, then the car waits. Use semaphores to synchronize the n passenger threads and the m car threads. Why is Program 4.16 (page 381 of the on-line appendix) not correct?

```
CountingSemaphore carAvail = new CountingSemaphore(0);
CountingSemaphore carTaken = new CountingSemaphore(0);
CountingSemaphore carFilled = new CountingSemaphore(0);
CountingSemaphore passengerReleased = new CountingSemaphore(0);
...
class Passenger implements Runnable {...
   public void run() {                            // thread
      while (true) {
         nap(1+(int)random(1000*wanderTime));
         P(carAvail);  V(carTaken);  P(carFilled);
         P(passengerReleased);
      }
   }
}
class Car implements Runnable {...
   public void run() {                            // thread
      while (true) {
         V(carAvail);  P(carTaken);  V(carFilled);
         nap(1+(int)random(1000*rideTime));
         V(passengerReleased);
```

```
            }
        }
    }
```

Correct the program and write a complete Java program simulating Jurassic Park. Now suppose each car holds C passengers, $C < n$, instead of just 1. Modify your code to reflect this change in the simulation.

12. **Amusement Park Bumper Cars.** Many amusement parks in the United States have bumper car rides. Each car holds one person. People who want to ride a bumper car line up and wait for a free car. When a car is returned and the previous rider gets out, a new rider gets in the car from the head of the waiting line and rides around on the bumper ride floor, bumping into the other cars. After riding around for a while, the rider in the bumper car decides that enough is enough and returns the car to the area where new riders line up. A new rider gets in and takes a ride in the bumper car. The rider who just got out of a bumper car wanders around the amusement park, perhaps getting something to eat. After wandering for a while, the rider decides to take another bumper car ride, returns to the rider waiting area, and gets in line. If there are more free cars than people wishing to ride, the free cars are kept in a line. A person wishing to ride a bumper car gets in the car at the head of this line and returning cars go to the end of this line.

There are N_{riders} rider threads (default 10) and N_{cars} bumper car threads (default 5). Each car takes a (different) random amount of time between 0 and T_{bump} seconds (default 5) to bump around on the floor (simulated with the **nap** method) each time a rider gets into the car. The bump time is a random number regenerated each time a car goes onto the bumper floor. After getting a ride, each rider wanders around the amusement park (**nap**) for a random amount of time between 0 and T_{wander} seconds (default 10) before returning to the waiting area to get in line for another bumper car ride. The wander time is a random number regenerated each time a rider leaves a car and goes into the amusement park.

Develop code for a multiclass multithreaded Java program simulating the bumper car ride operations, the rider threads, and the car threads. Use semaphores for synchronization. Run the simulation for T_{total} seconds (default 60). Each of the N_{riders} riders is simulated with an object containing one thread, created from a common class. Each bumper car is simulated with an object containing one thread, created from a common class. Finally, there is a driver class whose **main** method starts everything going.

The waiting area where riders get in line is implemented with a bounded buffer. Each rider who finishes wandering around the amusement park gets in line by depositing its rider identifier into the bounded buffer and then waits on its slot in an array of semaphores, P(rideBegin[rid]). When a bumper car is ready to pick up a rider, it fetches an identifier from the bounded buffer and executes V(rideBegin[rid]). This releases the rider from waiting in line so it can take a seat. The rider executes P(rideOver[rid]), blocking it until the ride is over. When the bumper car's **nap** simulating the ride is over, the car thread executes V(rideOver[rid]) so the rider

```
class Coordinator                      class Car extends Thread {
    extends Thread {                     private Coordinator
  public Coordinator(...)                  coord = null;
  public ... getInLine(...)              private int cid = -1;
  public ... takeAseat(...)              public Car
  public ... takeAride(...)                (int id, Coordinator c)
  public ... load(...)                     { cid = id;  coord = c; }
  public ... unload(...)                 public void run() {
}                                          while (true) {
class Rider                        // car waits until full
    extends Thread {                       coord.load(...);
  private Coordinator               // full car so bump on floor
    coord = null;                          nap(...);
  private int rid = -1;                    coord.unload(...);
  public Rider                           }
    (int id, Coordinator c)            }
    { rid = id;  coord = c; }         }
  public void run() {               class Bump {
    while (true) {                     public static void main
// wander around the park                (...) {
     nap(...);                            Coordinator c = new ...
     coord.getInLine(...);                for (int i = 0; ...
     coord.takeAseat(...);                 new Rider(i, c);
     coord.takeAride(...);               for (int j = 0; ...
    }                                     new Car(j, c);
  }                                    }
}
```

Figure 4.6: Skeleton Code for the Bumper Car Amusement Park Ride.

can wander around the amusement park again. Make sure that you have eliminated all race conditions.

Here is one way to organize the program. A rider class and a car class are instantiated multiple times. A coordinator class containing all the semaphores is instantiated. It implements the service methods invoked by the riders and cars. Each time a rider wants to get in line, it calls the getInLine(rid) method in the coordinator object. When this returns, the rider's identifier rid has been placed into the bounded buffer by the coordinator. The rider then calls the takeAseat(rid) and takeAride(rid) methods in the coordinator. These block the rider until the ride starts and finishes, respectively. When a car is ready to load a rider, it calls the coordinator's load(cid) method. When the ride is over, the car calls the coordinator's unload(cid) method. In contrast to the explicit queue of the bounded buffer for riders waiting to be loaded into empty cars, there need not be an explicit queue of empty cars waiting to load riders; car threads blocking on a semaphore form an implicit queue. Skeleton code is shown in Figure 4.6.

All default values should be overridable with command line arguments:

```
javac bumperCars.java
java BumperCars -r Nriders -c Ncars -b Tbump -w Twander -R Ttotal
```

Make sure that your program works correctly when N_{cars} is one and/or when N_{riders} is one.

13. Amusement Park Multirider Bumper Cars. This exercise is a modification of the previous one: instead of each bumper car holding exactly one rider, each car holds some fixed number of riders greater than one (one rider per car is a special case equivalent to the previous exercise). Since these cars are bigger and weigh more, at most two cars are allowed out on the bumper floor at any one time.

Suppose there are N_{riders} rider threads (default 20) and N_{cars} bumper car threads (default 5). The riders repeatedly wait to take rides in a bumper car. Each bumper car holds exactly N_{fits} riders (default 3). When a car returns from a ride on the bumper floor and empties, the first N_{fits} riders in line to take a ride take a seat in the car. If there are not enough waiting riders, then the car waits until it is completely filled to capacity before going out onto the bumper floor. If there are already cars waiting to load, then each free car waits its turn to load riders from the head of the rider waiting line. Should more than one car be allowed to load at a time?

Each time a rider wants to get in line, it calls the `getInLine(rid)` method in the coordinator object. When this returns, the rider's identifier has been placed into the bounded buffer by the coordinator. The rider then calls the `takeAseat(rid)`, `waitCarFull(rid)`, and `takeAride(rid)` methods in the coordinator. These block the rider until the rider is seated, the ride starts, and the ride finishes, respectively. When a car is ready to load riders, it calls the coordinator's `load(cid)` method. When the ride is done, the car calls the coordinator's `unload(cid)` method to release its riders.

All default values should be overridable with command line arguments. Make sure that your program works correctly when N_{cars} is one, when N_{riders} is one, or when N_{fits} is one.

14. Haunted House with One Touring Car. Suppose there are N_{pass} passenger threads (default 10) and one Haunted House touring car thread. The passengers repeatedly wait to take rides in the car to tour the Haunted House. The car holds only so much weight, W_{car} pounds (default 1000). When the car returns from a tour of the Haunted House and empties, the first passengers in line to take a Haunted House tour take seats in the car, up to the weight capacity of the car. However, the car goes out on tour only when it is full, so if there are not enough passengers in line when the car returns, the car waits until it fills. Passengers weigh a random number of pounds between W_{min} and W_{max} (default values 50 and 400, respectively; no small children are allowed into the Haunted House). The car is considered filled when the next person in line would cause the total passenger weight to exceed the car's capacity. That passenger cannot go, though, so waits at the head of the line for the car to go out on tour, return, and start filling again. If, when the car returns and empties, the waiting passengers all fit, the car must wait until the first passenger comes along who does not fit.

The car takes a random amount of time between 0 and T_{tour} seconds (default 5) to tour the Haunted House (simulated with a nap) each time it fills up. After getting a ride, each passenger wanders around the Haunted House grounds (nap) for a random amount of time between 0 and T_{wander} seconds (default 10) before returning to the car stand to wait in line for another tour of the Haunted House.

Develop code for a multiclass multithreaded Java program simulating the Haunted House operations, the passenger threads, and the car thread. Use semaphores for synchronization (no busy waiting). Run the simulation for T_{total} seconds (default 30). Each of the N_{pass} passengers is an object containing one thread, created from a common class. The touring car is represented by a single object having one thread.

There is a coordinator object whose methods are invoked by the passengers and the touring car. The car calls methods load(cid, capacity) and unload(cid, passengers). The passengers call methods getInLine(pid, weight), takeA-seat(pid), waitCarFull(pid), and takeAride(pid). When takeAseat returns, the passenger is seated in the touring car, but the car is not yet full and not yet touring. If the car is not loading or if a passenger does not fit when it calls takeAseat, then the passenger blocks until the car comes back and reloads. When waitCarFull returns, the car is full and going on a tour of the Haunted House. When takeAride returns, the tour is over and the passenger gets out of the car.

All default values should be overridable with command line arguments:

```
javac hauntedHouse.java
java HauntedHouse \
    -c Wcar -t Ttour -p Npass -m Wmin -M Wmax -w Twander -T Ttotal
```

15. **Haunted House with Multiple Touring Cars.** Modify your Haunted House car tour program so there are multiple touring cars, each with the same maximum weight capacity. The cars wait in line to fill up. The cars are allowed to tour the Haunted House simultaneously. Since the cars tour for a random time, they do not necessarily return to fill up in the order they leave. Make the number of cars, N_{cars}, a parameter of the simulation (default value 3) overridable from the command line. Each of the N_{cars} touring cars is an object containing one thread, created from a common class. Should more than one car be allowed to load at a time?

It is very important to make sure that when a car returns to unload, the passengers released are the ones who boarded the car. Also make sure your program works correctly when N_{cars} is 1.

16. **Counting Semaphores From Binary.** Section 4.6 looked at several implementations of counting semaphores using only binary ones. Analyze the following one ([13], page 184). Are there any trouble-causing context switches or V's on a binary semaphore whose value is already 1?

```
import Utilities.*;
import Synchronization.*;

class CountingSemaphoreFromBinary extends MyObject {
   private int count = 0;
   private BinarySemaphore mutex = new BinarySemaphore(1);
   private BinarySemaphore delay = null;

   public CountingSemaphoreFromBinary(int n) {
      if (n < 0) throw new IllegalArgumentException();
      count = n;  // initial value of delay is 0 if count is 0 else 1
      delay = new BinarySemaphore(count>0 ? 1 : 0);
   }

   public void down() {
      P(delay);
      P(mutex);
      count--;
      if (count > 0) V(delay);
      V(mutex);
   }

   public void up() {
      P(mutex);
      count++;
      if (count == 1) V(delay);
      V(mutex);
   }
}
```

17. **Algorithm Animation.** Animate one of Class 4.4, Program 4.8, or Class 4.13 (bounded buffer producer and consumer, sleeping barber, or database readers and writers, respectively).

Chapter 5

Monitors

Semaphores are like `gotos` and pointers in that programming with them is prone to mistakes. Semaphores work but they lack structure and discipline. For example, a disastrous easy-to-make coding mistake is the following.

> `V(S);` *critical section*; `V(S);`

And, as described in Section 4.5, the following mistake leads to deadlock.

> `P(S);` *critical section*; `P(S);`

Even when semaphores are used correctly in a program for mutual exclusion and condition synchronization, it is difficult to distinguish the two uses without a thorough examination of all the code.

Monitors were devised to help avoid these kinds of mistakes and to provide a higher level programming language construct than semaphores. Monitors are related to objects and object-oriented programming, to abstract data types and data encapsulation. They are the built-in synchronization primitive of Java.

In this chapter, we define monitors and condition variables and describe two signaling disciplines that monitors use: signal and exit and signal and continue. An experiment shows that Java monitors uses the latter. We look at signal-and-exit monitor solutions to the bounded buffer, dining philosophers, and readers and writers classic synchronization problems, using a Java-like pseudocode. Then we look at Java programs having signal-and-continue monitors that also solve the three problems. An examination of the code for the `BinarySemaphore` and `CountingSemaphore` library classes was deferred from the previous chapter. We now see how they are implemented as monitors. A lock is like a binary semaphore with the restriction that the thread releasing a lock must be the one that acquired it. We look at a monitor implementation.

Even though Java lacks individually named condition variables, notification objects substitute for them in many situations. We see the three classic synchronization problems solved with notification objects. Since monitors can be implemented with semaphores, as will be shown, the two tools are equal in power in that they solve the same types of problems. Last, we look at the implementation of the `XtangoAnimation` algorithm animation package. It starts several threads when used, and its code raises many synchronization issues. After reading this chapter, you will understand the advantages monitors have as a higher level construct than semaphores. You will also be aware of the precautions a programmer must take when using Java's signal-and-continue monitors.

5.1   Definitions

A *monitor* ([15], Section 5.3), ([34], Section 6.7), ([36], Section 4.5), ([41], Section 2.2.7), ([43], Section 2.2.6) is a programming language module or object that encapsulates several service or access methods and their global and local variables. The only way to manipulate or access the variables inside the monitor is to call one of the service methods. Only one thread at a time is allowed to be active inside the monitor, that is, executing one of the service methods. This mutually exclusive access prevents race conditions involving the variables inside the monitor that could otherwise occur if several threads were active inside service methods at the same time. Each monitor object has a lock. The compiler generates code at the beginning of each service method to acquire the lock and at the end to release the lock. If the monitor is locked when a thread calls one of the monitor's service methods, the thread blocks and is added to the set of threads waiting to acquire the lock.

Mutual exclusion synchronization is therefore implicit in monitors, guaranteed by the compiler. To provide a mechanism for event or condition synchronization, a monitor may contain *condition variables*. The two operations on a condition variable are *signal* and *wait*. These are analogous to the "up" and "down" operations on binary semaphores. A thread that waits on a condition variable temporarily leaves the monitor and blocks, releasing the lock and joining the set of threads blocked on that condition variable. Each signal on a condition variable awakens one thread from the condition variable's set of blocked threads, not necessarily the one that has been blocked the longest. If the set is empty, the signal is not saved and has no effect, in contrast to the way semaphores work. Since releasing the monitor lock and joining the condition variable queue is an atomic action, there is no danger of lost wakeup signals (Section 3.5.4). A thread awakened by a signal is removed from the set of threads blocked on the condition variable and added to the set of threads waiting to acquire the monitor's lock. Once the lock is reacquired, the thread continues execution of the service method it had called earlier. See Figure 5.1. A monitor condition variable has no value and is best thought of as the name of the set of threads blocked on that condition variable. Note that condition variables and semaphores differ in two ways: a signal on an empty condition variable has no effect whereas a V increments a semaphore on which no thread is blocked, and a wait on a condition variable always blocks the thread until a subsequent signal whereas a P decrements a semaphore whose value is positive without blocking.

Monitor condition variables are implemented with one of several signaling disciplines: *signal and exit*, *signal and wait*, and *signal and continue*. In signal and exit, if a thread executing inside the monitor signals on a condition variable, it is required to leave the monitor immediately after generating the signal by executing a return statement in the service method it invoked. A thread from the wait set

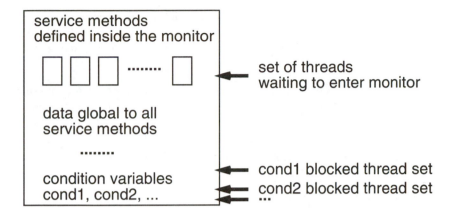

Figure 5.1: Monitor Service Methods, Condition Variables, and Sets.

of that condition variable is awakened and continues executing inside the monitor. It gets priority to execute inside the monitor over all threads waiting to enter the monitor via one of its service methods. In signal and wait, the signaled thread executes inside the monitor while the signaler waits for it to leave the monitor; then the signaler continues. In signal and continue, the signaled thread waits for the signaler to leave the monitor before it resumes execution inside the monitor. Neither signal and wait nor signal and continue requires a thread to execute a return statement after generating a signal. See ([1], Chapter 6) and [12] for much more thorough treatments of monitors and their various signaling disciplines.

Java monitors use the signal-and-continue discipline. We look first at signal and exit since it is easier to understand, particularly for those working with monitors for the first time. Solutions to the classical problems are shown in a Java-like pseudocode. Monitor service methods are indicated with the keyword **synchronized**; only one active thread at a time is permitted. Nonsynchronized methods in a monitor are of a private utility nature or make a sequence of synchronized method calls. The **wait**(*condVar*) method is used to wait on a condition variable; **notify**(*condVar*) is used to signal. Section 5.3 examines signal and continue, illustrated with Java solutions to the classical problems.

5.2 Signal and Exit

In this section, we make the following two assumptions about condition variables and their signaling discipline.

1. After signaling on a condition variable, the signaler must exit the monitor immediately by executing a return statement so that no variables change before the signaled thread wakes up and continues executing inside the monitor. In this way the signaled thread finds the condition that led to the signal still true when it resumes execution inside the monitor.

2. The signaled thread is given priority to proceed inside the monitor over those
   threads waiting to enter the monitor through a service method call. Again,
   the signaled thread finds the condition still true when it resumes execution
   inside the monitor.

We will see in Section 5.3 that Java does not work like this. However, for convenience
we use a pseudocode that resembles Java to express the signal-and-exit monitor
examples in this section.

5.2.1   The Bounded Buffer Producer and Consumer

The bounded buffer monitor in Class 5.1 synchronizes a single producer thread and
single consumer thread. It is written in a Java-like pseudocode.

```
public synchronized void deposit(double data) {
    if (count == size) wait(notFull);
    buf[rear] = data;
    rear = (rear+1) % size;
    count++;
    if (count == 1) notify(notEmpty);
}
public synchronized double fetch() {
    double result;
    if (count == 0) wait(notEmpty);
    result = buf[front];
    front = (front+1) % size;
    count--;
    if (count == size-1) notify(notFull);
    return result;
}
```

Only one thread executes at a time in the monitor, having called the fetch or
deposit synchronized method. If the buffer is full, the producer thread blocks with
the wait method on the condition variable notFull; the producer is later unblocked
by the consumer with notify when it frees up a buffer slot. If the buffer is empty,
the consumer thread blocks on the condition variable notEmpty; the consumer is
later unblocked when the producer fills a slot with an item.

The monitor in Class 5.1 could be used, if it were real Java code, with the driver
code in Program 3.9 with no changes to either. It is important to note that the
BoundedBuffer class in Class 4.4 is not the same thing as a monitor; more than one
thread at a time may be active inside its methods. We used semaphores inside the
methods of that class for synchronization and to prevent race conditions. Mutual
exclusion synchronization is implicit in a monitor and condition variables are used
for condition synchronization.

5.2.2 The Dining Philosophers

The monitor in Class 5.2 coordinates the dining philosophers.

```
public void takeForks(int i) { hungryAndGetForks(i); }
public void putForks(int i) {
    finishedEating(i);
    checkForkDown(left(i)); checkForkDown(right(i));
}
private void seeIfStarving(int k) {
    if (state[k] == HUNGRY && state[left(k)] != STARVING
            && state[right(k)] != STARVING) {
        state[k] = STARVING;
    }
}
private void test(int k, boolean checkStarving) {
    if (state[left(k)] != EATING && state[left(k)] != STARVING
            && (state[k] == HUNGRY || state[k] == STARVING) &&
        state[right(k)] != STARVING && state[right(k)] != EATING)
        state[k] = EATING;
    else if (checkStarving)
        seeIfStarving(k); // simplistic naive check for starvation
}
private synchronized void hungryAndGetForks(int i) {
    state[i] = HUNGRY;
    test(i, false);
    if (state[i] != EATING) wait(self[i]);
}
private synchronized void finishedEating(int i) {
    state[i] = THINKING;
}
private synchronized void checkForkDown(int i) {
    test(i, checkStarving);
    if (state[i] == EATING) notify(self[i]);
}
```

The monitor has an array of condition variables, one array entry for each philosopher
to block on if its forks are not both available. A naive form of starvation detection
and prevention is implemented. A hungry philosopher enters the "starving" state
if it cannot pick up both forks to eat whenever one of its neighbors puts down its
forks. A hungry philosopher is not allowed to eat if it has a starving neighbor.
The monitor in Class 5.2 could be used, if it were real Java code, with the driver
code in Program 4.10 (modified to process a -S command line option that turns on
starvation checking).

Since the signal-and-exit discipline requires a thread to exit the monitor immediately after signaling on a condition variable, a thread cannot perform two signal

operations on two condition variables during one call to a monitor service method. To handle this situation, the philosopher code calls the public nonsynchronized method `putForks` when the philosopher puts down its forks. This method makes two calls to the monitor's private synchronized method `checkForkDown`; each such call generates at most one signal.

5.2.3 The Readers and Writers

The monitor in Class 5.3 solves the readers and writers problem and is based on ([6], Figure 5.5).

```
public synchronized void startRead(int i) {
    if (isWriting) wait(OKtoRead);
    else if (!empty(OKtoWrite)) {
        // new incoming readers cannot starve writers
        wait(OKtoRead);
    }
    numReaders++;
    // when a writer finishes, all waiting readers start
    notify(OKtoRead);
}
public synchronized void endRead(int i) {
    numReaders--;
    if (numReaders == 0) notify(OKtoWrite);
}
public synchronized void startWrite(int i) {
    if (numReaders != 0 || isWriting) wait(OKtoWrite);
    isWriting = true;
}
public synchronized void endWrite(int i) {
    isWriting = false;
    if (!empty(OKtoRead)) notify(OKtoRead);
    else notify(OKtoWrite); // nor do writers starve readers
}
```

It implements a fair, starvation-free solution; that is, a continual stream of arriving readers cannot delay for an arbitrary amount of time a writer from writing. The Boolean method `empty(`*condVar*`)` returns true if the condition variable's queue of waiting threads is empty. Whenever a writer finishes, it sweeps into the database **all** waiting readers, called a platoon or batch, even those that arrived after any waiting writer. (The other approach to preventing starvation is strict serialization. See Exercise 4.6.) The monitor in Class 5.3 could be used, if it were real Java code, with the driver code in Program 4.14 with no changes to either.

5.3 Signal and Continue

The signal-and-continue discipline does not require the signaling thread to leave the monitor after a signal on a condition variable. Nor does the signaled thread have priority to proceed in the monitor over other threads waiting to enter through a service method call. Relaxing the first requirement simplifies the coding of some monitors. In Class 5.2 we were forced to introduce a service method, `putForks`, that invokes two potentially signal generating private methods in the monitor whenever a philosopher puts down its forks. With signal and continue, only one call is needed, as we will see in Class 5.6 below.

There are disadvantages in relaxing the second requirement on page 132, the one giving signaled threads priority to proceed in the monitor over threads trying to enter through a service method ([12], page 99). We cannot guarantee that the condition leading to the signal is still true when the signaled thread reenters the monitor: before leaving the monitor, the signaling thread could change data fields and alter the state of the monitor after generating the signal. Also threads trying to enter the monitor through a service method can "barge" ahead of signaled threads that were waiting on condition variables, resulting in an unbounded waiting time on a condition variable, a form of starvation.

For example, consider a signal-and-continue bounded buffer monitor for multiple producer and multiple consumer threads. A producer that wants to deposit into a full buffer waits on a condition variable for a signal from a consumer. After getting such a signal, it is possible for another producer to "barge" into the monitor and fill the just-emptied slot. Since we no longer guarantee that the condition leading to the signal is still true when the signaled thread proceeds in the monitor, we need to take the precaution of changing the `if` statement containing the wait,

    if (condition) wait();

to a `while` loop,

    while (condition) wait();

Since potentially more than one thread is signaled before the signaler leaves the monitor, the signal condition may no longer be true when a signaled thread reenters the monitor ([12], page 100). Further, some other thread may have entered the monitor through a service method and modified the condition before the signaled thread reenters the monitor.

If a `while` loop is used instead of an `if` by a thread to wait on a condition variable, then a broadcast signal becomes feasible. The signaler broadcasts a signal to all threads waiting on the condition variable as a hint if the signaler thinks but is not positively sure that a waiting thread can proceed. Java supports a broadcast signal with the `notifyAll` method.

5.3.1 Java Monitors

To construct a Java monitor, use the modifier **synchronized** for all methods in which only one thread should be executing at a time. These methods are usually public, but may be private if the public access to the monitor consists of calls to several private **synchronized** methods, as was done in the pseudocode example Class 5.2.

Each Java object has a lock associated with it. A thread invoking a synchronized method in an object must obtain the object's lock before executing the method's code. The thread blocks if the lock is currently held by some other thread. A synchronized method in an object

```
class Name {
    synchronized type method() {
        ...
    }
}
```

is equivalent to a method whose code consists of a single block synchronized on the object.

```
class Name {
    type method() {
        synchronized (this) {
            ...
        }
    }
}
```

Static methods in a class may also be declared **synchronized**; in this case, a class lock must be obtained. For example, the constructor in class B

```
class B {
    private static int numConstructed = 0;
    private synchronized void inc() {
        numConstructed++;
    }
    public B() {
        inc();
    }
}
```

increments a counter by calling a static synchronized method to avoid lost updates.

Unfortunately, each Java monitor has just one (anonymous) condition variable; all waits and signals refer to it automatically. Use **wait()** and **notify()** to wait for and generate a signal, respectively; use **notifyAll()** to wake up or send signals to all the threads waiting on the anonymous condition variable (broadcast signal).

Java monitors use the signal-and-continue signaling discipline, as the experiment set up in Program 5.4 demonstrates. The sample output illustrates the following differences between the signal-and-exit and signal-and-continue signaling disciplines.

- Java allows a thread trying to get in the monitor through a service method to "barge" ahead and enter before a signaled thread continues inside the monitor.

- A `notify()` moves to the ready queue one of the waiting threads, an arbitrary one and not necessarily the one that has waited the longest.

- A `notifyAll()` moves all waiting threads to the ready queue, from which they are scheduled to run on the CPU in an unspecified order.

5.3.2 The Bounded Buffer Producer and Consumer

The Java monitor in Class 5.5 solves the bounded buffer single producer and single consumer problem.

```
public synchronized void deposit(double value) {
   while (count == numSlots)
      try { wait(); } catch (InterruptedException e) {}
   buffer[putIn] = value;
   putIn = (putIn + 1) % numSlots;
   count++;              // wake up the consumer since
   if (count == 1) notify();   // it might be waiting
}
public synchronized double fetch() {
   double value;
   while (count == 0)
      try { wait(); } catch (InterruptedException e) {}
   value = buffer[takeOut];
   takeOut = (takeOut + 1) % numSlots;
   count--;                     // wake up the producer since
   if (count == numSlots-1) notify(); // it might be waiting
   return value;
}
```

This monitor is used with the classes (`ProducerConsumer`, `Producer`, and `Consumer`) in Program 3.9 with no changes. The producer thread waits if the buffer is full, and the consumer thread waits if the buffer is empty. Whenever the producer puts an item into an empty buffer, it signals since the consumer might be waiting. Whenever the consumer extracts an item from a full buffer, it signals since the producer might be waiting. Notice there are no race conditions or lost updates involving the variable `count`.

5.3.3 The Dining Philosophers

The Java monitor in Class 5.6 coordinates the dining philosophers.

```
class DiningServer ...
public synchronized void takeForks(int i) {
   state[i] = HUNGRY;
   test(i, false);
   while (state[i] != EATING)
```

```
            try {wait();} catch (InterruptedException e) {}
    }
    public synchronized void putForks(int i) {
        state[i] = THINKING;
        test(left(i), checkStarving);
        test(right(i), checkStarving);
        notifyAll();
    }
    private void seeIfStarving(int k) {
        if (state[k] == HUNGRY && state[left(k)] != STARVING
               && state[right(k)] != STARVING) {
            state[k] = STARVING;
        }
    }
    private void test(int k, boolean checkStarving) {
        if (state[left(k)] != EATING && state[left(k)] != STARVING
               && (state[k] == HUNGRY || state[k] == STARVING) &&
              state[right(k)] != STARVING && state[right(k)] != EATING)
            state[k] = EATING;
        else if (checkStarving)
            seeIfStarving(k); // simplistic naive check for starvation
    }
```

The simple starvation prevention scheme of Class 5.2 is used. This monitor is used
with the classes in Program 4.10 (modified to process a -S command line option
that turns on starvation checking).

Since Java supports only a single anonymous condition variable in its monitors,
we cannot use an array of condition variables, one per philosopher, for blocking a
hungry philosopher that cannot eat. Instead, a notifyAll() unblocks all waiting
philosophers when any philosopher puts down its forks. This is very inefficient since
at most two waiting philosophers need be signaled to check their forks.

Two sample runs are shown in Class 5.6. In the first, the thinking and eating
times are set up so that philosophers 0 and 2 alternate their eating cycles, in effect
starving philosopher 1 between them. The second run turns on starvation checking
with -S on the command line; philosopher 1 eats and does not starve.

```
% java DiningPhilosophers \
      -S -R120 1 100 10 1 1 100 1000000 1 1000000 1
DiningPhilosophers:
    numPhilosophers=5, checkStarving=true, runTime=120
DiningServer: checkStarving=true
Philosopher 0 is alive, napThink=1000, napEat=100000
Philosopher 1 is alive, napThink=10000, napEat=1000
Philosopher 2 is alive, napThink=1000, napEat=100000
Philosopher 3 is alive, napThink=1000000000, napEat=1000
Philosopher 4 is alive, napThink=1000000000, napEat=1000
```

```
All Philosopher threads started
age()=110, Philosopher 0 is thinking for 623 ms
age()=170, Philosopher 1 is thinking for 739 ms
age()=170, Philosopher 2 is thinking for 304 ms
age()=220, Philosopher 3 is thinking for 625066794 ms
age()=220, Philosopher 4 is thinking for 852766912 ms
age()=550, Philosopher 2 wants to eat
age()=550, Philosopher 2 is eating for 92594 ms
age()=880, Philosopher 0 wants to eat
age()=880, Philosopher 0 is eating for 30529 ms
age()=990, Philosopher 1 wants to eat
philosopher 1 is STARVING
age()=31360, Philosopher 0 is thinking for 545 ms
age()=31910, Philosopher 0 wants to eat
age()=93150, Philosopher 2 is thinking for 462 ms
age()=93150, Philosopher 1 is eating for 59 ms
age()=93260, Philosopher 1 is thinking for 8682 ms
age()=93260, Philosopher 0 is eating for 22245 ms
age()=93650, Philosopher 2 wants to eat
age()=93650, Philosopher 2 is eating for 92309 ms
age()=101940, Philosopher 1 wants to eat
philosopher 1 is STARVING
age()=115510, Philosopher 0 is thinking for 614 ms
age()=116110, Philosopher 0 wants to eat
age()=120120, time to stop the Philosophers and exit
```

5.3.4 The Readers and Writers

The Java monitor in Class 5.7 synchronizes the database readers and writers and is based on ([6], Figure 5.5).

```
public synchronized void startRead(int i) {
    long readerArrivalTime = 0;
    if (numWaitingWriters > 0 || numWriters > 0) {
        numWaitingReaders++;
        readerArrivalTime = age();
        while (readerArrivalTime >= startWaitingReadersTime)
            try {wait();} catch (InterruptedException e) {}
        numWaitingReaders--;
    }
    numReaders++;
}
public synchronized void endRead(int i) {
    numReaders--;
    okToWrite = numReaders == 0;
    if (okToWrite) notifyAll();
```

```
    }
    public synchronized void startWrite(int i) {
        if (numReaders > 0 || numWriters > 0) {
            numWaitingWriters++;
            okToWrite = false;
            while (!okToWrite)
                try {wait();} catch (InterruptedException e) {}
            numWaitingWriters--;
        }
        okToWrite = false;
        numWriters++;
    }
    public synchronized void endWrite(int i) {
        numWriters--;                       // ASSERT(numWriters==0)
        okToWrite = numWaitingReaders == 0;
        startWaitingReadersTime = age();
        notifyAll();
    }
```

It implements a fair, starvation-free solution: a continual stream of arriving readers cannot delay for an arbitrary amount of time a writer from writing. A reader wishing to read the database must wait if there is a writer currently accessing the database or a waiting writer. The reader's time of arrival at the database is saved in a local variable. Whenever a writer finishes, it sweeps into the database a platoon of **all** waiting readers. (See Exercise 4.6 for the strict serialization approach.) The platoon consists of all those waiting readers who arrived at the database before the current writer finished writing. This monitor is used with the classes (ReadersWriters, Reader, and Writer) in Program 4.14 with no changes.

From the sample output at times 1210 and 4390, we see that if a reader wants to read the database when there is a waiting writer, the reader must wait. Therefore, writers do not starve.

```
    All threads started
    age=440, Reader0 wants to read
    age=440, Reader0 reading for 1530 ms
    age=490, Reader1 wants to read
    age=490, Reader1 reading for 93 ms
    age=600, Reader1 finished reading
    age=600, Reader1 napping for 1931 ms
    age=1040, WRITER1 wants to write
    age=1210, Reader2 wants to read    reader 2 waits to go after writer 1
    age=1320, WRITER0 wants to write
    age=1430, Reader3 wants to read
    age=1590, WRITER2 wants to write
    age=1760, Reader4 wants to read
    age=1980, Reader0 finished reading
```

```
age=1980, Reader0 napping for 329 ms
age=1980, WRITER1 writing for 1144 ms
age=2310, Reader0 wants to read
age=2530, Reader1 wants to read
age=3130, WRITER1 finished writing    now all waiting readers can go
age=3130, WRITER1 napping for 774 ms
age=3130, Reader4 reading for 985 ms
age=3180, Reader2 reading for 1007 ms
age=3240, Reader3 reading for 472 ms
age=3240, Reader0 reading for 1436 ms
age=3240, Reader1 reading for 1894 ms
...
```

However, the readers and writers do not enter the database to perform their operations in exactly the same order they arrived and queued up at the database. In other words, the servicing order is not strictly FIFO. When a writer exits the database, **all** waiting readers enter, even those that arrived after a waiting writer.

5.4 Deadlock

Section 4.5 warns that care must be taken to avoid deadlock when semaphores are used to protect nested critical sections or allocate different types of resources. Nested monitor calls and nested synchronized blocks are also subject to deadlock. Suppose class S has the structure

```
class S {
  synchronized void f(T t) {
    ... t.g(...); ...
  }
}
```

and class T has the structure

```
class T {
  synchronized void g(S s) {
    ... s.f(...); ...
  }
}
```

Here s and t are references to two monitor objects created from classes S and T, respectively, and shared by two threads A and B. If the following sequence of events occurs,

A: calls s.f(t)
B: calls t.g(s)
A: blocks on call to t.g
B: blocks on call to s.f

the two threads deadlock.

The deadlock prevention scheme described in Section 4.5 can also be used with monitors: globally order all monitor objects and require all threads to lock monitor objects (through synchronized method calls) in the same order. In the case of synchronized code blocks (implicit binary semaphores), the same ordering idea can be used with the objects locked by each block.

5.5   Binary and Counting Semaphore Monitors

Chapter 4 on semaphores uses two classes from this book's Synchronization package, BinarySemaphore and CountingSemaphore, to create semaphore objects for mutual exclusion and condition synchronization. The JDK does not include either a binary or counting semaphore class. However, they are easily implemented as Java monitors with P and V methods. Both the binary and counting semaphore classes extend the abstract class Semaphore, shown in Library Class 5.1.

```
public abstract class Semaphore {
    protected int value = 0;
    protected Semaphore() {value = 0;}  // constructors
    protected Semaphore(int initial) {value = initial;}
    public synchronized void P() {
        value--;
        if (value < 0)
            try { wait(); } catch (InterruptedException e) {}
    }
    public synchronized void V() {
        value++;   if (value <= 0) notify();
    }
}
```

The semaphore's value field ranges over both positive and negative integers. A positive or zero value corresponds to the conventional value of a semaphore. A negative value means there are threads blocked on the semaphore, waiting to be released with a V; the absolute value of the value field is the number of blocked threads. This implementation prevents barging: a thread calling P always waits if there are other waiting threads (negative value), even if it obtains the semaphore object lock before a signaled thread. When a V is done, the JVM does not guarantee that the thread waiting the longest is the next one active in the monitor

The Semaphore class P method uses a wait() that is part of an if statement instead of a while loop, in contrast to the recommendation of Section 5.3. This is because a thread blocked in a P is not waiting for some condition to become true but is waiting for permission to proceed, which comes from the notify() in the V method. The code handling an InterruptedException is not shown.

This class provides several methods, not shown above, for semaphores in addition to P and V: the toString method converts the semaphore into a string for System. out.println, the value method reads the semaphore's value, and the nonblocking

tryP method decrements the semaphore's value, if possible, but throws an exception instead of blocking otherwise. The code for the binary and counting semaphore classes extended from **Semaphore** in shown in Library Classes 5.2 and 5.3.

```
public class BinarySemaphore extends Semaphore {
    public BinarySemaphore() {super();}  // constructors
    public BinarySemaphore(int initial)
        {super((initial!=0) ? 1:0);}
    public BinarySemaphore(boolean initial)
        {super(initial ? 1:0);}
    public final synchronized void V() {
        super.V();
        if (value > 1) value = 1; // cap the value
    }
}
public class CountingSemaphore extends Semaphore {
    public CountingSemaphore() {super();}  // constructors
    public CountingSemaphore(int initial) {super(initial);}
}
```

5.6 Locks

In contrast to an implicit binary semaphore in the form of a **synchronized** block, an explicit binary semaphore may be released by any thread, not necessarily the one that acquired it. The lock implemented in Program 5.8 acts like an explicit binary semaphore except only the owner of the lock is permitted to unlock it and every lock's initial state is unlocked.

```
public synchronized void lock() {
    Thread who = Thread.currentThread();
    if (owner == who) return; // allow owner to relock silently
    else if (owner == null) {
        owner = who;
        return;
    } else /* owner != who && owner != null */ {
        while (owner != null) { // since ''barging'' is possible
            try {    // in Java monitors, a while loop is needed
                wait(); // even though only one thread is awakened
            } catch (InterruptedException e) {}
            // here 'owner' can be null or
            // another thread if it barged in
        }
        owner = who;
        return;
    }
}
```

```
public synchronized void unlock()
      throws IllegalMonitorStateException {
   Thread who = Thread.currentThread(); // allow an unlocked
   if (owner == null) return;  // lock to be unlocked silently
   else if (owner != who) {
      throw new IllegalMonitorStateException();
   } else /* owner == who */ {
      owner = null;
      notify(); // at most one thread can proceed if
   }               // any are waiting so notifyAll() not
}                  // needed
```

If a thread not owning the lock tries to unlock it, an `IllegalMonitorStateException` object is thrown. An unlocked lock may be unlocked and a lock owner may relock the lock it owns, both without generating an exception. One of these locks should be used instead of a **synchronized** block (implicit binary semaphore) if the lock is acquired in one method and released in another method, both by the same thread.

5.7 Notification Objects

It is possible to use an object somewhat like a (named) condition variable in a Java monitor.

```
shared object:
   Object obj = new Object();
in one thread:
   synchronized (obj) {...
      if (!condition)
         try { obj.wait(); }
         catch (InterruptedException e) {}
      ...
   }
in another thread:
   synchronized (obj) {...
      if (condition) obj.notify();
      ...
   }
```

The shared object `obj` is used as a *notification* object by the two threads. While inside a synchronized block on `obj`, one thread checks conditions to see if it should continue; if not, it waits. Another thread changes conditions and notifies the waiting thread. When used inside a monitor, a notification object plays the role of a named condition variable.

```
class Name {
```

```
Object obj = new Object();
other data fields;
public type method1(...) {...
    synchronized (obj) {...
        if (!method2(...))
            try { obj.wait(); }
            catch (InterruptedException e) {}
        ...
    }
    ...
}
private synchronized boolean method2(...) {...}
public type method3(...) {...
    synchronized (obj) {...
        if (method4(...)) obj.notify();
        ...
    }
    ...
}
private synchronized boolean method4(...) {...}
}
```

A thread calls a nonsynchronized service method in the monitor, enters a synchronized block on a notification object, and then calls a private synchronized method. If conditions are not right to continue, the thread waits inside the notification object for a signal. Since the threads are performing nested object locking, the programmer must take care to prevent deadlock, as described in Section 5.4. In the above code skeleton, the locks are always requested in the same order.

Class 5.9 moves the code inside the **elements** and **spaces** semaphores of Class 4.4 into the bounded buffer implementation.

```
private Object conveyD = new Object();
private Object conveyF = new Object();
...
public void deposit(double value) {
    synchronized (conveyD) {
        spaces--;    // grab a space or wait behind others
        if (spaces < 0) {
            try { conveyD.wait(); }
            catch (InterruptedException e) {}
        }
        buffer[putIn] = value;
        putIn = (putIn + 1) % numSlots;
    }
    synchronized (conveyF) {
        elements++; // signal a waiting consumer if there is one
```

```
            if (elements <= 0) conveyF.notify();
    }
}
public double fetch() {
    double value;
    synchronized (conveyF) {
        elements--; // grab an element or wait behind others
        if (elements < 0) {
                try { conveyF.wait(); }
                catch (InterruptedException e) {}
        }
        value = buffer[takeOut];
        takeOut = (takeOut + 1) % numSlots;
    }
    synchronized (conveyD) {
        spaces++;   // signal a waiting producer if there is one
        if (spaces <= 0) conveyD.notify();
    }
    return value;
}
```

This class works with multiple producer threads and multiple consumer threads. There are two notification objects, one for waiting producers and one for waiting consumers. Notice there are no synchronized methods in this example. The code handling an InterruptedException is not shown.

Class 5.10 shows a DiningServer class with an array of notification objects, convey, one array entry per philosopher.

```
private Object[] convey = new Object[numPhils];
    for (int i = 0; i < numPhils; i++) convey[i] = new Object();
...
public void takeForks(int i) {
    synchronized (convey[i]) {
        if (hungryAndGetForks(i)) return;
        else try { convey[i].wait(); }
            catch (InterruptedException e) {}
    }
}
public synchronized void putForks(int i) {
    state[i] = THINKING;
    test(left(i), checkStarving);
    test(right(i), checkStarving);
    if (state[left(i)] == EATING) forksAvailable(left(i));
    if (state[right(i)] == EATING) forksAvailable(right(i));
}
private synchronized boolean hungryAndGetForks(int i) {
```

```
      state[i] = HUNGRY;
      test(i, false);
      return state[i] == EATING;
   }
   private void forksAvailable(int i) {
      synchronized (convey[i]) { convey[i].notify(); }
   }
   private void test(int k, boolean checkStarving) {
      if (state[left(k)] != EATING && state[left(k)] != STARVING
            && (state[k] == HUNGRY || state[k] == STARVING) &&
          state[right(k)] != STARVING && state[right(k)] != EATING)
         state[k] = EATING;
      else if (checkStarving)
         seeIfStarving(k); // simplistic naive check for starvation
   }
   private void seeIfStarving(int k) {
      if (state[k] == HUNGRY && state[left(k)] != STARVING
            && state[right(k)] != STARVING) {
         state[k] = STARVING;
      }
   }
}
```

If the forks are not available when the philosopher gets hungry, it waits inside its notification object for a signal. This is an example of a notification: the philosopher registers its request with the server, and if the resources are not available, waits for a notification signal inside an object created for this use. An InterruptedException is not handled (Exercise 10).

Class 5.11 implements a starvation-free synchronization algorithm for the readers and writers. It uses a local notification object, convey, for each thread to wait inside until it can access the database.

```
   private int numReaders = 0;
   private boolean isWriting = false;
   private Vector waitingReaders = new Vector();
   private Vector waitingWriters = new Vector();
   ...
   public void startRead(int i) {
      Object convey = new Object();
      synchronized (convey) {
         if (cannotReadNow(convey))
            try { convey.wait(); }
            catch (InterruptedException e) {}
      }
   }
   private synchronized boolean cannotReadNow(Object convey) {
      boolean status;
```

```
      if (isWriting || waitingWriters.size() > 0) {
         waitingReaders.addElement(convey);   status = true;
      } else {
         numReaders++;   status = false;
      }
      return status;
   }
   public void startWrite(int i) {
      Object convey = new Object();
      synchronized (convey) {
         if (cannotWriteNow(convey))
            try { convey.wait(); }
            catch (InterruptedException e) {}
      }
   }
   private synchronized boolean cannotWriteNow(Object convey) {
      boolean status;
      if (isWriting || numReaders > 0) {
         waitingWriters.addElement(convey);   status = true;
      } else {
         isWriting = true;   status = false;
      }
      return status;
   }
   public synchronized void endRead(int i) {
      numReaders--;
      if (numReaders == 0 && waitingWriters.size() > 0) {
         synchronized (waitingWriters.elementAt(0)) {
            waitingWriters.elementAt(0).notify();
         }
         waitingWriters.removeElementAt(0);
         isWriting = true;
      }
   }
   public synchronized void endWrite(int i) {
      isWriting = false;
      if (waitingReaders.size() > 0) {
         while (waitingReaders.size() > 0) {
            synchronized (waitingReaders.elementAt(0)) {
               waitingReaders.elementAt(0).notify();
            }
            waitingReaders.removeElementAt(0);
            numReaders++;
         }
      } else if (waitingWriters.size() > 0) {
```

```
        synchronized (waitingWriters.elementAt(0)) {
            waitingWriters.elementAt(0).notify();
        }
        waitingWriters.removeElementAt(0);
        isWriting = true;
    }
}
```

The platoon strategy, as opposed to strict serialization, is used in preventing starvation. A finishing writer signals the notification objects of all waiting readers. Two vectors, `waitingReaders` and `waitingWriters`, are used as queues for the notification objects of waiting readers and writers. An `InterruptedException` is not handled (Exercise 10).

In contrast to the named condition variables of Section 5.2, it is not possible with this notification scheme to wait in the middle of a synchronized monitor service method for a signal and then continue executing inside the monitor service method at that point after receiving the signal. To avoid deadlock, the thread must leave the synchronized method with a return statement before waiting inside the notification object. After a signal, the thread reenters the monitor via a service method call. The notification code closely resembles the Java implementation of semaphores, shown in Section 5.5.

5.8   Implementing Monitors with Semaphores

Semaphores can be implemented with monitors, as shown in Section 5.5. Conversely, monitors can be implemented with semaphores, making the two synchronization techniques equivalent in power. Monitors, though, as mentioned at the beginning of this chapter, are a higher level concept. The implementation shown here is based on ([1], Section 6.6) for signal-and-continue and ([6], Section 5.4) for signal-and-exit. The description in ([6], Section 5.4) for signal and continue is not correct; the one in ([41], pages 52–53) for signal-and-exit is not correct. See Exercise 17.

Each monitor includes a binary semaphore that permits only one thread at a time to be active in the monitor.

    semaphore mutex = 1
        · · ·
    service method$i$ {
            P(mutex);
            · · ·
            V(mutex);
            exit the monitor, i.e., return
    }
        · · ·

Each condition variable $cond_i$ is implemented with a semaphore SEM_i and an integer counter $COUNT_i$, both initially zero. The following implements the signal-and-continue signaling discipline.

wait($cond_i$):
      $COUNT_i + +;$
      V(mutex);
      P(SEM_i);
      P(mutex);

signal($cond_i$):
      if $(COUNT_i > 0)$ { $COUNT_i - -;$ V(SEM_i); }
      ... continue in the monitor, perhaps send more signals

As mentioned earlier, when a signal is generated a thread waiting at P(mutex) to enter the monitor via a service method call may barge in (as a result of a context switch or faster CPU) and enter the monitor before the signaled thread executes P(mutex). The thread that barged in may change the condition; when the signaled thread's P(mutex) succeeds, the condition may no longer be true. To protect against this, waiting threads should recheck the condition after waking up from a signal and reentering the monitor.

The above is not correct for signal and exit because a signaled thread does not have priority to reenter the monitor. To implement signal and exit, we change the above to

wait($cond_i$):
      $COUNT_i + +;$
      V(mutex);
      P(SEM_i);

signal($cond_i$):
      if $(COUNT_i > 0)$ { $COUNT_i - -;$ V(SEM_i); }
      else V(mutex);
      exit the monitor, i.e., return

A signaled thread gets priority to proceed in the monitor over any threads waiting to enter the monitor via a service method call. This subtlety is easily overlooked.

5.8.1 Named Condition Variables for Java

The methods for condition variables in Library Class 3.1, MyObject,

```
protected static void wait(ConditionVariable cv) {
    cv.waitCV();
}
protected static void notify(ConditionVariable cv) {
    cv.notifyCV();
}
protected static boolean empty(ConditionVariable cv) {
    return cv.emptyCV();
}
```

and the ideas in the pseudocode of Section 5.8 for implementing monitors with semaphores can be used to complete the implementation of the class `ConditionVariable`
in Library Class 5.4 (Exercise 20).

```
public class ConditionVariable { // not yet implemented
   public void waitCV(Object monitor) {}
   public void notifyCV(Object monitor) {}
   public boolean emptyCV(Object monitor) {return true;}
}
```

5.9   Algorithm Animation

Library Class 5.5 is a Java implementation of the XTANGO animator command set
described in Section 2.7. This package has many thread synchronization issues. The
animation surface is implemented with a Java AWT frame having several buttons
along the top and a canvas in the center for drawing. All window events, such as
button clicks, are handled in the frame's `actionPerformed` method.

All of the public methods in the `XtangoAnimator` class, such as `coords`, `line`,
`circle`, and `move`, create an object and call the `doCommand` method in the frame.

```
// Create a circle with the given radius centered at the
// given position.
public void circle(String id, float xpos, float ypos,
      float radius, Color colorval, int fillval) {
   Icircle c =
      new Icircle(id, xpos, ypos, radius, colorval, fillval);
   af.doCommand(c);
}
```

The `XtangoAnimator` class has a `main` method that tests all of these methods. The
objects created in the `XtangoAnimator` public methods are instantiated from the
`AnimatorCommand` class. It has two subclasses: `AnimatorAction` for commands like
`coords` and `move`, and `AnimatorIcon` for icons to be drawn like lines and circles.
`AnimatorShape` is a subclass of `AnimatorIcon` for drawn icons with shapes, like
circles, triangles, and rectangles.

An `AnimatorIcon` object has **add** and **draw** methods. The **add** method accesses
an `icons` vector of all icons to be drawn during the animation and a hash table that
associates the object's identifying string with the object's entry in the vector. After
checking the hash table for a duplicate string, the method adds the object to the
`icons` vector.

```
protected String id;
...
void add(Hashtable ht, Vector icons) {
   Object old = null;
   synchronized (ht) {
```

```
    if (ht.containsKey(id)) {
       System.err.println("duplicate id=" + id);
       return;
    }
    old = ht.put(id, this);
 }
 if (old == null) {
    synchronized (icons) { icons.addElement(this); }
 } else { System.err.println("should not happen!"); }
}
```

The **draw** method is called by a thread in the canvas. The method is **abstract**
in the **AnimatorIcon** class and must be implemented by each particular icon class,
such as **Iline**.

```
synchronized void draw(AnimatorCanvas ac, Graphics g) {
   g.setColor(colorval);
   if (widthval == XtangoAnimator.THIN) {
      g.drawLine(
          ac.scaleX(position.x), ac.scaleY(position.y),
          ac.scaleX(position.x+size.w),
          ac.scaleY(position.y+size.h));
   } else if (widthval == XtangoAnimator.MEDTHICK) {...}
   else if (widthval == XtangoAnimator.THICK) {...}
}
```

An **AnimatorAction** object has a **perform** method that uses the identifying
string of the icon being manipulated to retrieve a reference to that icon from the
hash table. For example, to move an icon its position, stored inside the icon object,
is changed by the **perform** method.

```
void perform(AnimatorCanvas ac, Hashtable ht, Vector icons) {
   AnimatorIcon icon = null;
   synchronized (ht) {
      if ((icon = (AnimatorIcon) ht.get(id)) == null) {
         System.err.println("no such id=" + id);
         return;
      }
   }
   synchronized (icon.position) { icon.position(xpos, ypos); }
}
```

The frame's **doCommand** method checks the object passed by the public methods
in **XtangoAnimator** to see if the object is an **AnimatorAction** or an **AnimatorIcon**.

```
void doCommand(AnimatorCommand command) {
   if (XtangoAnimator.debug)
```

```
        System.out.println("doCommand: command " + command);
    if (command instanceof AnimatorAction) {
        ((AnimatorAction) command).perform(ac, ht, icons);
    } else if (command instanceof AnimatorIcon) {
        ((AnimatorIcon) command).add(ht, icons);
    } else {
        System.err.println("doCommand: illegal command");
    }
//  try {
//      int frameDelay = ac.frameDelay;  Thread.sleep(frameDelay);
//  } catch (InterruptedException e) {}
    synchronized (this) {
        if (singleStep)
            try { wait(); } catch (InterruptedException e) {}
    }
}
```

If the former, doCommand calls the object's **perform** method, moving an icon for example; if the latter, doCommand calls the object's add method so the object is drawn on the canvas. The doCommand method is not synchronized, permitting commands to be processed in parallel, such as two threads moving icons at the same time. The sleep(frameDelay) is commented out in the current version to allow a group of commands to be done nearly instantaneously. Invoke

```
xa.delay(frames);
```

after an animation command if its action should be performed as a distinct step in the algorithm animation.

Single-stepping is implemented with a wait() near the end of doCommand, shown above, and a notifyAll() in the actionPerformed method of the frame.

```
    public void actionPerformed(ActionEvent evt) {
        Object o = evt.getSource();
        if (o instanceof Button) {
            String label = ((Button) o).getLabel();
            if (label.equals("Start")) {...
            } else if (label.equals("Single Step Off")) {
                synchronized (this) { singleStep = true; }
                singleStepButton.setLabel("Single Step On");
            } else if (label.equals("Single Step On")) {
                synchronized (this) {
                    singleStep = false; // now that single stepping is
                    this.notifyAll();   // off, clear out any waiting
                }                       // threads
                singleStepButton.setLabel("Single Step Off");
            } else if (label.equals("Step")) {
                synchronized (this)
```

```
                    { if (singleStep) this.notifyAll(); }
               } else if ...
          } ...
     }
```

All drawing is done by a thread in the canvas.

```
public void run() {
    while (true) {
        try {
            Thread.sleep(frameDelay);
        } catch (InterruptedException e) {}
        repaint();                  // tell AWT to call paint()
    }
}
public synchronized void paint(Graphics g) {
        // activated by repaint()
    offscreenGraphics.setColor(getBackground());
    offscreenGraphics.fillRect(0, 0, widthCanvas, heightCanvas);
    synchronized (icons) {
        int howMany = icons.size();
        for (int i = 0; i < howMany; i++) { ((AnimatorIcon)
            icons.elementAt(i)).draw(this, offscreenGraphics);
        }
    }
    g.drawImage(offscreenImage, 0, 0, this);
}
```

After a delay time determined by the magnitude of frameDelay, the canvas thread uses the hash table and icons vector to call each AnimatorIcon object's draw method. To avoid flicker, the drawing is done in an off-screen image.

To avoid race conditions and corrupted data structures, the drawing thread and the user threads invoking doCommand through the public methods in XtangoAnimator must be synchronized so that only one thread at a time accesses the hash table and the icons vector. An icon should be drawn before or after but not while any of its attributes is being changed by a command. Look for all occurrences of the keyword synchronized in the code!

Summary

The monitor is Java's built-in synchronization primitive, specifically, object locks, synchronized blocks, wait(), notify(), and notifyAll(). Monitors are usually easier and safer to use than semaphores because all shared variables and synchronization constructs are encapsulated into a single class definition. Recall from the previous chapter that related semaphore operations may be widely separated, scattered among many classes. Nonetheless, deadlock is a major concern when using either semaphores or monitors.

In this chapter we defined the monitor, its condition variables, and several signaling disciplines that are in use: signal and exit, signal and continue, and signal and wait. Since Java uses signal and continue, a Java monitor designer must be aware of the behavior of this particular signaling discipline. Barging is possible, more than one signal may be generated by a thread active in a monitor, and waiting threads nearly always need to recheck the monitor condition on which they are waiting each time they reenter the monitor after a signal.

`BinarySemaphore` and `CountingSemaphore`, the binary and counting semaphore classes used extensively in Chapter 4, are implemented as Java monitors. We examined their implementation, deferred from the earlier chapter.

We looked at monitor solutions to the three classic synchronization problems (bounded buffer producer and consumer, dining philosophers, database readers and writers) using signal and exit and signal and continue. The latter two problems were solved with a starvation-free algorithm.

Java synchronized blocks and our explicit binary semaphores are closely related. We defined a class, `Lock`, that combines the features of both.

Each Java monitor has only a single nameless condition variable, in contrast to the conventional definition of a monitor. This complicates the design of some monitor synchronization solutions or makes the resulting code less efficient because a `notifyAll()` must be used instead of a signal targeted to a specific group of waiting threads. Consequently, most Java monitor methods follow this design pattern:

```
public synchronized type method(...) {
    ...
    notifyAll(); // if any wait conditions altered
    while (!condition)
        try { wait(); } catch (InterruptedException e) {}
    ...
    notifyAll(); // if any wait conditions altered
}
```

Using notification objects helps somewhat in coping with this situation; however, the code may be convoluted and hard to understand because of nested synchronization blocks inside the monitor. And deadlock is of even more concern. We implemented solutions to the three classic synchronization problems using notification objects.

Monitors and semaphores are of equal power in the theoretical sense that each can be implemented with the other. In this chapter, we showed how to do both.

Several algorithm animations were shown in previous chapters, using the `XtangoAnimation` package. We concluded the chapter with a sketch of how the package is implemented, appropriate at this point because of the many synchronization concerns in the package.

5.10 Exercises

1. **Test and Set.** Write a Java monitor that implements the test-and-set instruction described in Section 3.5.3.

2. **Producers and Consumers.** Class 5.1 is a signal-and-exit monitor for a single producer thread and a single consumer thread. It has two condition variables, `notFull` and `notEmpty`, and is written in a Java-like pseudocode. Analyze the correctness of this monitor if one or more of the following changes are made (there are eight combinations in all): there are multiple producer and consumer threads instead of one of each, the signaling discipline is signal and continue instead of signal and exit, there is one nameless (anonymous) condition variable instead of two.

Class 5.5 is a Java bounded buffer monitor for a single producer thread and a single consumer thread. The signaling discipline is signal and continue and there is one nameless (anonymous) condition variable. Explain exactly why the `wait` is part of a `while` loop instead of an `if` statement. The `notifys` in `deposit` and `fetch` are part of `if` statements so that signals are not wasted, that is, not generated when it is impossible any thread is waiting. On the other hand, using this `if` may mean that a needed signal does not get generated. Is this possible? Why or why not?

Modify Class 5.5 so that it can be used with multiple producer and consumer threads, as was done in Exercise 4.2 for the semaphore version. Think carefully about whether `notifys` should be changed to `notifyAlls` and whether signals should be generated unconditionally instead of inside an `if` statement. Explain your decisions.

3. **Bounded Buffer Fetch with Timeout.** Modify your bounded buffer monitor from the previous exercise (works for multiple producer and consumer threads) so that it has an additional method:

```
public double fetch(long maxMillisecondsWait)
    throws WaitTimeoutException
```

Use the `wait(long ms)` method that blocks at most *ms* milliseconds for a `notify()` or `notifyAll()`. Be sure to recheck the number of full buffer slots and the elapsed milliseconds each time the `wait` returns in order to determine which event occurred. Throw an exception if the `wait` timed out. Why can we not return 0 or –1? Explain why we must check the elapsed milliseconds each time the `wait` returns?

4. **Fair Baboons.** Write a monitor for the fair baboons program done in Exercise 4.7. Pick either strict serialization or platooning as your strategy.

5. **Sleeping Barbers.** Write a monitor for the sleeping barbers program done in Exercise 4.4.

6. **Fair Dining Philosophers.** Enhance the starvation detection in the monitor in Class 5.2 or 5.6 for the fair dining philosophers so that the two neighbors must alternate their eating three times before the one in the middle becomes starving.

7. **Readers and Writers.** Modify Class 5.7 so that the strict serialization strategy is used to prevent starvation. Modify Class 5.11 in the same way.

8. **Bounded Buffer Notification Monitor.** In Classes 3.8 and 3.19, each buffer slot has an `occupied` field used by the threads for busy waiting and suspend/resume

synchronization, respectively. Write a bounded buffer monitor, valid for multiple producer threads and multiple consumer threads, that uses each buffer slot as a notification object in a similar way. Make `notify()` and `if...wait()` feasible by using nested synchronization blocks so that at most one producer or consumer is waiting on a buffer slot at a time.

```
synchronized (buffer[putIn]) {  // executed by a producer
    if (buffer[putIn].occupied) buffer[putIn].wait();
    buffer[putIn].value = value;
    buffer[putIn].occupied = true;
    buffer[putIn].notify();
}
```

9. **Readers and Writers Notification Monitor.** Class 5.11 uses a `convey` object for each reader to wait inside if it has to delay reading the database due to a waiting writer. For the platoon approach, it is necessary to use only one such object in which all delayed readers wait. A writer exiting the database does a `notifyAll` in this object to release all waiting readers, if any. Make this modification.

10. `InterruptedException` **in Notification Objects.** If a thread calls some object's `wait` method, the thread blocks and waits until removed from the wait set by a call to the object's `notify` method. Invoking the thread's `interrupt` method also removes the thread from the wait set. The `wait` method then throws an `InterruptedException` object. One way to handle an `InterruptedException` object in a monitor having `wait` inside a `while` loop is to check the condition and `wait` again.

```
while (condition) {
    try { wait(); }
    catch (InterruptedException e) { }
}
```

If the `wait` is part of an `if` statement, this technique is not correct: an `interrupt` has the same effect as a `notify`. Instead, we use a `while` loop in conjunction with the `if` statement.

```
if (condition) {
    while (true) {
        try { wait(); break; }
        catch (InterruptedException e) { continue; }
    }
}
```

The only way a waiting thread proceeds in the monitor is after a `notify`; an `interrupt` causes the thread to `wait` again. After leaving the wait set, due to a `notify` or `interrupt`, the thread must compete with other threads to reacquire the object's lock. The `wait` method returns when the lock is obtained after a `notify`. In the case of an `interrupt`, the `catch` block is executed when the lock is obtained. An object's lock must also be acquired to call its `notify` method.

Suppose that the waiting set of the object contains exactly one thread. A race condition occurs in the second technique above for handling an `InterruptedException` if some thread tries to lock the object to call `notify` and, at about the same time, some other thread invokes `interrupt`. If the `interrupt` occurs first, then the interrupted waiting thread and the notifying thread compete to obtain the object's lock. If the interrupted thread succeeds, it will execute `wait` again and be notified. However, if the notifying thread obtains the lock first, the signal is lost because the wait set is empty. Both Library Class 5.1 and Program 5.9 contain code to check for this race condition.

```
// code that waits
   value--;
   if (value < 0) {
       while (true) { // we must be notified not interrupted
           try { wait(); break; }
           catch (InterruptedException e) {
               if (value >= 0) break;
               else continue;
           }
       }
   }
...
// code that notifies
   value++;
   if (value <= 0) notify();
```

The waiting thread examines `value` to see if it missed a signal while trying to lock the object after an `interrupt`.

This race condition is not detected in the notification objects of Section 5.7, such as in Program 5.10.

```
synchronized (convey[i]) {
   if (hungryAndGetForks(i)) return;
   else while (true)    // we must be notified not interrupted
       try { convey[i].wait();  break; }
       // notify() after interrupt() race condition ignored
       catch (InterruptedException e) { continue; }
}
```

Correct this deficiency.

11. **Deadlock.** Classes 5.10 and 5.11 use nested synchronization blocks that are not always locked in the same order. Is deadlock possible, as discussed in Section 5.4?

12. **Fraternity Party.** Write a monitor for the fraternity party program done in Exercise 4.8.

13. **Bakery.** Write a monitor for the bakery program done in Exercise 4.3.

14. **Amusement Park Multirider Bumper Cars.** Modify your multiple rider bumper car program from Exercise 4.13 so that the coordinator class is coded as a Java monitor instead of with semaphores; that is, all the methods for condition synchronization are synchronized and use wait(), notify(), and/or notifyAll(). Your monitor will have the following service methods called by the rider and car threads: getInLine(rid), takeAseat(rid), waitCarFull(rid), takeAride(rid), load(cid), and unload(cid).

Remember that Java monitors use signal and continue, so think about the ramifications of this as you design your monitor, in particular, the use of while rather than if with wait() and the use of notifyAll() instead of notify(). Remember that "barging" is possible with signal and continue. Do not use nap within a monitor synchronized method. Do you see why?

Here is one approach to such a monitor class. Think of the monitor as maintaining the state of the system and the synchronized methods as making atomic changes to the state of the system. For example, takeAseat checks to see if there is a car loading (or ready to load). If not, it sets a Boolean variable riderWaiting and then calls wait(). If there is a car loading (or ready to load), it adds the rider to the car and checks if the car is full. If the car is full, it signals with notify() or notifyAll(). Similarly, load checks to see if any riders are waiting. If so, it signals with notify() or notifyAll(). If not, it sets a Boolean variable carReadyToLoad and calls wait(). Do not let two cars load at the same time. Do you see why?

A totally different approach is to use a bounded buffer. Remember to use a bounded buffer that is safe for multiple producers and multiple consumers and that has no semaphores. A rider enters the monitor, puts its identifier into a bounded buffer maintained inside the monitor, and then waits. A car enters the monitor to get enough riders out of the bounded buffer to fill it. If not enough riders are currently in the buffer to fill the car, the car waits. If you use this approach, be careful about nested monitor method calls leading to deadlock, that is, a rider or car calling a synchronized coordinator method that calls a synchronized bounded buffer method. Do you see why?

15. **Haunted House with Multiple Touring Cars.** Modify your multiple car Haunted House program from Exercise 4.15 so that the coordinator class is coded as a Java monitor.

16. **Implementing Semaphores with Java Monitors.** Compare the performance of

```
class AnotherBinarySemaphore {

    private boolean locked = false;
```

```
    public AnotherBinarySemaphore() {}  // constructors
    public AnotherBinarySemaphore(boolean initial) {locked = initial;}
    public AnotherBinarySemaphore(int initial) {
        if (initial < 0 || initial > 1)
            throw new IllegalArgumentException("initial<0 || initial>1");
        locked = (initial == 0);
    }

    public synchronized void P() {
        while (locked) {
            try { wait(); } catch (InterruptedException e) {}
        }
        locked = true;
    }

    public synchronized void V() {
        if (locked) notify();
        locked = false;
    }
}
```

with Library Class 5.2. Then compare the performance of Library Class 5.2 with Program 5.8.

Modify **AnotherBinarySemaphore** so that it is **AnotherCountingSemaphore**, as follows.

```
    class AnotherCountingSemaphore {

        private int value = 0;

        public AnotherCountingSemaphore() {}  // constructors
        public AnotherCountingSemaphore(int initial) {
            if (initial < 0) throw new IllegalArgumentException("initial<0");
            value = initial;
        }

        public synchronized void P() {
            while (value == 0) {
                try { wait(); } catch (InterruptedException e) {}
            }
            value--;
        }

        public synchronized void V() {
            if (value == 0) notify();
            value++;
        }
    }
```

Then compare the performance of the latter with Library Class 5.3, in particular, discover how barging might lead to an inconsistent semaphore state.

17. **Implementing Monitors with Semaphores.** Section 5.8 shows how monitors are implemented with semaphores. The implementation

> wait($cond_i$):
> > $COUNT_i + +$;
> > V(mutex);
> > P(SEM_i);
> > P(mutex);
> > $COUNT_i - -$;

> signal($cond_i$):
> > if ($COUNT_i > 0$) V(SEM_i);
> > ...continue in the monitor, perhaps send more signals

shown in ([6], Section 5.4) for signal and continue is not correct. Why? Think about what happens if two successive signals are done on a condition variable on which one thread is waiting.

The description in ([41], pages 52–53) for signal and exit is not correct. Why? Think about what happens if the up(c) is done in procedure leave_with_signal when there are no threads blocked on the semaphore c.

18. **FIFO Semaphores.** If a thread calls notify() and the set of waiting threads is not empty, an arbitrary thread from the set is awakened to reacquire the monitor's lock. Using the notification idea from Section 5.7, modify Library Class 5.1 so that threads blocked inside P are released in first-come-first-served order by calls to V. Use the Vector class to contain the waiting threads' notification objects, as is done in Class 5.11.

19. **Flawed Condition Variables.** Consider the following attempt to implement named condition variables in Java. For each condition, create a Condition object whose wait and notify methods are used in a Monitor object for synchronization.

```
public class Condition {
}

public abstract class Monitor {

    protected static void wait(Condition c) {
        synchronized (c)
            { try { c.wait(); } catch (InterruptedException e) {} }
    }

    protected static void signal(Condition c) {
        synchronized (c) { c.notify(); }
    }
}
```

The following extends the Monitor class to implement a bounded buffer. Are there any problems with this approach? Look for race conditions and the potential for deadlock.

```
class BoundedBuffer extends Monitor {

    private int numSlots = 0;
    private double[] buffer = null;
    private int putIn = 0, takeOut = 0, count = 0;
    private Condition elements =
        new Condition(), spaces = new Condition();

    public BoundedBuffer(int numSlots) {
        if (numSlots <= 0)
            throw new IllegalArgumentException("numSlots<=0");
        this.numSlots = numSlots;
        buffer = new double[numSlots];
    }

    public synchronized void deposit(double value) {
        while (count == numSlots) wait(spaces);
        buffer[putIn] = value;
        putIn = (putIn + 1) % numSlots;
        count++;
        if (count == 1) signal(elements);
    }

    public synchronized double fetch() {
        double value;
        while (count == 0) wait(elements);
        value = buffer[takeOut];
        takeOut = (takeOut + 1) % numSlots;
        count--;
        if (count == numSlots-1) signal(spaces);
        return value;
    }

    public static void main(String[] args) {
        BoundedBuffer bb = new BoundedBuffer(5);
        bb.deposit(Math.PI);
        System.out.println("fetched " + bb.fetch() + " from bb");
    }
}
```

How about this version?

```
class BoundedBuffer extends Monitor {

    private int numSlots = 0;
    private double[] buffer = null;
    private int putIn = 0, takeOut = 0, count = 0;
```

```
      private Condition elements =
         new Condition(), spaces = new Condition();

      public BoundedBuffer(int numSlots) {
         if (numSlots <= 0)
            throw new IllegalArgumentException("numSlots<=0");
         this.numSlots = numSlots;
         buffer = new double[numSlots];
      }

      public void deposit(double value) {
         while (true) {
            synchronized (this) {
               if (count < numSlots) {
                  buffer[putIn] = value;
                  putIn = (putIn + 1) % numSlots;
                  count++;
                  if (count == 1) signal(elements);
                  return;
               }
            }
            wait(spaces);
         }
      }

      public double fetch() {
         double value;
         while (true) {
            synchronized (this) {
               if (count > 0) {
                  value = buffer[takeOut];
                  takeOut = (takeOut + 1) % numSlots;
                  count--;
                  if (count == numSlots-1) signal(spaces);
                  return value;
               }
            }
            wait(elements);
         }
      }

      public static void main(String[] args) {
         BoundedBuffer bb = new BoundedBuffer(5);
         bb.deposit(Math.PI);
         System.out.println("fetched " + bb.fetch() + " from bb");
      }
   }
```

20. **Named Condition Variables for Java.** Complete the implementation of the class `ConditionVariable` in Library Class 5.4 so that it can be used in Java monitors (classes with `synchronized` methods). See Section 5.8.1. Using the `Vector`

class, associate a queue with each condition variable; waitCV adds the thread to the condition variable's queue before doing a wait() inside the monitor, which is why this is passed to waitCV in MyObject and why waitCV is not static. When the waiting thread is awakened, it checks to see if it has reached the head of the queue; if not, it waits again. A call to notifyCV invokes notifyAll() inside the monitor; all the waiting threads check to see if they are at the head of the queue. Compare the performance of the technique outlined here with the one in Section 5.7.

The preceding implements signal and continue. Is it possible to implement signal and exit? If so, do it. If not, why not?

Why can we not just call the condition variable object's wait() instead of the monitor's wait(cv)?

21. **More Named Condition Variables.** The condition variable class CondVar, adapted from [33], is designed for use in semaphore programs and resembles a notification object.

```
import Utilities.*;
import Synchronization.*;

public class CondVar extends MyObject {

    public synchronized void wait(BinarySemaphore mutex) {
        V(mutex);                // release the monitor
        try { wait(); }          // atomically before waiting
        catch (InterruptedException e) {}
        P(mutex);                // reacquire the monitor
    }

    public synchronized void signal() {
        notify();                // release a waiting thread
    }

    public synchronized void signalAll() {
        notifyAll();             // release all waiting threads
    }
}
```

The following example creates a condition variable from this class.

```
import Utilities.*;
import Synchronization.*;

class Allocator extends MyObject {

    private BinarySemaphore mutex =
        new BinarySemaphore(1);
    private int available = 0;
    private CondVar cv = new CondVar();
```

```
    public Allocator(int initial) {
        if (initial <= 0)
            throw new IllegalArgumentException();
        available = initial;
    }

    public void want(int w) {
        P(mutex);           // acquire the monitor
        while (w > available) cv.wait(mutex);
        available -= w;
        V(mutex);           // release the monitor
    }

    public void done(int d) {
        P(mutex);           // acquire the monitor
        available += d;
        cv.signalAll();
        V(mutex);           // release the monitor
    }
}
```

The `Allocator` class is functionally equivalent to a monitor, using an explicit semaphore `mutex` instead of synchronized methods for mutual exclusion. The semaphore is passed as a parameter to the condition variable's wait method. Compare the performance of this technique with the ones in Sections 5.7, 5.8, and 5.8.1. Will these condition variables work inside a Java monitor (a class all of whose methods are synchronized)? Why?

22. **Semaphore with a Timeout.** Modify Library Class 5.1 so that the P method is overloaded with one having an argument of type integer that represents a millisecond timeout option. If the P(*ms*) call is still blocked after the timeout period expires, throw an exception.

23. **Four-of-a-Kind Game.** ([25], page 107) Write a monitor that is used in a multithreaded Java program simulating the four-of-a-kind game. The game is played with a deck of cards containing six suits of four cards each. Four players sit around a table, each holding four cards. There are piles of cards between each pair of players, alternating with them around the table. At the start of the game, each pile contains two cards. Each player repeatedly discards a card into the left-hand pile and draws a card from the right-hand pile. The first player to obtain four-of-a-kind wins the game.

24. **Locks.** The lock on a Java object acting as a monitor is obtained by entering a synchronized block on that object or entering a synchronized method in the object. The lock is released when the block or method is exited. Java allows the same thread to lock a monitor object multiple times. This occurs in two nested synchronized blocks on the same object or when a synchronized method in an object invokes another synchronized method in the same object. The Java virtual machine counts the number of times the lock is locked in this fashion and only releases the lock when

the same number of unlocking events occurs. Modify the Lock class in Program 5.8 so that it behaves this way. Every time the thread currently owning the lock calls lock, increment a counter; every time it calls unlock, decrement the counter; if the counter reaches zero, release the lock.

Add a tryLock method that obtains the lock if currently free but throws a Would-BlockException object if the lock is not free.

Modify the Lock class in Program 5.8 so that it does not allow barging. This occurs if a thread calls lock after other threads have entered their wait() loops and gets the lock before the waiting threads. Also make the lock fair by granting the lock in a first-come-first-served order. Add a Vector to contain references to the threads waiting to obtain the lock. Instead of notifyAll(), use notify() and the notification technique of Section 5.7.

25. Time Slicing Scheduler Class. Modify Library Class 3.2, the Scheduler class that introduces time slicing, so that at most one object can be instantiated from this class during a program execution. Add a static variable to the class that counts instantiations. Call a static method in the class constructor that increments this count. Does this method need to be synchronized?

26. Algorithm Animation. Find all remaining race conditions, if any, in Library Class 5.5 and fix them. Give a specific sequence of events that leads to each race condition you find.

Add an Iimage icon class to Library Class 5.5 that associates a string id with an image stored in a GIF or JPEG file.

Add a Cgroup command class that associates a string id with a group (an array) of other ids so that commands such as move and change color can be applied to the whole group.

Add a CnewId command class that gives an icon a new string id.

Add a Cwidth class that changes the widthval of a line icon.

Add a Crotate class that rotates an icon.

Add an arrow option to the Iline class.

The vis, raise, and lower methods deal with viewing planes and the order icons are drawn on top of one another. Add a Chide class and a hide method that toggles the visibility of an icon in the sense of drawing the icon or not, regardless of its viewing plane. Add a Boolean field to the AnimatorIcon class; if it is false, the drawing loop in the canvas thread skips the icon.

Chapter 6

Message Passing and the Rendezvous

The previous two chapters show how a collection of threads sharing one address space in a uniprocessor or shared-memory multiprocessor uses semaphores or monitors for mutual exclusion and event synchronization. Even though two threads in two different address spaces cannot interfere with each other's variables and are therefore not subject to race conditions, they may still need to synchronize their execution or communicate data. Suppose in the bounded buffer producer and consumer problem, the producer and consumer threads are in separate address spaces. Items built by the producer need to be delivered (communication) to the consumer. The consumer needs to block if the buffer is empty, and the producer needs to block if the buffer is full (synchronization). As another example, suppose a client thread executing on a diskless workstation wants to read some data from a file on a disk attached to a file server machine. The client must somehow send its request to the file server and then block until the data are returned.

However, two threads in two different address spaces cannot share semaphores or monitors for synchronization or communication. For example, threads spread across a distributed system, such as a collection of machines, each with its own CPU and memory, connected together on a LAN, cannot share semaphores or monitors. Computer science researchers are devising *distributed shared memory* (DSM) systems ([42], Chapter 6), so one day such sharing might be possible; however, DSM systems are not yet practical. Therefore, we must use another technique for thread communication and synchronization in distributed systems. This chapter describes message passing and two tools implemented with message passing, the rendezvous and the remote procedure call. Message passing may be used by threads within one address space as an alternative to semaphores and monitors.

We examine several varieties of message passing: synchronous, asynchronous, capacity controlled, and conditional. Message types supported are integer numbers (`int`), floating-point numbers (`double`), and objects. Within one address space, a pipe holds sent but not yet received messages. Between address spaces, particularly between machines, a socket is used. Two message passing applications are presented, distributed mutual exclusion and the distributed dining philosophers. We next see

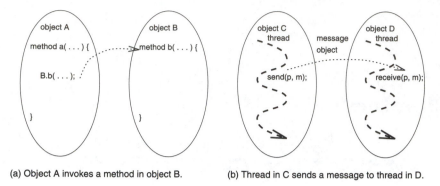

(a) Object A invokes a method in object B.   (b) Thread in C sends a message to thread in D.

Figure 6.1: Method Invocation Compared to Message Passing.

how two threads in the same address space or in different address spaces establish a rendezvous and then perform one or more transactions. This is the basis of client-server interaction. A conditional or guarded rendezvous is also implemented. Java's remote method invocation package handles remote procedure calls. A simple example illustrates how to use this package. The chapter concludes with two message passing animations, the distributed dining philosophers and a parallel version of quicksort.

6.1   Message Passing Definitions

Sometimes the phrase "sending a message to an object" is used in object-oriented programming to describe a thread in an object calling or invoking a method in another object. However, this is inaccurate. "Passing" or "sending a message" should be used to describe a thread in one object sending a message to a *thread* executing in another object, where the message itself is an object. Figure 6.1 illustrates the difference.

Primitive operations executed by threads to perform message passing are send(to, message) and receive(from,message), where from and to specify some sort of source and destination addressing, respectively, and message is a reference to the object containing the message. The terms *port*, *channel*, and *mailbox* are used to describe where messages are sent and from where they are received.

Message passing is *blocking* or *nonblocking*, These design choices are also called *synchronous* and *asynchronous*, respectively. If receives are blocking and there is no message available, the receiver blocks until one arrives. If sends are blocking, the sender blocks if there is no receiver ready to receive the message. If sends are nonblocking, a send returns control immediately after the message is queued by the messaging system. If receives are nonblocking, a receive returns a failure indicator if no message is available. Instead of sharing variables, threads in different address spaces share message passing channels implemented by the messaging system. Sending a message is analogous to a thread making a remote assignment of a value to a variable in another address space. If sends are blocking, then the sending thread delays until the remote assignment is made. Asynchronous message passing is an extension or enhancement of the semaphore P and V operations to include data. In fact, asynchronous message passing of empty messages is equivalent to (potentially remote) semaphore P and V operations.

If both send and receive are blocking, then a *simple rendezvous* occurs when the message is transferred or copied from the sender to the receiver. Both the sending thread and the receiving thread are at known points in their code at the same time and a unidirectional flow of information takes place.

We also have *buffered* and *nonbuffered* design choices. A nonbuffered send blocks until a receiver executes a receive. A buffered send usually implies nonblocking. But there is probably an upper limit on the buffer size above which the sender blocks. There is not much functional difference between blocking buffered and blocking nonbuffered sends.

So we really have three varieties of each. All send/receive design choice combinations below are feasible except 2/3, 3/2, and 3/3. For send,

1. Blocking: waits for receiver or receiver is already waiting;

2. Buffered, nonblocking: message is buffered but the receiver has not necessarily gotten it yet;

3. Nonbuffered, nonblocking: returns an error if no receiver is ready or waiting, returns okay if message is sent and received.

For receive,

1. Blocking: waits for message, i.e., sender to send;

2. Buffered, nonblocking: returns an error if no message is waiting, else returns okay;

3. Nonbuffered, nonblocking: returns an error if no sender is ready or waiting, returns okay if message is sent and received.

Two other design considerations are naming or addressing and the sharing of channels by multiple threads. How does the sending thread address the destination thread? How does the receiving thread specify the desired message source? Instead of the sender and receiver addressing each other directly, a channel, also called a port or mailbox, may be used. The sender and receiver refer to the channel in their message passing operations.

```
shared by sender and receiver:
    channel chan;
sender:
    send(chan, message);
receiver:
    message = receive(chan);
```

client   server

...   ...

send (request)   receive (service request)

... [wait]   ... [do requested service]

receive (results)   send (back results)

...   ...

Figure 6.2: Client-to-Server Remote Procedure Call.

A channel shared by a single sender and a single receiver is called a *one-to-one* communication link between the two threads. If several senders share a channel to communicate to a single receiver, the channel is *many-to-one*. Channels may also be *one-to-many* and *many-to-many*.

An *extended rendezvous* occurs if

- the sender does a blocking send followed by a blocking receive,

- and the receiver does a blocking receive followed by a blocking send.

Both threads are at known points in their code, and a bidirectional flow of information takes place. See Figure 6.2. Typically a *client* thread uses this technique to communicate with a *server* thread and request a service to be performed on its behalf. A similar situation is a *worker* thread contacting a coordinator, administrator, or *master* thread, asking for more work to do.

An extended rendezvous is sometimes called a *remote procedure call* (RPC), particularly if the sender and receiver are on two different machines connected by a LAN and if a new thread is created on the remote machine to execute the code in the remote procedure on behalf of the sender. In this case, tools may be provided to the programmer to make the code for the rendezvous look like a simple procedure call. Such tools are called RPC libraries or packages. For more information, see ([34], Section 16.3.1), ([36], Section 12.5), ([41], Section 10.3), ([42], Section 2.4). The extended rendezvous and remote procedure call are ideal tools for client-server programming. They appear functionally equivalent to the client: the client blocks while the server performs some steps to handle the client's request. The difference is in the implementation on the server side. A rendezvous is accepted by an explicit server thread, programmed by the designer of the server application; the thread waits in a loop for such rendezvous request messages. Whenever a remote procedure call is made by a client, the RPC package or library creates a new thread to execute the server procedure, transparently to the programmer.

6.2   Message Passing in Java

Several forms of message passing are implemented in this book's `Synchronization` package, using the synchronization tools provided by Java: synchronized methods, synchronized blocks, and monitor waiting and signaling. If all the threads are in the same JVM (and necessarily on the same physical machine), a reference or handle to an object is passed from one thread to the other through a message passing object used as a port, mailbox, or channel. Both synchronous and asynchronous message passing are implemented, as shown in Library Classes 6.1

```java
public final class SyncMessagePassing
        extends MessagePassingRoot {
    private Object theMessage = null;
    private final Object sending = new Object();
    private final Object receiving = new Object();
    private final BinarySemaphore senderIn =
        new BinarySemaphore(0);
    private final BinarySemaphore receiverIn =
        new BinarySemaphore(0);
    public final void send(Object m) {
        if (m == null) throw new NullPointerException();
        synchronized (sending) {
            theMessage = m;
            V(senderIn);
            P(receiverIn);
        }
    }
    public final Object receive() {
        Object receivedMessage = null;
        synchronized (receiving) {
            P(senderIn);
            receivedMessage = theMessage;
            V(receiverIn);
        }
        return receivedMessage;
    }
}
```

and 6.2.

```java
public final class AsyncMessagePassing
        extends MessagePassingRoot {
    private int numMessages = 0; // negative if waiting receivers
    private final Vector messages = new Vector();
    public final synchronized void send(Object m) {
        if (m == null) throw new NullPointerException();
        numMessages++;
        messages.addElement(m); // at end
        if (numMessages <= 0) notify();  // unblock a receiver
    }
    public final synchronized Object receive() {
        Object receivedMessage = null;
```

```
            numMessages--;
            if (numMessages < 0)
                try { wait(); } catch (InterruptedException e) {}
            receivedMessage = messages.firstElement();
            messages.removeElementAt(0);
            return receivedMessage;
        }
    }
```

The synchronous message passing class uses semaphores to coordinate the transfer of the message from the sender to the receiver, blocking one until the other arrives, then releasing both. Thus, the two threads rendezvous. The asynchronous message passing class uses a `Vector` to retain or buffer sent but not yet received messages; if the counter `numMessages` is negative, then there are receivers waiting for a message.

These classes implement the `MessagePassing` interface and extend the MessagePassingRoot class, shown in Library Classes 6.3

```
    public interface MessagePassing {
        public abstract void send(Object m)
            throws NotImplementedMethodException;
        public abstract void send(int m)
            throws NotImplementedMethodException ;
        public abstract void send(double m)
            throws NotImplementedMethodException;
        public abstract Object receive()
            throws NotImplementedMethodException;
        public abstract int receiveInt()
            throws ClassCastException, NotImplementedMethodException;
        public abstract double receiveDouble()
            throws ClassCastException, NotImplementedMethodException;
        public abstract void close()
            throws NotImplementedMethodException;
    }
```

and 6.4.

```
    public abstract class MessagePassingRoot
            implements MessagePassing {
        public abstract void send(Object m)
            throws NotImplementedMethodException;
        public void send(int m) {
            send(this, new Integer(m));
        }
        public void send(double m) {
            send(this, new Double(m));
        }
        public abstract Object receive()
```

```
           throws NotImplementedMethodException;
    public int receiveInt() throws ClassCastException {
       return ((Integer) receive(this)).intValue();
    }
    public double receiveDouble() throws ClassCastException {
       return ((Double) receive(this)).doubleValue();
    }
 }
```

The `MessagePassing` interface includes abstract methods for sending and receiving objects and the `int` and `double` base data types. Class `MessagePassingRoot` provides an implementation for sending and receiving `ints` and `doubles` as objects using the wrapper classes `Integer` and `Double`. Both the `AsyncMessagePassing` and `SyncMessagePassing` classes provide implementations for sending and receiving objects. Thus, these two classes may also be used to send and receive `int` and `double` messages since they inherit the `MessagePassingRoot` methods. All of the abstract methods in the `MessagePassing` interface throw `NotImplementedMethodException`. A class extending `MessagePassingRoot` should override some of the methods with an implementation that just throws the exception if the class designer chooses to restrict the kinds of messages that may be passed.

The capacity of the asynchronous channel is limited only by the JVM memory since a `Vector` is used. The constructor argument for Library Class 6.5 specifies the amount of buffering, restricting the capacity of the channel. Its implementation uses a circular array of object references to retain unreceived messages.

```
public final class BBMessagePassing
        extends MessagePassingRoot {...
    public final void send(Object value) {
       if (value == null) throw new NullPointerException();
       synchronized (mutexS) {
          P(spaces);
          buffer[putIn] = value;
          putIn = (putIn + 1) % numSlots;
          V(elements);
       }
    }
    public final Object receive() {
       Object value = null;
       synchronized (mutexR) {
          P(elements);
          value = buffer[takeOut];
          takeOut = (takeOut + 1) % numSlots;
          V(spaces);
       }
       return value;
    }
```

```
    }
```

If the circular array fills up, senders block. Note the resemblance to the bounded buffer implemented with semaphores and monitors in earlier chapters. The synchronized blocks on objects `mutexS` and `mutexR` are required because this bounded buffer is accessed by multiple producer threads (message senders) and multiple consumer threads (message receivers); see Exercise 4.2.

The input-output streams `PipedInputStream` and `PipedOutputStream` are used to send data values of type `int` and `double` that represent messages through a pipe, as shown in Library Class 6.6. From a pipe created in the class constructor, `DataInputStream` and `DataOutputStream` objects are created whose `readInt` and `writeInt` methods are used to read and write integer messages through the pipe. Messages of type `double` are passed using similar code, not shown.

```
    public final class PipedMessagePassing
            extends MessagePassingRoot {...
      public final void send(int m) {
        synchronized (sending) {
            try { outData.writeInt(m); }
            catch (IOException e)
              { throw new MessagePassingException(); }
        }
      }
      public final int receiveInt() {
        int value = 0;
        synchronized (receiving) {
            try { value = inData.readInt(); }
            catch (IOException e)
              { throw new MessagePassingException(); }
        }
        return value;
      }
    }
```

Objects may be serialized, that is converted into a stream of bytes, through a pipe, as shown in Library Class 6.7. From a pipe created in the class constructor, `ObjectInputStream` and `ObjectOutputStream` objects are created whose `readObject` and `writeObject` methods are used to read and write serialized object messages through the pipe.

```
    public final class ObjPipedMessagePassing
            extends MessagePassingRoot {...
      public final void send(Object m) {
        synchronized (sending) {
            try { outObj.writeObject(m); }
            catch (IOException e)
              { throw new MessagePassingException(); }
```

```
            }
        }
    public final Object receive() {
        Object o = null;
        synchronized (receiving) {
            try { o = inObj.readObject(); }
            catch (Exception e)
                { throw new MessagePassingException(); }
        }
        return o;
    }
}
```

These two classes correspond to sending a message by value rather than by reference. Sending messages is buffered and nonblocking until the pipe fills up. Receiving messages is the blocking kind in these classes.

If the threads are in different JVMs (and possibly on different physical machines), a socket is set up between two threads wishing to communicate. A socket is a communication end point connected to a socket on another machine for two threads to send data back and forth using the TCP/IP networking protocol. See ([39], Chapter 6) for more information. The socket works very much like a pipe. Both Library Classes 6.6 and 6.7 have constructors that use a socket passed as an argument instead of an internal pipe. We will see examples of this in Section 6.3.

Program 6.1 is a simple example of sending and receiving messages that are object references within the same JVM.

```
class Problem { public int x, y;
    public Problem(int x, int y) { this.x = x;  this.y = y; }
}
...
AsyncMessagePassing gs = new AsyncMessagePassing();
SyncMessagePassing ca = new SyncMessagePassing();
...
class GenerateProblem extends MyObject implements Runnable {...
    public void run () {
        nap(1000);
        send(gs, new Problem(1, 2));
        nap(4000);
        int z = ((Integer) receive(ca)).intValue();
    }
}
class ComputeAnswer extends MyObject implements Runnable {...
    public void run () {
        nap(2000);
        Problem p = (Problem) receive(gs);
        nap(1000);
```

```
        send(ca, new Integer(p.x + p.y));
    }
}
```

If an error occurs, a `MessagePassingException` (Library Class 6.8) is thrown. The two filter classes `MessagePassingSendOnly` (Library Class 6.10) and `MessagePassingReceiveOnly` (Library Class 6.11) may be wrapped around a message passing channel to permit only sending or receiving on that channel. This is done by overriding the restricted method with one that just throws `NotImplementedMethodException` (Library Class 6.9).

6.2.1 Synchronization Using Message Passing

Two threads in different address spaces needing to synchronize or communicate data cannot use semaphores or monitors; they must use message passing. Two threads in the same address space may use message passing as an alternative to semaphores and monitors. Program 6.2, whose threads share an address space, sets up message passing channels used by a producer thread and a consumer thread for synchronization and communication. The consumer thread receives items built by the producer thread through one of the channels, an example of communication. The consumer extracts the item from the message and sends the empty message back to the producer. Since the number of messages is finite, they act like a bounded buffer. The consumer blocks when the buffer is empty and the producer when the buffer is full, an example of synchronization.

```
class Buffer {
    public String who; public double value; public long when;
    public Buffer() { who = null; value = 0.0; when = 0; }
    public String toString() {
        return
            " who="+ who + " value=" + value + " when=" + when;
    }
}
...
MessagePassing mpEmpty = new AsyncMessagePassing();
MessagePassing mpFull = new AsyncMessagePassing();
...
class Producer extends MyObject implements Runnable {...
    public void run() {
        int napping;  double value;
        while (true) {
            napping = 1 + (int) random(pNap);
            nap(napping);
            value = random();
            Buffer buffer = (Buffer) receive(mpEmpty);
            buffer.who = getName();
```

```
                buffer.value = value;
                buffer.when=age();
                send(mpFull, buffer);
            }
        }
    }
    class Consumer extends MyObject implements Runnable {...
        public void run() {
            int napping;
            while (true) {
                napping = 1 + (int) random(cNap);
                nap(napping);
                Buffer buffer = (Buffer) receive(mpFull);
                buffer.who = null;
                buffer.value = 0.0;
                buffer.when = 0;
                send(mpEmpty, buffer);
            }
        }
    }
```

The driver sends a number of empty messages

```
    for (int i = 0; i < numSlots; i++) send(mpEmpty, new Buffer());
```

to the producer that represent the empty buffer slots of the initial bounded buffer
([41], Figure 2-15), ([43], Figure 2-15). After filling a slot, the producer sends it to
the consumer, who empties it and sends it back to the producer. The output of the
first sample run shows the producer thread filling up the buffer and then waiting
for a free-slot message before inserting any more items into the buffer. The second
sample run shows the consumer emptying the buffer and waiting for new items from
the producer. Thus message passing synchronizes the producer and the consumer
threads, just as the semaphores elements and spaces do in Class 4.4.

The next example, Program 6.3, tests each of the message passing channel types
we have looked at: synchronous, asynchronous, controlled capacity, piped, and object piped.

```
    mp = new AsyncMessagePassing();          // or
    mp = new BBMessagePassing(5);            // or
    mp = new SyncMessagePassing();           // or
    mp = new PipedMessagePassing();          // or
    mp = new ObjPipedMessagePassing();
    ...
    class Producer extends MyObject implements Runnable {...
        public void run() {
            double item;
            int napping;
```

```
        while (true) {
            napping = 1 + (int) random(pNap);
            nap(napping);
            item = random();
            send(mp, item);
        }
    }
}
class Consumer extends MyObject implements Runnable {
    public void run() {
        double item;
        int napping;
        while (true) {
            napping = 1 + (int) random(cNap);
            nap(napping);
            item = receiveDouble(mp);
        }
    }
}
```

This program has two types of threads sharing one address space: those that produce work and those that perform or consume the produced work. A producer thread puts some work to be done into a message passing channel that is called a *bag of tasks*. Consumer threads reach into the bag to extract the next piece of work to do. Note that the threads are sharing a many-to-many channel in this example. Such worker threads are called a *worker crew*. If just a single coordinator or administrator thread produces work while many worker threads reach into the bag, this technique is called *master/worker*. The channel used for the bag of tasks is one-to-many. Sometimes the worker threads put partially completed work back into the bag for other workers to do later. We will see an example of a worker crew in Program 6.14 of Section 6.5.

6.2.2   Distributed Mutual Exclusion

The next message passing example is the distributed mutual exclusion algorithm, described in ([6], Chapter 11) and implemented in Program 6.4. See also ([34], Section 18.2.2), ([36], page 554), ([41], Section 11.2.2), ([42], Section 3.2.2). A collection of threads that share memory may use any of the following for mutual exclusion and condition synchronization: the bakery algorithm of Section 3.5, semaphores, monitors, and message passing (messages sent through the shared memory). Suppose, though, that the threads do not share memory but have private memories and are connected to a local area network. Suppose they need mutually exclusive access to some shared resource like a printer or tape drive. If all we have is message passing, can we implement some sort of *distributed mutual exclusion* algorithm? Furthermore, suppose we do not want to use a central server in order to avoid a bottleneck.

To recap, we want to solve the N-thread mutual exclusion problem with an algorithm that works in a distributed environment and does not involve a central server. We have N nodes connected by a network or point-to-point communication channels, and we assume

- error-free communication between all nodes, that is, no lost or garbled messages;

- messages sometimes arrive in a different order than they were sent; and

- nodes do not fail or halt, either inside or outside their critical sections.

In other words, nodes eventually respond to all query messages sent to them. The basic idea of the algorithm is

> do forever {
>   noncritical section code
>   choose a sequence number
>   send it to all other nodes
>   wait for a reply message from all other nodes
>   enter critical section
>   postprotocol
> }

Each of the N nodes has three threads executing concurrently (the three threads are executing on the CPU and memory of the node). One thread executes the above "do forever" loop. Another thread handles requests from other nodes. And the third waits for replies from all other nodes. A node, say node i, sends a reply or acknowledgment message to another node, say node j, that has sent node i a request message. Node i sends the reply immediately if node j has a lower sequence number (higher priority) in its message or if node i is not trying to enter its critical section. Node i defers the reply (until node i gets into and then out of its critical section) if node j has a higher sequence number (lower priority) in its message. Ties are broken by node identifiers. A node chooses its sequence number by adding one to the highest sequence number it has seen so far in incoming messages from other nodes. The following activities occur in each node.

> execute noncritical section code
>
> preprotocol:
>   choose sequence number as highest seen so far $+ 1$
>   send it to all other nodes as a request to enter critical section
>
> wait for replies
> while waiting,
>   reply to other nodes if their sequence number is lower
>
> enter critical section

postprotocol:
     reply to others (the deferreds) if their sequence number was higher

This algorithm enforces mutual exclusion because a node does not enter its critical section until it receives replies to its request message from all other nodes. There is no deadlock since ties are broken by node identifiers, as shown in Program 6.4. There is no starvation in the absence contention: if none of the other nodes wants to enter its critical section, replies are immediate. There is no starvation in the presence contention: after a node exits its critical section, it chooses a new sequence number the next time it wants to enter its critical section; that number will be higher than those of other contending nodes.

```
private void chooseNumber() {
    P(s); requesting = true; number = highNumber + 1; V(s);
}
private void sendRequest() {
    replyCount = 0;
    for (int j = 0; j < numNodes; j++) if (j != id)
        send(requestChannel[j], new Message(number, id));
}
private void waitForReply() { P(wakeUp); }
private void replyToDeferredNodes() {
    P(s); requesting = false; V(s);
    for (int j = 0; j < numNodes; j++) {
        if (deferred[j]) {
            deferred[j] = false; send(replyChannel[j], id);
        }
    }
}
private void outsideCS() {
    int napping;
    napping = ((int) random(napOutsideCS)) + 1;
    nap(napping);
}
private void insideCS() {
    int napping;
    napping = ((int) random(napInsideCS)) + 1;
    nap(napping);
}
private void main() {                    // node main thread
    while (true) {
        outsideCS();
        chooseNumber();                  // PRE-PROTOCOL
        sendRequest();                   //        "
        waitForReply();                  //        "
        insideCS();
```

```
            replyToDeferredNodes();            // POST-PROTOCOL
        }
    }
    private void handleRequests() {  // thread to handle requests
        while (true) {
            Message m = (Message) receive(requestsToMe);
            int receivedNumber = m.number;
            int receivedID = m.id;
            highNumber = Math.max(highNumber, receivedNumber);
            P(s);
            boolean decideToDefer = requesting
                && (number < receivedNumber
                || (number == receivedNumber && id < receivedID));
            if (decideToDefer) deferred[receivedID] = true;
            else send(replyChannel[receivedID], id);
            V(s);
        }
    }
    private void handleReplies() {   // thread to handle requests
        while (true) {
            int receivedID = receiveInt(repliesToMe);
            replyCount++;
            if (replyCount == numNodes - 1) V(wakeUp);
        }
    }
```

Three features of the algorithm necessary for its correctness are

1. Putting sequence numbers into outgoing request-to-enter messages,

2. Keeping track of the highest sequence number seen in incoming request-to-enter messages, and

3. Choosing a sequence number higher than any seen so far.

Putting sequence numbers into messages is equivalent to running a local clock and time-stamping outgoing messages with the clock's value. Choosing a sequence number for an outgoing message higher than any incoming sequence number seen so far is equivalent to using Lamport's method ([41], Section 11.1.1), ([42], Section 3.1.1) to correct clock skew.

If outgoing messages are not time-stamped, deadlock may result in the distributed mutual exclusion algorithm. If the arrival time of a message is used to determine when a remote node decided it wanted to enter its critical section, two nodes might send request-to-enter messages to each other at about the same time and both think they have priority. The two nodes then deadlock.

If time-stamped messages are used to determine priority but clock skew is not corrected with Lamport's method, then starvation may occur. A node with a faster

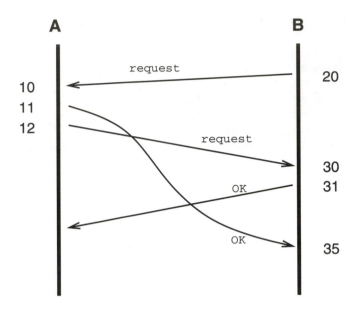

Figure 6.3: Clock Skew Allows Mutual Exclusion Violation.

running clock gets lower priority than one with a slower clock and starves. Worse, mutual exclusion can fail as the example in Figure 6.3 shows. At time 35, node B thinks node A has entered and exited its critical section because B gets an OK message with time stamp 11, causing B to think this is A's deferred reply to B's earlier request-to-enter message. So B enters its critical section. Since A is currently in its critical section, mutual exclusion is violated.

While interesting from a theoretical point of view, this algorithm has several serious practical problems. Many more messages are sent and received for a node to get permission to enter its critical section, compared to a central server algorithm in which one node arbitrates critical section entries for all other nodes. Instead of the single point of failure that a central server algorithm has, the distributed mutual exclusion algorithm described here depends on all of its nodes never crashing.

6.2.3   Conditional Message Passing

In *conditional* message passing, the message remains queued until some condition, specified by the receiver, becomes true. At that time, the message is passed to the receiver, unblocking it. The message may be sent synchronously or asynchronously. A simple conditional message passing example is Program 6.5, a variation of the producers and consumers with bounded buffer.

```
if (synchronous) cmp = new SyncConditionalMessagePassing(true);
else             cmp = new AsyncConditionalMessagePassing(false);
    ...
```

```
class ConsumerCondition extends MyObject implements Condition {
    private double value = 0;
    public ConsumerCondition(double value)
        { this.value = value; }
    public boolean checkCondition(Object message) {
        return ((Double) message).doubleValue() < value;
    }
}
class Producer extends MyObject implements Runnable {...
    public void run() {
        double item;
        int napping;
        while (true) {
            napping = 1 + (int) random(pNap);
            nap(napping);
            item = random();
            cmp.send(new Double(item));
        }
    }
}
class Consumer extends MyObject implements Runnable {...
    public void run() {
        double item;
        int napping;
        while (true) {
            napping = 1 + (int) random(cNap);
            nap(napping);
            double limit = random();
            item = ((Double) cmp.receive(
                new ConsumerCondition(limit))).doubleValue();
        }
    }
}
```

The consumers are "picky" and accept only producer messages whose data items are smaller than some limit specified as a condition in each consumer receive operation. Section 6.2.4 contains another conditional message passing example.

Program 6.5 tests both the asynchronous (Library Class 6.14) and synchronous (Library Class 6.15) conditional message passing classes. Both of these classes implement the interface in Library Class 6.12.

```
public interface ConditionalMessagePassing {
    public abstract void send(Object message);
    public abstract Object receive(Condition condition);
}
```

The condition object created by the receiver and passed as an argument in its receive request must implement the interface in Library Class 6.13. The condition object must contain a checkCondition method used by the channel to determine which messages sent are eligible to be received.

```
public interface Condition {
    public abstract boolean checkCondition(Object m);
}
```

The AsyncConditionalMessagePassing class uses three Vector queues to hold blocked receivers, their associated conditions, and messages that have been sent but not yet received. Each receive operation activates the private matchedMessage-WithReceiver method, which scans the queue of sent messages for one meeting the receiver's condition. If one is found, it is returned to the receiver; otherwise the receiver is left blocked. Each send operation also activates the same method to see if the new message meets any blocked receiver's condition. If so, the receiver is unblocked and given the message; if not, the message is added to the queue of unreceived messages. The class starts an internal thread that calls the private method matchedMessageWithReceiver on every send and receive.

```
public class AsyncConditionalMessagePassing
        implements ConditionalMessagePassing, Runnable {...
    Vector blockedMessages = new Vector();
    Vector blockedConditions = new Vector();
    Vector blockedReceivers = new Vector();
    Thread me = new Thread(this);
    ...
    private boolean matchedMessageWithReceiver() {
        int numMessages = blockedMessages.size();
        int numReceivers = blockedReceivers.size();
        if (numMessages == 0 || numReceivers == 0) return false;
        for (int i = 0; i < numReceivers; i++) {
            for (int j = 0; j < numMessages; j++) {
                Object m = blockedMessages.elementAt(j);
                Condition c = (Condition)
                    blockedConditions.elementAt(i);
                if (c.checkCondition(m)) {
                    blockedMessages.removeElementAt(j);
                    blockedConditions.removeElementAt(i);
                    SyncMessagePassing mp = (SyncMessagePassing)
                        blockedReceivers.elementAt(i);
                    blockedReceivers.removeElementAt(i);
                    mp.send(m);
                    return true;
                }
            }
        }
```

```
      }
      return false;
   }
   public void run() {              // internal thread
      synchronized (me) {
         while (true) {
            while (matchedMessageWithReceiver()) ;
            try { me.wait(); } catch (InterruptedException e) {}
         }
      }
   }
   public void send(Object message) {
      if (message == null) throw new NullPointerException();
      synchronized (me) {
         blockedMessages.addElement(message);
         me.notify();
      }
   }
   public Object receive(Condition condition) {
      if (condition == null) throw new NullPointerException();
      SyncMessagePassing mp = new SyncMessagePassing();
      synchronized (me) {
         blockedConditions.addElement(condition);
         blockedReceivers.addElement(mp);
         me.notify();
      }
      return mp.receive();
   }
}
```

The `SyncConditionalMessagePassing` class is similar; it has an additional queue to hold senders since they must block until a conditional receive operation succeeds.

6.2.4 The Distributed Dining Philosophers

The next example, Program 6.6, uses conditional asynchronous message passing. It solves the distributed dining philosophers problem, implementing the dining philosophers without a central server thread. If there are a large number of philosophers, say millions, then a central server most likely becomes a bottleneck. In the distributed version, each philosopher communicates only with its two neighbors and negotiates the use of a fork with the neighbor sharing that fork.

```
   class ServantCondition implements Condition {...
      private boolean hungry = false;
      private boolean dirtyL = false, dirtyR = false;
      ...
```

```java
   public boolean checkCondition(Object m) {
      if (m instanceof Hungry) return true;
      else if (!hungry) return true;
      else if (m instanceof PassL || m instanceof PassR)
         return true;
      else if (m instanceof NeedL && dirtyL) return true;
      else if (m instanceof NeedR && dirtyR) return true;
      else return false;
   }
}
class Servant implements Runnable {...
   private BinarySemaphore eat = new BinarySemaphore(0);
   private BinarySemaphore releaseForks =
      new BinarySemaphore(0);
   ...
   public void takeForks(int id)
      { myChannel.send(new Hungry()); P(eat); }
   public void putForks(int id) { V(releaseForks); }
   public void run() {                   // servant thread
      Object message = null;
      ServantCondition sc = null;
      boolean hungry = false;
      while (true) {
         sc = new ServantCondition(hungry, dirtyL, dirtyR);
         message = myChannel.receive(sc);
         if (message instanceof Hungry) {
            hungry = true;
            if (!haveR) rightServantChannel.send(new NeedL());
            if (!haveL) leftServantChannel.send(new NeedR());
            while (!(haveR && haveL)) {
               sc =
                  new ServantCondition(hungry, dirtyL, dirtyR);
               message = myChannel.receive(sc);
               if (message instanceof PassL) {
                  haveL = true; dirtyL = false;
               } else if (message instanceof PassR) {
                  // right servant sends fork
                  haveR = true; dirtyR = false;
               } else if (message instanceof NeedL) {
                  haveL = false; dirtyL = false;
                  leftServantChannel.send(new PassR());
                  leftServantChannel.send(new NeedR());
               } else if (message instanceof NeedR) {
                  haveR = false; dirtyR = false;
                  rightServantChannel.send(new PassL());
```

```
                    rightServantChannel.send(new NeedL());
                }
            }
            V(eat); dirtyR = true; dirtyL = true;
            P(releaseForks);
            hungry = false;
        } else if (message instanceof NeedR) {
            haveR = false; dirtyR = false;
            rightServantChannel.send(new PassL());
        } else if (message instanceof NeedL) {
            haveL = false; dirtyL = false;
            leftServantChannel.send(new PassR());
        }
    }
}
}
```

Each philosopher has a servant thread that does the fork negotiation; the philosophers devote maximal time to philosophizing. In the central server version, the central server keeps track of the forks and hands them out to a hungry philosopher if both its forks are not currently in use. In the distributed version, the servants pass needL, needR, passL, and passR messages back and forth. Each fork is always in the possession of some philosopher (or its servant), one of the two on either side of the fork. When a philosopher finishes eating, it labels its two forks as used (soiled or dirty as seen by the other philosophers). As a courtesy to its neighbors, a philosopher (or its servant) wipes clean a soiled fork, one the philosopher was last to use, before passing the fork to a neighbor.

Starvation is prevented by requiring a philosopher to give up, when asked, a fork it holds that is dirty, i.e., that it was the last one to use. The algorithm allows a hungry philosopher to hold onto a clean fork while waiting for its other fork, even if a neighbor requests the fork. Deadlock is prevented by distributing the forks initially in an asymmetric pattern: philosopher 1 gets both forks in the dirty state, philosophers 2 through $n - 1$ get one clean fork (the right one) each, and the last philosopher gets no forks. In general, if philosopher p is the most recent philosopher to eat, then it possesses both forks in the dirty state. If a circular chain starts to develop around the table, the chain breaks when it tries to pass through philosopher p. Either philosopher $p - 1$ or $p + 1$ eats and deadlock does not occur.

6.3 Rendezvous

Synchronous message passing is an example of the rendezvous: two threads reaching specific points in their code at the same time and communicating information. In synchronous message passing, the information flows in one direction only, from sender to receiver, called a simple rendezvous. In the full-fledged general or extended rendezvous, the information flows in both directions.

An extended rendezvous is sometimes called a *remote procedure call* from a client to a server (or a worker to the master) because it resembles a call to a procedure on a remote machine that is executed there. Interface definition language preprocessors make the syntax nearly identical. Typically the call represents a request for service, such as reading a file that resides on the remote machine. The server may handle the request in its main thread or the server may spawn a new thread to handle the request while the server's main thread handles additional requests for service from other clients. The latter gives greater throughput and efficiency since a lengthy request would otherwise delay the handling of requests from the other clients.

An addressing mechanism is needed for the client to contact an appropriate server. In the local case (all threads in the same JVM), an object (Library Class 6.17) is used as the place for the client and server to "meet" and establish a rendezvous.

```
public class EstablishRendezvous {...
    private MessagePassing in = new SyncMessagePassing();
    private ServerSocket serverSocket =
      new ServerSocket(portNum, 50);
    ...
    public Rendezvous serverToClient()
        throws MessagePassingException {
        if (portNum < 0)
            return (Rendezvous) receive(in);      // local case
        Socket socket = null;
        try { socket = serverSocket.accept(); } // remote case
        catch (IOException e)
            { throw new MessagePassingException(); }
        Rendezvous r = new ExtendedRendezvous(socket);
        return r;
    }
    public Rendezvous clientToServer()
        throws MessagePassingException {
        if (portNum < 0) {                        // local case
            Rendezvous r = new ExtendedRendezvous();
            send(in, r);
            return r;
        } else {                                  // remote case
            Socket socket = null;
            try { socket = new Socket(machineName, portNum); }
            catch (IOException e)
                { throw new MessagePassingException(); }
            Rendezvous r = new ExtendedRendezvous(socket);
            return r;
        }
    }
}
```

The server calls method `serverToClient` in this object and blocks until the client calls method `clientToServer`. At this point in time, both methods return a newly created `ExtendedRendezvous` object (Library Class 6.18) that the client and server subsequently use for bidirectional communication.

```
public class ExtendedRendezvous implements Rendezvous {...
    private MessagePassing in = new SyncMessagePassing();
    private MessagePassing out = new SyncMessagePassing();
                    // or
    out = in = new ObjPipedMessagePassing(socket);
    ...
    public Object clientMakeRequestAwaitReply(Object m) {
        send(in, m);   return receive(out);
    }
    public Object serverGetRequest() { return receive(in); }
    public void serverMakeReply(Object m) { send(out, m); }
```

Since the `clientMakeRequestAwaitReply` method is not synchronized, a particular `ExtendedRendezvous` object should be used by only one client thread. This object contains message passing channels shared by the client and server and implements the interface in Library Class 6.16.

```
public interface Rendezvous {
    public abstract Object clientMakeRequestAwaitReply(Object m);
    public abstract Object serverGetRequest();
    public abstract void serverMakeReply(Object m);
}
```

In the local case, one `EstablishRendezvous` object is shared by both client and server. In the remote case (between two threads in different JVMs that might be on different physical machines), a client creates an `EstablishRendezvous` object, passing the server's machine name and TCP/IP port number (see [39]) to the object's constructor; the server also creates an `EstablishRendezvous` object, passing only the port number to the constructor.

When the rendezvous occurs, an `ExtendedRendezvous` object is constructed by `EstablishRendezvous` and returned to both the client and server. In the local case (within the same JVM), the client and server share the `ExtendedRendezvous` object and use it to transact (synchronous message passing of object references). In the remote case (between JVMs), each gets its own `ExtendedRendezvous` object containing a socket (see [39]) to the other JVM (and machine). Objects are serialized through the socket. The case of sending raw data types through a pipe (same JVM) or a socket (different JVMs) is not implemented.

Program 6.7 is a local case example.

```
class Client implements Runnable {...
    private EstablishRendezvous er = // shared with server
        ...
```

```
    public void run() {
        int napping;
        RendezvousRequestReply rrr;
        while (true) {
            napping = 1 + (int)random(napTime);
            nap(napping);
            rrr = new RendezvousRequestReply(getName());
            rrr = (RendezvousRequestReply)
                er.clientToServer().clientMakeRequestAwaitReply(rrr);
        }
    }
}
class ServerThread implements Runnable {...
    private Rendezvous r = // from server
    ...
    public void run() {
        RendezvousRequestReply rrr =
            (RendezvousRequestReply) r.serverGetRequest();
        rrr.doRequest();
        r.serverMakeReply(rrr);
    }
}
class MultiThreadedServer implements Runnable {...
    private EstablishRendezvous er = // shared with client
    ...
    public void run() {
        while (true) {
            Rendezvous r = er.serverToClient();
            if (threadedServer) {
// spawn a new thread to handle the request asynchronously
                new ServerThread(r);
            } else {
// do it here and now before handling any more clients
                RendezvousRequestReply rrr =
                    (RendezvousRequestReply) r.serverGetRequest();
                rrr.doRequest();
                r.serverMakeReply(rrr);
            }
        }
    }
}
```

The command line option -t controls whether or not the server spawns off a new thread to handle the request. The second run in the sample output shows the server can handle more requests per second if it spawns off a new thread to handle each incoming request. Depending on the characteristics of the incoming requests and the architecture the server is running on, this is generally the case, for example IO-bound requests or multiple CPUs available to the server.

In this local case example, the clients and server share an `EstablishRendezvous` object for addressing. Each time a client wants to rendezvous with the server, it calls the `clientToServer` method to get an `ExtendedRendezvous` object whose `clientMakeRequestAwaitReply` method it uses to transact with the server. The client passes a reference to a `RendezvousRequestReply` object to the server. This object contains the data and a method, `doRequest`, for the server to call. The `ExtendedRendezvous` object is used only once by the client; however, it could be reused for multiple `clientMakeRequestAwaitReply` calls as is done in the next example, the remote dining philosophers.

Program 6.8, the multiple machine dining philosophers, is a remote case example.

```
class Philosopher implements Runnable {...
   private static Rendezvous r = null;  // one per philosopher
   ...
   public void run() {            // thread for each philosopher
      while (true) {
         think();
         // takeForks(id);
         r.clientMakeRequestAwaitReply(new Integer(id));
         eat();
         // putForks(id);
         r.clientMakeRequestAwaitReply(new Integer(-id-1));
      }
   }
   public static void main(String[] args) {...
      EstablishRendezvous er =
         new EstablishRendezvous(diningServer, port);
      r = er.clientToServer();
      // tell the dining server that this philosopher is alive
      r.clientMakeRequestAwaitReply(new Integer(id));
   }
}
class DiningServer implements Runnable {...
   private Rendezvous r = null;  // one per philosopher
   ...
   public void run() {            // one of these threads for
      int message = 0;           // each philosopher
      while (true) {
         message = ((Integer) r.serverGetRequest()).intValue();
         if (message == -philosopherID-1) {
            putForks(philosopherID);
            // acknowledge the release of the forks
            r.serverMakeReply(new Integer(0));
         } else if (message == philosopherID) {
```

```
            takeForks(philosopherID);
            // release the philosopher when forks available
            r.serverMakeReply(new Integer(0));
        }
    }
}
public static void main(String[] args) {...
    // accept connections from the philosophers
    // and start a message passing thread for each philosopher
    EstablishRendezvous er = new EstablishRendezvous(port);
    Rendezvous[] r = new Rendezvous[numPhils];
    for (int i = 0; i < numPhils; i++) {
        r[i] = er.serverToClient();
        int id =
            ((Integer) r[i].serverGetRequest()).intValue();
        new DiningServer(id, r[i]);
    }
    // let the philosophers start eating
    for (int i = 0; i < numPhils; i++)
        r[i].serverMakeReply(new Integer(0));
}
```

Suppose there are machines named bander, cheshire, humpty, queen, and king connected together on a LAN and used as clients in this example, along with a machine named jubjub used as the server. The example compile and run in the comment at the end of the program shows how (on UNIX) to run each philosopher in its own JVM on a different physical machine.

```
% java DiningServer -n5 -R20 &
% sleep 5; rsh bander "java Philosopher -s jubjub -i0" &
% sleep 5; rsh cheshire "java Philosopher -s jubjub -i1" &
% sleep 5; rsh humpty "java Philosopher -s jubjub -i2" &
% sleep 5; rsh queen "java Philosopher -s jubjub -i3" &
% sleep 5; rsh king "java Philosopher -s jubjub -i4"
```

Each philosopher sends an Integer object containing its *id* value to the server when it is hungry. Since this is a rendezvous, the philosopher is blocked until it gets a reply indicating that its forks are available. The server spawns a new thread for each philosopher to handle the transactions. The server uses semaphores internally to keep track of the forks. Each philosopher sends an Integer object containing its $-id - 1$ value to indicate it is putting down its forks. Each philosopher has its own ExtendedRendezvous object whose clientMakeRequestAwaitReply method it calls over and over again (in contrast to the previous example, in which the clients obtained a new ExtendedRendezvous object for each transaction with the server).

How much does message passing cost? How much time does it take? Program 6.9 attempts to measure the amount of time the client and server take to transact

Number	Array	Average Time (ms) Per Call			
		intra-JVM	inter-JVM		
of Calls	Size	(by reference)	localhost	LAN	WAN
10	1	3.0	138.8	2136	1813
10	10	4.9	143.8	1312	1115
10	100	3.8	183.8	2237	2697
10	1000	16.7	628.7	1372	9507

Table 6.1: Communication Times.

in a rendezvous. A client sends a message containing an array of length N to the server. The server adds one to each entry of the array and sends it back. The client does this M times and calculates the number of bytes sent per millisecond. The program is run in two ways. The local run passes the message as a reference from the client to the server within the same JVM. The remote run serializes the message containing the array through a socket over the network to the server running in a different JVM, possibly on another physical machine. Program 6.9 calculates the time it takes to call a method (indirectly via an extended rendezvous) with an object argument in several different situations:

intra-JVM The invoked method is in a class in the same JVM as the calling thread and the object is passed as a reference (JDK 1.1 on Solaris 2.5).

localhost The invoked method is in a class in a different JVM on the same machine as the calling thread; the object is serialized through a socket (JDK 1.1 on Solaris 2.5).

LAN The invoked method is in a class in a different JVM on a different machine connected to the machine of the calling thread by a departmental LAN (standard ethernet); the object is serialized through a socket (JDK 1.1 on Solaris 2.5).

WAN The invoked method is in a class in a different JVM on a different machine connected to the machine of the calling thread by a wide area network (WAN; modem, multiple Internet gateways and routers); the object is serialized through a socket (JDK 1.1 and Windows 95 calling Solaris 2.5).

The object passed as an argument to the invoked method contains an array of double-precision floating-point numbers (Java type `double`). The method adds one to each element of the array. The times in milliseconds are shown in Table 6.1 for four different sizes of the array. Each time is the average of ten trials for over and back serialization (except the intra-JVM case) of the object passed to the method. The times for the LAN and WAN cases vary considerably because of random network delays.

6.3.1   Conditional Rendezvous

Synchronous conditional message passing corresponds to a conditional simple rendezvous, that is, once the condition is met information in the form of a message object flows in one direction from the client to the server. Library Class 6.20 implements an extended *guarded* or *conditional* rendezvous, in which information flows in both directions once a server finds a client message meeting the condition. This class is a combination of `EstablishRendezvous` and `ExtendedRendezvous` with condition checking added; its implementation is very similar to `SyncConditionalMessagePassing`, Library Class 6.15. The client calls the `clientTransactServer` method of the `ConditionalRendezvous` object; the server first calls `serverGetClient` to obtain a client meeting the condition and then uses the `Rendezvous` object returned to interact with the client (`serverGetRequest` and `serverMakeReply` methods). The condition interface, Library Class 6.19, is enhanced with more information passed to the `checkCondition` method, compared to Library Class 6.13, so the condition check can be based on information gathered about all outstanding messages.

```
public interface RendezvousCondition {
/*
 * The information available to the checkCondition method is:
 *    the particular message being evaluated,
 *       blockedMessages.elementAt(messageNum);
 *    the queue of blocked messages itself, blockedMessages;
 *    and the number of blocked servers, numBlockedServers.
 * This is the state of the ConditionalRendezvous object.  The
 * particular message can be checked to see if it meets the
 * condition and this test may involving counting how many
 * blocked messages meet some other criterion and/or the number
 * of blocked servers.
 */
    public abstract boolean checkCondition(int messageNum,
        Vector blockedMessages, int numBlockedServers);
}
```

An example using a condition that depends only on the message passed and not on other queued messages is the dining philosophers classical problem, Class 6.10.

```
class EatCondition implements RendezvousCondition {...
    public boolean checkCondition(int messageNum,
        Vector blockedMessages, int numBlockedServers) {
        Object message = blockedMessages.elementAt(messageNum);
        int id = ((Integer) message).intValue();
        if (id < 0) return true;                // putForks()
        else if (state[left(id)] != EATING
            && state[right(id)] != EATING)
            return true;                        // takeForks()
```

```
              else return false;
      }
   }
   class DiningServer implements Runnable {...
      private ConditionalRendezvous cr =
         new ConditionalRendezvous();
      state = new int[numPhils];
      for (int i = 0; i < numPhils; i++) state[i] = THINKING;
      ...
      public void takeForks(int id) {
         cr.clientTransactServer(new Integer(id));
      }
      public void putForks(int id) {
         cr.clientTransactServer(new Integer(-id-1));
      }
      public void run() {  // makes atomic state changes
         while (true) {
            Rendezvous r = cr.serverGetClient(
               new EatCondition(state, EATING));
            int id = ((Integer) r.serverGetRequest()).intValue();
            if (id < 0) state[-id-1] = THINKING;
            else state[id] = EATING;
            r.serverMakeReply(new Integer(0));
         }
      }
   }
}
```

A particular ConditionalRendezvous object can be shared by several servers; multiple calls by servers to the serverGetClient method can be outstanding, that is, blocked, waiting for a client message meeting the condition. Furthermore, after calling serverGetClient and before completing the rendezvous with that client, a server might call serverGetClient again; such a server is handling several rendezvous with different clients simultaneously. A banking example, Program 6.11, illustrates this. A bank with a single account is accessed by a number of threads making deposit and withdrawal requests to the account. The bank is created with an initial balance. The deposit and withdrawal threads make requests for random amounts at random times using the clientTransactServer method of a ConditionalRendezvous object they share with the bank.

```
   class WithdrawCondition implements RendezvousCondition {...
      public boolean checkCondition(int messageNum,
            Vector blockedMessages, int numBlockedServers) {
         Object message = blockedMessages.elementAt(messageNum);
         int amount = ((Integer) message).intValue();
         int size = blockedMessages.size();
         // count number waiting deposits
```

```
        if (allDepositsBeforeAnyWithdrawals) {
            if (amount > 0) return true; // deposit is okay
            int numBlockedDeposits = 0;
            // count number waiting deposits
            for (int i = 0; i < size; i++) {
                Object m = blockedMessages.elementAt(i);
                int a = ((Integer) m).intValue();
                if (a > 0) numBlockedDeposits++;
            }
            if (numBlockedDeposits > 0 /* && amount < 0 */)
                return false;
            else return -amount < balance;
        } else {
    // special case (-1): any deposit or withdrawal is okay
            if (balance < 0) return true;
    // any deposit is okay but withdrawals must pass next test
            else if ( /* balance >= 0 && */ amount > 0)
                return true;
    // if we get here then balance >= 0 and amount <= 0,
    // so a |withdrawal| < balance is okay;
    // but if balance==0 (special flag value) then
    // no withdrawals are allowed
            else return -amount < balance;
        }
    }
}
class Depositor implements Runnable {...
    private ConditionalRendezvous cr = // from driver
    ...
    public void run() {                    // thread
        int deposit, napping, put;
        while (true) {
            napping = 1 + (int) random(dNap);
            nap(napping);
            deposit = 1 + (int) random(dNap);
            put = ((Integer) cr.clientTransactServer(
                    new Integer(deposit))).intValue();
        }
    }
}
class Withdrawer implements Runnable {...
    private ConditionalRendezvous cr = // from driver
    ...
    public void run() {                    // thread
        int withdraw, napping, got;
```

```
        while (true) {
            napping = 1 + (int) random(wNap);
            nap(napping);
            withdraw = 1 + (int) random(wNap);
            got = ((Integer) cr.clientTransactServer(
                new Integer(-withdraw))).intValue();
        }
    }
}
class Bank implements Runnable {...
    private ConditionalRendezvous cr = // from driver
    ...
    public void run() {                    // thread
        int balance = initialBalance;
        while (true) {
            if (starvationFree) {
                // take anything
                // (-1 is special flag value for this)
                RendezvousCondition c =
                    new WithdrawCondition(-1, false);
                Rendezvous r = cr.serverGetClient(c);
                int amount =
                    ((Integer) r.serverGetRequest()).intValue();
                if (amount > 0) {                // deposit
                    balance += amount;
                    nap(1 + (int) random(1000));
                    r.serverMakeReply(new Integer(amount));
                } else if (-amount < balance) {
                    // allowed withdrawal
                    balance += amount;
                    nap(1 + (int) random(1000));
                    r.serverMakeReply(new Integer(-amount));
                } else {
                    // withdrawal too big; take deposits until okay
                    while (-amount >= balance) {
                        // deposits only
                        // (0 is special flag value for this)
                        RendezvousCondition nc =
                            new WithdrawCondition(0, false);
                        Rendezvous nr = cr.serverGetClient(nc);
                        int deposit = ((Integer)
                            nr.serverGetRequest()).intValue();
                        balance += deposit;
                        nap(1 + (int) random(1000));
                        nr.serverMakeReply(new Integer(deposit));
```

```
            }
            balance += amount;
            nap(1 + (int) random(1000));
            r.serverMakeReply(new Integer(-amount));
        }
    } else {
        // take only deposits and allowed withdrawals
        // but a large withdrawal may "starve" in the queue
        RendezvousCondition c =
            new WithdrawCondition(balance,
                allDepositsBeforeAnyWithdrawals);
        Rendezvous r = cr.serverGetClient(c);
        int amount =
            ((Integer) r.serverGetRequest()).intValue();
        balance += amount;
        nap(1 + (int) random(1000));
        r.serverMakeReply(new Integer(Math.abs(amount)));
    }
        }
      }
    }
  }
```

If `starvationFree` is false, a large withdrawal might sit in the queue and starve while smaller withdrawals continue to be processed. In contrast, if **starvation-Free** is true (set with the -s option), the server (bank thread) accepts only deposits and no withdrawals until the bank balance is large enough to process the waiting large withdrawal. The -a option sets the requirement that all queued deposits are processed unconditionally by the bank before any queued withdrawals. In this case, the condition checking depends not only on the message passed but also on the characteristics of the other messages in the queue. Each time the bank calls the `serverGetClient` method, it passes a `WithdrawCondition` object whose `checkCondition` method counts the number of queued deposits. A withdrawal is processed only if this count is zero. The -B option adds additional banks to test simultaneously executing servers, making the simulation less realistic in the sense that deposits and withdrawals are handled by the first available bank. How the request is processed depends on the handling bank's balance and not on the balances in the other banks.

Table 6.2 summarizes the message passing and rendezvous techniques we have considered, showing the types of messages passed.

6.4   Remote Method Invocation

Sun Microsystems has added a *remote method invocation* (RMI) package to Java, providing the ability to make remote procedure calls. We used the phrase "remote procedure call" in Section 6.3 to describe an extended rendezvous between two threads in different JVMs, perhaps on different physical machines. Sun's RMI is

Class Constructor	Blocking	Message Type	Medium
`SyncMessagePassing()`	synchronous	object	reference
`BBMessagePassing(int)`	bounded buffer	object	reference
`AsyncMessagePassing()`	asynchronous	object	reference
`PipedMessagePassing()`	asynchronous	`int,` `double`	pipe
`PipedMessagePassing(Socket)`	asynchronous	`int,` `double`	socket
`ObjPipedMessagePassing()`	asynchronous	serialized object	pipe
`ObjPipedMessagePassing(Socket)`	asynchronous	serialized object	socket
`SyncConditionalMessagePassing()`	conditional synchronous	object	reference
`AsyncConditionalMessagePassing()`	conditional asynchronous	object	reference
`ExtendedRendezvous()`	client/server	object	reference
`ExtendedRendezvous(Socket)`	client/server	serialized object	socket
`ConditionalRendezvous()`	conditional client/server	object	reference

Table 6.2: Message Passing Classes.

similar: a collection of classes, the `java.rmi` package, that allows a thread in one JVM to invoke (call) a method in an object in another JVM, perhaps on a different physical machine. A new thread is created in the other (remote) JVM to execute the called method. Parameters to the remote method and the method's return result, if any, are passed from one JVM to the other using object serialization (object streams) over the network.

Using RMI, a Java programmer writes *distributed computing* applications. Program 6.12 is an example.

```
public interface Compute extends Remote {
   public abstract Work compute(Work w) throws RemoteException;
}
class Work implements Serializable {...
   private final int N = 5;
   private double[]
      a = new double[N], b = new double[N], c = new double[N];
   for (int i = 0; i < N; i++)
      { a[i] = random(-N, N); b[i] = random(-N, N); }
   ...
   public void doWork() {
      // simulate some computation time
      nap(1+(int)random(1000*N));
      for (int i = 0; i < N; i++) c[i] = a[i] + b[i];
   }
```

```
    }
    class ComputeServer extends UnicastRemoteObject
          implements Compute {...
      public Work compute(Work w) throws RemoteException {
        w.doWork();
        return w;
      }
      public static void main(String args[])  {
        System.setSecurityManager(new RMISecurityManager());
        try {    // register this server
          ComputeServer server = new ComputeServer(serverName);
          Naming.bind("rmi://" + serverMachine + "/"
              + serverName, server);
        } catch (Exception e) {}
      }
    }
    class Client extends MyObject implements Runnable {
      private Compute server = // from main()
      ...
      public void run() {
        Work w = null;
        while (true) {
          nap(1 + (int) random(napTime));
          w = new Work(getName());
          try { w = server.compute(w); } catch (Exception e) {}
        }
      }
      public static void main(String[] args) {
        Compute server = null;
        try { server = (Compute)
          Naming.lookup("rmi://" + serverMachine + "/"
              + serverName);
        } catch (Exception e) {}
        for (int i = 0; i < numClients; i++)
          new Client(i, server, 1000*napTime);
      }
    }
```

Suppose a client on one machine wants to send two vectors to be added to a server
on another machine. Presumably the server executes on a computer architecture
that performs the operation more quickly and efficiently. The client is thus using
the remote server to have work performed on its behalf (adding vectors). The two
vectors are placed in a Work object by the client; the server invokes the object's
doWork method to perform the vector addition. The server is accessed through a
Compute interface known to the client and implemented by the server. Such interfaces must extend Remote from the java.rmi package. In our example, the Compute

interface contains a single method, `compute`, that takes a `Work` object parameter and returns a `Work` object result. All such interface methods must have a `throws RemoteException` clause. Note that the `Work` class implements the `Serializable` interface, required of objects that are serialized through the network as part of a remote method invocation. Library Class 3.1, `MyObject`, must also implement `Serializable` since the `Work` class extends it.

The `ComputeServer` remote server object implements the `Compute` interface and extends the `UnicastRemoteObject` class from the `java.rmi.server` package. The server registers itself with the `rmiregistry` program by calling the `Naming.bind` method from the `java.rmi` package, passing a string that resembles a URL and shows where the server is. (A URL is a World Wide Web uniform resource locator, for example `http://...`, `ftp://...`, and `mailto:...`.) This URL optionally specifies an IP port number to be used by the client and server. The client accesses the server by calling `Naming.lookup`, passing the server's URL; this call returns a reference to an object on the client side that implements the `Compute` interface. Each time the client calls this object's `compute` method, the `Work` object passed as the method's parameter is serialized through the network to the server side. A server thread is created to call `compute`, which then calls the `Work` object's `doWork` method. The object, now containing the sum of the two vectors, is serialized back to the client.

The sample run attached as a comment to the end of Program 6.12 was produced by executing the client and server on two Sun workstations (named `cheshire` and `jubjub`, respectively) running Solaris 2.5 and connected by a LAN, with port 7777 specified by the user. In a directory accessible to both the client and server, we compile the program, create the "stubs" with the `rmic` command, and start the RMI registry program. For security reasons, Sun requires that the server and registry program be on the same machine.

```
% javac Compute.java
% rmic ComputeServer
% rmiregistry 7777 &
```

Then we start the server and the client.

```
% java ComputeServer -M jubjub:7777 &
% rsh cheshire "java Client -M jubjub:7777 -R10"
```

6.5 More Animation with Java

We conclude this chapter with animations of two message passing programs. Program 6.13 is an enhanced version of the distributed dining philosophers, Program 6.6; statements are added to drive the animation interpreter. The philosophers are represented by circles equally spaced around a large circle representing the table. A bowl of spaghetti rests in the center of the table, represented by a half-tone orange circle. Forks are represented with thick lines. The state of each philosopher is indicated by a different color: outline black for thinking, green for hungry, and

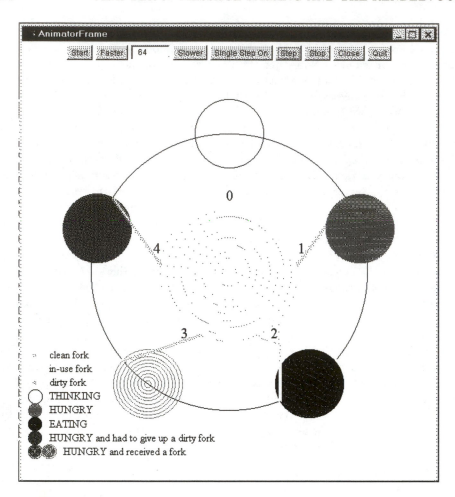

Figure 6.4: Animation Snapshot of the Distributed Dining Philosophers.

blue for eating. Forks used by a philosopher to eat are yellow; when the philosopher finishes eating, the forks are dirty and become orange. Each fork moves back and forth between the two philosophers who use it to eat. See the comments in the program for an explanation of the animation statements. Figure 6.4 is a snapshot of the window during the animation.

The quicksort algorithm is parallelized for a shared memory multiple CPU machine by dedicating to a worker thread each CPU allocated to the program and using a message passing channel as a bag of tasks.

```
AsyncMessagePassing task = new AsyncMessagePassing();
```

The main method of Program 6.14 puts the whole array to be sorted into the bag. A worker extracts a task (a segment of the array) from the bag,

```
while (true) {
```

```
    m = (Task) receive(task);
    quickSort(id, m.left, m.right);
}
```

chooses a pivot point, and partitions the array segment. Each of the two resulting partitions is put back into the bag for one of the workers to extract later.

```
if (right-(l+1) > 0) send(task, new Task(l+1, right));
if ((l-1)-left > 0) send(task, new Task(left, l-1));
```

This is an example of the worker crew paradigm, first described in Section 6.2.1. Even though message passing is used for the bag of tasks, this program requires shared memory because the array is sorted "in place" and the work requests put into the bag are array index pairs and not copies of parts of the array. During the animation, each array segment extracted by a worker thread is enclosed in a box and the circles representing the array values in that segment are colored to match the worker thread partitioning the segment. Figure 6.5 is a snapshot of an animation of 100 random numbers between 1 and 10,000 sorted by six threads. After watching several of these animations, we see the effects of a poor pivot value and the reason the algorithm has limited speedup.

Summary

Threads in different address spaces that want to synchronize and communicate cannot use semaphores and monitors. Instead they use message passing and two tools based on message passing, the rendezvous and the remote procedure call. We looked at two design parameters for the send and receive message passing primitives: blocking versus nonblocking and buffered versus nonbuffered. We said two threads participate in a simple rendezvous when one executes a blocking send, the other a blocking receive, and a message is sent.

The Synchronization package includes a variety of message passing classes for Java programs, in particular, synchronous, asynchronous, and their conditional versions. In conditional message passing, a message must satisfy a condition specified by the receiver to be acceptable. Messages may be integers, floating-point numbers, or objects. The latter are passed by reference within one JVM and serialized (passed by value) between JVMs, using a pair of sockets. Two major examples illustrated message passing in Java, distributed mutual exclusion and the distributed dining philosophers.

An extended rendezvous is a pair of messages between two threads, a request for service by a client and a reply by a server, performed with send/receive and receive/send in the two threads. The client and server thus carry out a transaction. The rendezvous is implemented in the Synchronization package with two classes, one for addressing and one for communicating. If the client and server execute in different JVMs on different machines, the addressing mechanism uses an IP address/port number to set up a socket pair through which serialized object messages are passed. The remote dining philosophers example showed how to start each philosopher on

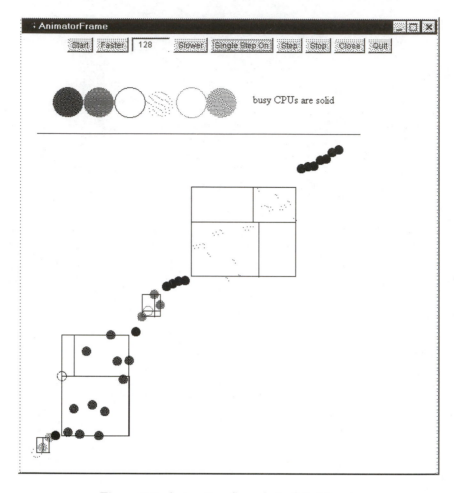

Figure 6.5: Animation Snapshot of Quicksort.

its own workstation. The philosophers communicate with the dining server over the LAN connecting the machines. A conditional version of the rendezvous allows servers to specify the kinds of transactions they are willing to accept.

A remote procedure call is a transaction or extended rendezvous that appears to the programmer as a local procedure call. Sun Microsystems has added a remote procedure call package, called RMI, to the JDK that allows a thread in one JVM to invoke a method in an object in a different JVM, perhaps on a different machine. Transparently to the programmer, a new thread is spawned in the remote JVM to execute the method invoked by the local thread.

The last examples in the chapter are two animations, the distributed dining philosophers and parallel quicksort. In the former, forks move back and forth between the philosophers in response to their messages negotiating the use of shared forks. Two or more forks can move concurrently, a feature of the animation. The quicksort algorithm is parallelized for a shared-memory multiprocessor with a worker crew, one worker per CPU allocated to the program. The bag of tasks is implemented with a message passing channel.

6.6 Exercises

1. **Send/Receive Design Choices.** Section 6.1 gives three design choices for send and three for receive. Explain why combinations 2/3, 3/2, and 3/3 are not feasible.

2. **Message Passing Bounded Buffer.** Will Program 6.2 work correctly if there are multiple producer threads and multiple consumer threads?

3. **Distributed Bag of Tasks.** Modify Program 6.3 so that all producer threads execute on one machine and all consumer threads execute on another machine. Recall that classes `PipedMessagePassing` (Library Class 6.6) and `ObjPipedMessagePassing` (Library Class 6.7) have constructors with a socket argument. You will need to borrow some code from the second and third constructors of Library Class 6.17, `EstablishRendezvous`.

Do you think it is possible to modify Program 6.3 so that each thread, producer or consumer, executes on its own machine? Why, or why not?

4. **Distributed Mutual Exclusion.** Answer the following questions (based on [6], page 123).

   a. Program 6.4 has a binary semaphore s, local to each node. Why is it necessary?

   b. Suppose the binary semaphore s is deleted from method `replyToDeferredNodes` and the `V(s)` in thread `handleRequests` is moved up to just before the `if` statement. Show that deadlock is possible.

   c. Does the `V(s)` in `replyToDeferredNodes` need to be moved to the end of the method? In other words, why have a `P(s)...V(s)` bracket the single assignment statement `requesting = false`? Where is the race condition?

   d. Suppose node m decides to enter its critical section and sends a request message to node n. Node n sends a reply message to node m indicating that node n does not want to enter its critical section. Suppose further that node n later decides to enter its critical section and sends a request message to node m (and to all the other nodes). What happens if node n's request message is received by node m before the earlier-sent reply message of node n to node m?

5. **Distributed Dining Philosophers.** After reading Section 6.2.4, answer the following questions.

   a. Does the solution to the dining philosophers shown in Program 6.6 have the desirable "maximal parallelism" property?

   b. Show that deadlock is possible if philosopher 1 is initially given both forks in the clean state (that is, all forks are handed out initially clean).

c. Does the program work correctly if synchronous conditional message passing is used instead of asynchronous?

6. **The Classical Problems Using Rendezvous.** Implement the bounded buffer multiple producers and consumers with a (possibly conditional) rendezvous.

In the exercises for Chapters 4 and 5, you implemented starvation-free versions of the dining philosophers and database readers and writers. Add code to the dining philosophers conditional rendezvous, Class 6.10, to prevent starvation. Implement the database readers and writers with a (possibly conditional) rendezvous so it is fair to both readers and writers; that is, neither readers nor writers starve. Pick either strict serialization or platooning as your strategy.

First, take the version that allows starvation, seed the random number generator with a constant, and determine parameters for the command line that show starvation occurring in the simulation. With the random number generator seeded and the random numbers reproducible, you will have an easier time debugging. Then modify the code to prevent starvation.

7. **Fair Baboons.** Write a (possibly conditional) rendezvous version of the fair baboons program done in Exercise 4.7. Pick either strict serialization or platooning as your strategy.

8. **Sleeping Barbers.** Write a (possibly conditional) rendezvous version of the sleeping barbers program done in Exercise 4.4.

9. **Fraternity Party.** Write a (possibly conditional) rendezvous version of the fraternity party program done in Exercise 4.8.

10. **Bakery.** Write a (possibly conditional) rendezvous version of the bakery program done in Exercise 4.3.

11. **Banker's Algorithm.** Write a Java program that simulates a computing system in which there are n resource types and $E = (e_1, e_2, \ldots, e_n)$ existing resources of each type. There are m threads in the system. To apply the Banker's Algorithm ([15], Section 6.8), ([34], Section 7.5), ([36], Section 5.4), ([41], Section 6.5), ([43], Section 3.3.6), we must know the total demands of the threads in advance, and this information is in the m by n matrix T. Your program simulates the threads requesting and returning resources from a central server thread. In order to avoid deadlock, your program needs to compute (using the Banker's Algorithm) if granting the request keeps the system in a safe state. Use message passing and/or the rendezvous.

When a thread submits a request for resources, $R = (r_1, r_2, \ldots, r_n)$, i.e., it wants r_i units of type i, the central server satisfies the request atomically, that is, the central server allocates either all or none of the requested resources to the thread, depending on whether or not the resulting state is safe. If the state would be unsafe, the thread blocks and the central server remembers the request. Also, a request by a thread for more resources than are currently available must be queued by the central server (the thread must block). Requests by a thread for more resources than exist or for more resources than its maximum demand aborts the thread.

Threads also release resources. If threads are blocked with outstanding requests, the freed resources may be used to satisfy outstanding requests, but only if the resulting state is safe.

Note that starvation is possible in this program. It could happen like this. You are keeping a FCFS queue of threads whose requests cannot be granted because the resulting state would be unsafe or the resources are currently not available. As other threads release resources, the central server scans the queue of blocked threads and grants resources to those for which it is safe. The problem is that threads possibly starve if they are repeatedly passed over as the central server scans the queue.

If, while trying to decide if a state is safe or not, you finish off as many threads as possible one by one, and there are some left, you do not have to backtrack and try a different order. In other words, one order of finishing off threads is good enough: either they all finish and the state is safe, or you end up with some potentially deadlocked ones, and the state is unsafe.

In order to test your program thoroughly, you need to drive the threads with input scripts. Use reasonable values for m, n, E, and T. Each thread has its own input file. The input data for each thread consist of lines of the following form.

> napTime   requestReleaseFlag $r_1 r_2 \ldots r_n$

A thread reads lines from its input file and first naps for the napping time input, then sends a request or release message to the central server (Banker) for resources $(r_1, r_2, \ldots, r_n)$. The thread then blocks until its request is granted (no need to block for a release of resources).

12. **Message Passing Empty Method.** Add a

```
public boolean empty() {...}
```

method to each of the message passing classes. It returns true if no messages are queued, waiting to be received, and false otherwise. Do you think this is a good idea? Why, or why not? Add

```
protected static final boolean empty(MessagePassing mp) {
    return mp.empty();
}
```

to Library Class 3.1, `MyObject`. Design and implement a test program.

13. **Conditional Message Passing.** Enhance the `ConditionalMessagePassing` classes (Library Classes 6.14 and 6.15) by adding constructors with a socket parameter so that two threads in different JVMs, perhaps on different physical machines, can use a socket to perform conditional message passing.

When either the send or receive method is invoked, the thread executing the run method awakes and checks all queued message objects from senders with all queued condition objects from blocked receivers, looking for a match. A more efficient approach when receive is called is to check just the receiver's condition with all queued messages and when send is called just the sender's message with all queued conditions. Implement this performance improvement.

14. **Sharing EstablishRendezvous Objects.** Modify Program 6.7 so that there is a fixed-size pool of server threads operating independently instead of a single server thread (that optionally spawns off a new thread to handle each client request). The servers share a single EstablishRendezvous object. Then modify the program so that the client threads execute on one machine and the server threads execute on another machine.

15. **Conditional Rendezvous.** Enhance the ConditionalRendezvous class (Library Class 6.20) by adding a constructor with a socket parameter so that two threads in different JVMs, perhaps on different physical machines, can use a socket to perform conditional rendezvous.

16. **Remote Method Invocation.** Convert one of the monitor or semaphore classical problem solutions (bounded buffer producer and consumer, dining philosophers, database readers and writers, sleeping barbers) from local method calls (all in one JVM) to inter-JVM method calls (RMI).

Chapter 7

Parallel Computing

So far, most of our Java examples deal with race conditions, critical sections, mutual exclusion, thread synchronization, and interthread communication in shared and distributed memory platforms. In this book, the term "concurrent programming" is used to describe these types of programs. Although there are no standard definitions for concurrent programming and parallel processing, we use the latter to describe programs that perform numerically intensive computations using a large number of processors. Specialized parallel architectures, other than uniform memory access (UMA) multiple-instruction multiple-data (MIMD) shared-memory multiprocessors and clusters of workstations on a LAN, may be involved, such as nonuniform memory access (NUMA) multiprocessors, single-instruction multiple-data (SIMD) CM-2 Connection Machines, Cray vector supercomputers, and systolic arrays. The amount of synchronization required is closely related to the problem being solved and the hardware involved. Synchronization is automatic and fine-grained when done by the hardware, as on an SIMD machine. It is infrequent and done in software in coarse-grained MIMD algorithms on shared-memory multiprocessors. Concurrent programming is more concerned with resource allocation and avoiding deadlock and starvation. Parallel processing is more concerned with distributing the work to be done across the available processing units.

This chapter is a brief introduction to the parallel computing capabilities of Java. There are many books on parallel computer architectures and parallel programming. See, for example, [10, 30, 32]. We have seen one example of parallelizing an algorithm to use multiple CPUs: the animated quicksort in Program 6.14. That algorithm requires shared memory since the array is sorted "in place" and needs to be accessed by all the worker threads. A bag of tasks implemented with a message passing channel is used to distribute the work. In this chapter, we look at additional examples of parallel processing programs. Some require shared memory; others use message passing in a distributed memory architecture. Some parcel out the computational work to a fixed number of threads, one per CPU allocated to the program; others create a varying number of threads based on the input data. We will see a variety of message passing channel connection patterns among the threads.

7.1 Definitions

We categorize parallel algorithms along several lines, using the abbreviations shown in parentheses:

- *coarse-grained* (**CG**) versus *fine-grained* (**FG**) concurrency or parallelism, determined by the frequency of thread synchronization or communication relative to the amount of computation done (sometimes the term *medium-grained* concurrency, **MG**, is used as well);

- shared-memory (**SM**) multiprocessor versus distributed memory (**DM**) CPUs, determined by the presence of shared data in shared memory directly accessible by all CPUs;

- message passing (**MP**) versus semaphore, monitor, barrier, or `join()` (**SY**) synchronization, where the latter set requires shared memory (note that message passing does not imply distributed memory if the channels and their buffers reside in shared memory);

- worker crew (**WC**) with a bag of tasks and a fixed number of workers, perhaps based on the number of CPUs allocated to the program, versus *data parallelism* (**DP**), where the amount of data to process or work to perform determines the number of worker threads spawned and dedicated CPUs needed for maximal parallelism;

- pattern of message passing communication that is *totally connected* (**TC**) if every thread needs to communicate with every other thread, or *star* shaped (**ST**) if there are worker or client threads that communicate only with a master or server thread, or *grid* shaped (**GR**) if each thread communicates only with its nearest neighbors (north, south, east, and west), or a *pipeline* (**PI**) if each thread communicates only with the threads to its left and right.

In a uniprocessor with multiple functional units (ones for branch prediction, integer addition, floating-point operations, operand address calculation), the concurrency is fine grained because synchronization is needed at the individual instruction level: one unit may need to wait for the result produced by another unit. A vector unit in a Cray computer is another fine-grained example. So is an SIMD (single instruction, multiple data) machine, such as the CM-2 Connection Machine, where each instruction is executed by all the processors in lockstep.

A shared-memory multiprocessor running a collection of threads that use semaphores or locks for thread synchronization is either medium grained or coarse grained, depending on how frequently the semaphores and locks are accessed. A collection of workstations on a LAN cooperating to solve some problem is an example of coarse-grained parallelism. Since communication and synchronization over the network are more expensive than through shared memory, it is more efficient and cost effective to do large amounts of computation between synchronization steps.

In some cases the need for shared memory can be relaxed. If the shared data are read-only, they can be replicated or broadcast to each distributed memory and the copies stored there. In other situations, it might be possible to pass the shared data around as a message, to be updated by the currently owning thread. For example, we might replace

```
/* shared */ int N;
/* shared */ Object mutex = new Object();
 ...
synchronized (mutex) { N = N + 1; }
```

with

```
/* local */ int N;
 ...
N = receive(channeli);
N = N + 1;
send(channelj, N);
```

FG has too much overhead and inefficiency unless the communication and synchronization tools are highly optimized, perhaps with hardware support. **DM** may consist of a network of workstations (NOW) or a specialized parallel architecture in which each CPU has its own memory and some kind of fast interconnect or switch connects them for message passing. The fast interconnect can be a grid, tree, or hypercube.

If a problem has a lot of data, or if it will take a lot of work (computation) to solve and if the data or work can be split up or subdivided into independent chunks, then a thread with its own CPU can be allocated to each chunk of data or work. These two styles or paradigms of parallel programming are called data parallelism (splitting up the data) and master/worker (splitting up the computational work), respectively. Closely related to the latter is the bag of tasks paradigm, introduced in Section 6.2.1, in which the size of the worker crew is determined by the number of CPUs. Several example Java programs in this chapter show parallel algorithms that split up the data: multiplying matrices, sorting numbers, and computing a function iteratively over a rectangular domain. Other examples are parallel algorithms that divides up the work: worker crew quicksort and solving the N-queens problem. Some of the programs require shared memory; others use message passing. The Java examples are categorized using the criteria described above: **CG/MG/FG**, **SM/DM**, **MP/SY**, **WC/DP**, and **TC/ST/GR/PI**. We start with some examples of data parallelism using message passing.

7.2 Data Parallel Message Passing

A parallel version of the Sieve of Eratosthenes is shown in Program 7.1 (**FG, MP, DP, PI**).

```
public static MessagePassing[] sieve = new MessagePassing[n];
public static int[] seenCount = new int[n];
sieve[0] = new SyncMessagePassing();  // blocking send
```

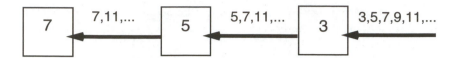

Figure 7.1: Parallel Sieve of Eratosthenes.

```
for (int i = 1; i < n; i++)
   sieve[i] = new AsyncMessagePassing();
for (int i = 0; i < n; i++) seenCount[i] = 1;
for (int i = 0; i < n; i++) new Filter(i);
int number = 3;
while (true) { send(sieve[0], number); number += 2; }
...
class Filter implements Runnable {...
   public void run () {                    // thread
       int prime = -1, number = -1;
       prime = receiveInt(sieve[id]);
       if (id == n-1) { System.exit(0); }
       else
          while (true) {
              number = receiveInt(sieve[id]);
              seenCount[id]++;
              if (number % prime != 0) send(sieve[id+1], number);
          }
   }
}
```

This program computes the first N prime numbers by creating N filter threads that run in parallel. The first filter is sent, using message passing, all odd numbers. Each filter prints out the first number it receives, which is prime, and then sends to the next filter all numbers it receives that are not multiples of the prime number it printed out. See Figure 7.1. Finally, filter N receives the Nth prime number, which it prints out, and then executes a System.exit(0) statement. The sample output shows that the first few filters do most of the computation, so there is limited speed-up unless the threads are distributed in a more load-balanced manner across the available CPUs. The input, N, determines the number of threads spawned.

```
% java ParallelSieve -n 100
ParallelSieve: debug=false, n=100
age()=0, generating the first 100 prime numbers greater than 2
age()=660 filter 0 received prime 3
age()=660 filter 1 received prime 5
   ...
age()=2960 filter 99 received prime 547
done
```

the filters each saw the following counts of numbers
320 213 169 144 131 120 113 108 106 105 103 102 101 100 99 98
97 96 95 94 93 92 91 90 89 88 87 86 85 84 83 82 81 80 79 78 77
76 75 74 73 71 70 67 66 64 63 62 61 60 59 58 57 56 55 54 51 50
49 48 47 46 44 43 42 41 40 39 37 36 35 34 33 32 31 30 27 26 25
24 23 21 20 19 18 17 16 15 14 13 12 11 10 9 8 7 6 5 4 1

Program 7.2 (**FG, MP, DP, PI**) contains a more complicated example of message passing, a program that sorts numbers using a pipeline. Instead of creating all the threads in advance, each one is created only when it first has work to do. The total number of threads is determined by the size of the array sorted.

```java
class Result { public int position, value;
    public Result(int p, int v) { position = p; value = v; }
}
class Worker implements Runnable {...
    public static AsyncMessagePassing create
            (int m, AsyncMessagePassing result) {
        AsyncMessagePassing myPipe = new AsyncMessagePassing();
        Worker worker = new Worker(m, result, myPipe);
        (new Thread(worker)).start();
        return myPipe;
    }
    public void run() {                    // thread
        int candidate, smallest;
        smallest = receiveInt(myPipe);
        if (m > 1) {
            AsyncMessagePassing nextWorker;
            nextWorker = Worker.create(m-1, result);
            for (int i = m-1; i > 0; i--) {
                candidate = receiveInt(myPipe);
                if (candidate < smallest) {
                    int temp = candidate;
                    candidate = smallest; smallest = temp;
                }
                send(nextWorker, candidate);
            }
        }
        send(result, new Result(m, smallest));
    }
}
class PipelineSort {...
    private static void sort(int[] a) {
        int position, value;
        AsyncMessagePassing result = new AsyncMessagePassing();
        if (a.length == 0) return;
```

```
            AsyncMessagePassing firstWorker = null;
            firstWorker = Worker.create(a.length, result);
            for (int i = 0; i < a.length; i++)
               send(firstWorker, a[i]);
            for (int i = 0; i < a.length; i++) {
                  Result r = (Result) receive(result);
                  a[a.length-r.position] = r.value;
            }
      }
      public static void main(String[] args) {
         nums = new int[N];
         sort(nums);
      }
   }
```

The `sort` method calls `create` to start the first worker thread. Then `sort` sends the numbers to be sorted, one at a time, to the worker. Meanwhile, the worker created by `sort` calls `create`. So the first worker, the one created by `sort`, itself creates a second worker thread. The second worker passes its `myPipe` message passing channel back to the first worker.

The first worker receives all the numbers from `sort` and sends all but the smallest to the second worker. Meanwhile, the second worker creates a third and sends all but the smallest it sees to the third. The sorting is carried out in parallel because each worker continually passes `candidate` numbers along to the next worker in the pipeline; before passing a number, a worker compares it to the `smallest` number it has seen so far and swaps the two if necessary. Workers are created until the last one receives a single number. Then the worker threads send their smallest retained numbers back to `sort`, which puts them into the proper spot of the array. As in the parallel Sieve of Eratosthenes, the threads created earlier do more work than threads created later, limiting the amount of speed-up.

Program 7.3 (**CG**, **MP**, **DP**, **ST**) solves the *N*-queens problem in parallel.

```
   class nQueens implements Runnable {...
      private static PipedMessagePassing channel =
         new PipedMessagePassing();
      private int inRow = // from main()
      ...
      public void run() {                              // thread
         int[] board = new int[N+1];
         for (int i = 0; i < board.length; i++) board[i] = 0;
         board[1] = inRow;
         int numFound = place(2, board);
         send(channel, numFound);
      }
      private static boolean safe(int row, int column, int[] board)
         {...}
```

```
      private static int place(int column, int[] board) {...}
      public static void main(String[] args) {
         for (int row = 1; row <= N; row++) new nQueens(row);
         for (int row = 1; row <= N; row++)
            numSolutions += receiveInt(channel);
      }
   }
```

The input data are the N different squares in the first column on which a queen can be placed. For each such square, a thread is created to compute how many ways the rest of the board can be filled with mutually nonattacking queens. Thus there are N threads in all. Each thread produces a separate count. Before terminating, each thread uses a message passing channel to send its count to the **main** method, where the counts are accumulated and printed out. In **DM**, the size of the board is broadcast to each thread.

As described in Section 3.1.1, a Java program with multiple threads runs on a uniprocessor with the concurrency simulated. The threads share the CPU in a round robin fashion through time slicing. The sample output shown in Program 7.3 was produced on a uniprocessor computer running Windows 95. If enough CPUs are allocated to the program, a CPU can be dedicated to each thread; otherwise several threads share each CPU. In an exercise, you are asked to run the code in Program 7.3 on a shared-memory multiprocessor using several different numbers of allocated CPUs, if supported by your version of Java. You are asked to observe and explain the differences in the output.

7.3 Worker Crew Message Passing

Instead of starting a number of threads based on the input data or size of the problem, as in Program 7.3, we start up a fixed number of threads, perhaps based on the number of CPUs allocated to the program. In Program 7.4 (**CG**, **MP**, **WC**, **ST**), the work to be done (counting the ways N queens can be placed on an N-by-N chessboard without attacking each other) is partitioned into chunks. Each chunk consists of counting the ways $N - 1$ additional queens can be placed on an N-by-N chessboard that already has one queen somewhere in the first column. There are N of these chunks of work to be done, forming a bag of tasks. For each CPU, a worker thread is started that reads a row number for the first column queen from the bag of tasks.

```
   class Nqueens implements Runnable {...
      private static PipedMessagePassing getWork =
         new PipedMessagePassing();
      private static PipedMessagePassing putCount =
         new PipedMessagePassing();
      ...
      public void run() {                        // thread
         while (true) {
```

```
            int inRow = receiveInt(getWork);
            int[] board = new int[N+1];  // 0 unused
            for (int i = 0; i < board.length; i++) board[i] = 0;
            board[1] = inRow;
            int numFound = place(2, board);
            send(putCount, numFound);
        }
    }
    public static void main(String[] args) {
        for (int j = 0; j < NCPU; j++) new Nqueens(j);
        for (int i = 1; i <= N; i++) send(getWork, i);
        for (int row = 1; row <= N; row++)
            numSolutions += receiveInt(putCount);
    }
}
```

When a thread finishes a chunk, it sends its count to the main driver thread and gets another chunk of work to do if any are left. This is an example of the master/worker or worker crew paradigm of parallel computing, also used in Program 6.14 in Section 6.5. The number of threads is usually less than the number of chunks of work to do, so each worker typically completes several chunks. Both of these programs are coarse- to medium-grained concurrency, depending on how long a thread takes to compute for each chunk.

Using the technique of Program 6.8, the above program can be modified to run on a distributed memory cluster of workstations. Each worker thread is assigned to a different machine, as shown in Program 7.5 (**CG, DM, MP, WC, ST**).

```
    class Message implements Serializable {...}
    class NqueensWorker implements Runnable {...
        private EstablishRendezvous er =
            new EstablishRendezvous(masterMachine, portNum);
        ...
        public void run() {                    // thread
            Message m = new Message(id, false, 0, false, 0, 0);
            while (true) {
                Rendezvous r = er.clientToServer();
                m = (Message) r.clientMakeRequestAwaitReply(m);
                r.close();
                if (!m.containsWork) System.exit(0);
                N = m.N;
                int inRow = m.inRow;
                int[] board = new int[N+1];  // 0 unused
                for (int i = 0; i < board.length; i++) board[i] = 0;
                board[1] = inRow;
                int numFound = place(2, board);
                m = new Message(id, true, numFound, false, 0, 0);
```

```
            }
        }
    }
    class NqueensMaster {...
        private static EstablishRendezvous er =
            new EstablishRendezvous(portNum);
        ...
        public static void main(String[] args) {
            Message m = null;
            int numResultsReceived = 0;
            for (int i = 1; i <= N; i++) {
                Rendezvous r = er.serverToClient();
                m = (Message) r.serverGetRequest();
                if (m.containsResult) {
                    numSolutions += m.numFound;
                    numResultsReceived++;
                }
                r.serverMakeReply(
                    new Message(-1, false, 0, true, i, N));
                r.close();
            }
            while (numResultsReceived < N) {
                Rendezvous r = er.serverToClient();
                m = (Message) r.serverGetRequest();
                if (m.containsResult) {
                    numSolutions += m.numFound;
                    numResultsReceived++;
                }
                r.serverMakeReply(
                    new Message(-1, false, 0, false, 0, 0));
                r.close();
            }
            er.close();
        }
    }
```

The rendezvous technique is used: each worker is a client that asks the server for more work to do. The program also runs entirely on one machine with the **-w** command line option. These two cases, with and without **-w** on the command line, test the three kinds (client, server, local) of **EstablishRendezvous** objects that can be constructed.

7.4   Shared Memory Parallelism

If many CPUs are available on a shared-memory machine for matrix multiplication, one CPU can be assigned to compute each entry of the product matrix. Programs 7.6 and 7.7 (both **CG, SM, SY, DP**) show two ways to do this in Java. Both programs start up as many threads as there are entries in the product matrix. Since we do not want to print the result before it is completely computed, the first program uses a semaphore **done** on which the **main** method blocks.

```
class MatrixMultiply implements Runnable {...
    private static CountingSemaphore done =
        new CountingSemaphore(0);
    private int l, n // from main()
    ...
    public void run() {                    // thread
        double innerProduct = 0.0;
        for (int m = 0; m < M; m++)
            innerProduct += a[l][m]*b[m][n];
        c[l][n] = innerProduct;
        V(done);
    }
    public static void main(String[] args) {
        // start a thread to compute each c[l,n]
        for (int l = 0; l < L; l++) for (int n = 0; n < N; n++)
            new MatrixMultiply(l, n);
        // wait for them to finish
        for (int l = 0; l < L; l++) for (int n = 0; n < N; n++)
            P(done);
    }
}
```

A semaphore used this way is called a *barrier*. The thread executing the top-level code cannot continue past the **for** loop containing **P(done)** until all of the multiply threads have completed. Note that the multiply threads are not started up until the input matrices have been read and initialized. This program needs shared memory to store the matrices since they are accessed by all the threads. It has coarse-grained concurrency.

Instead of a barrier semaphore to make sure the product matrix is not printed until computed, a **join** method call is used in Program 7.7.

```
class MatrixMultiply implements Runnable {...
    private Thread me;
    private int l, n // from main()
    ...
    private void join() {
        try { me.join(); } catch (InterruptedException e) {}
    }
```

```
      public void run() {              // thread
         double innerProduct = 0.0;
         for (int m = 0; m < M; m++)
            innerProduct += a[l][m]*b[m][n];
         c[l][n] = innerProduct;
      }
      public static void main(String[] args) {
         // start a thread to compute each c[l,n]
         MatrixMultiply[][] mm = new MatrixMultiply[L][N];
         for (int l = 0; l < L; l++) for (int n = 0; n < N; n++)
            mm[l][n] = new MatrixMultiply(l, n);
         // wait for them to finish
         for (int l = 0; l < L; l++) for (int n = 0; n < N; n++)
            mm[l][n].join();
      }
   }
```

The above two matrix multiplication programs spawn a fixed number of threads, dependent on the amount of data, for the duration of the computation. Program 7.8 (**MG, SM, SY, DP**) uses the quicksort algorithm; the two recursive calls to method **qs** are performed by two new threads. This is medium-grained concurrency, and the number of threads varies during the computation. The program requires shared memory since the original unsorted array is sorted in place, that is, it is passed by reference to all threads.

```
   class QuickSort implements Runnable {...
      private static int[] nums;
      ...
      private static Thread QuickSortThread(int left, int right) {
         QuickSort qs = new QuickSort(left, right);
         Thread qst = new Thread(qs);
         qst.start();
         return qst;
      }
      public void run() {              // thread
         int pivot = nums[left];
         int l = left, r = right;
         Thread qsl = null, qsr = null;
         boolean done = false;
         while (!done) {...}
         // when the above loop finishes, nums[left] is the pivot,
         // nums[left:l] <= pivot and nums[l+1,right] > pivot
         int temp = nums[left]; nums[left] = nums[l];
         nums[l] = temp;
         // start the "recursive" threads, if any
         if (right-(l+1) > 0) qsr = QuickSortThread(l+1, right);
```

```
            if ((1-1)-left > 0) qsl = QuickSortThread(left, 1-1);
            try {    // and wait for them to finish
                if (qsl != null) qsl.join();
                if (qsr != null) qsr.join();
            } catch (InterruptedException e) {}
        }
        public static void main(String[] args) {
            nums = new int[N];
            // start up the first thread and wait for it to finish
            Thread qst = QuickSortThread(0, N-1);
            try { qst.join(); }
            catch (InterruptedException e) {}
        }
    }
```

Many problems in physics are solved by repeated calculation of the values of some function over a rectangular domain until convergence is achieved. At each successive step, the new value of the function at a point is calculated from the old values of the nearest neighbors of the point. If all the new values are close to the old values, the computation converges and the algorithm terminates. We assign a thread and CPU to each point in the rectangular domain.

In Program 7.9 (**FG, SM, SY, DP**), the values of the function over the rectangular domain are stored in a two-dimensional array grid. A thread is created for each point in the array. The thread starts out with a random number as its current function value. An iteration or step of the computation consists of the thread at each interior point in the grid calculating its new function value, which in this example is the average of the values of its four nearest neighbors.

```
    class LaplaceGrid implements Runnable {...
        private static double[][] grid = new double[M][N];
        private static Barrier = new Barrier(M, N);
        private Thread thread;
        ...
        public void join() {
            try { thread.join(); } catch (InterruptedException e) {}
        }
        public void run() {                       // thread
            double value, total, average, correction;
            grid[id][jd] = value = random(10*M*N);
            b.gate(id, jd); // Why do we call the barrier here?
            for (int iter = 0; iter < numIterations; iter++) {
                if (id > 0 && jd > 0 && id < M-1 && jd < N-1) {
                    total  = grid[id+1][jd];
                    total += grid[id-1][jd];
                    total += grid[id][jd+1];
                    total += grid[id][jd-1];
```

```
                  average = total/4.0; correction = average - value;
                  value += correction;
                }
                b.gate(id, jd);
                if (id > 0 && jd > 0 && id < M-1 && jd < N-1)
                  grid[id][jd] = value;
                b.gate(id, jd); // Why do we call the barrier again?
              }
            }
            public static void main(String[] args) {
              LaplaceGrid[][] lg = new LaplaceGrid[M][N];
              // start the workers
              for (int m = 0; m < M; m++) for (int n = 0; n < N; n++)
                lg[m][n] = new LaplaceGrid(m, n);
              for (int m = 0; m < M; m++) for (int n = 0; n < N; n++)
                lg[m][n].join();              // wait for them to finish
            }
          }
```

After each interior thread uses the old values of the function from its nearest neighbors to compute a new value, it waits for all the other interior threads to finish their step before it stores its new value in the grid and continues to the next iteration. One way to implement this synchronization is with a barrier, similar to the one in Program 7.6. Instead of a single semaphore, we use a collection of semaphores inside a separate barrier object with its own daemon thread (Section 3.1.2), as shown in Library Class 7.1. No thread continues past the barrier until all threads arrive at the barrier; in other words, each thread arriving at the barrier blocks until all the other threads arrive.

```
          public class Barrier implements Runnable {...
            private CountingSemaphore arrive = new CountingSemaphore(0);
            private BinarySemaphore[][] release =
              new BinarySemaphore[m][n];
            for (int i = 0; i < m; i++) for (int j = 0; j < n; j++)
              release[i][j] = new BinarySemaphore(0);
            ...
            public void gate(int i, int j)
              { V(arrive); P(release[i][j]); }
            public void gate(int j) { this.gate(0, j); }
            public void run() {              // thread
              while (true) {
                for (int i = 0; i < m; i++) for (int j = 0; j < n; j++)
                  P(arrive);
                for (int i = 0; i < m; i++) for (int j = 0; j < n; j++)
                  V(release[i][j]);
              }
```

```
        }
    }
```

The barrier class has two constructors and two versions of the **gate** method for one-dimensional and two-dimensional organizations of the data and threads. In an exercise, you are asked to discover the race condition possible if the semaphore **release** is a simple semaphore rather than an array.

Program 7.9 requires shared memory since the threads share the grid array and semaphores. Program 7.11, described in the next section, uses message passing to perform the computation in a distributed memory environment.

7.5 Patterns of Communication

The following programs show additional patterns of thread communication. We have seen the star and pipeline patterns. Program 7.10 (**FG**, **MP**, **DP**, **TC**) implements the parallel radix sorting algorithm and uses the totally connected communication pattern. Every thread communicates with every other thread.

```
class RadixSort implements Runnable {...
    private static int[] nums = new int[N];
    private static MessagePassing[] channel =
        new MessagePassing[N];
    for (int i = 0; i < N; i++)
        channel[i] = new AsyncMessagePassing();
    private static MessagePassing reply =
        new AsyncMessagePassing();
    ...
    public void run() {                   // thread
        int count = 0, other = 0;
        // send my number to all the other workers
        for (int i = 0; i < N; i++)
            if (i != id) send(channel[i], mine);
        // of the numbers sent by the other workers,
        // count how many are less
        for (int i = 1; i < N; i++) { // receive only N-1 numbers
            other = receiveInt(channel[id]);
            if (other < mine) count++;
        }
        // send my count of less-than-seen back to main()
        send(reply, new Result(mine, count));
    }
    public static void main(String[] args) {
        // start the worker threads
        for (int i = 0; i < N; i++) new RadixSort(i, nums[i]);
        int[] tallyCounts = new int[N];
        for (int i = 0; i < N; i++) tallyCounts[i] = 0;
```

```
            for (int i = 0; i < N; i++) {  // gather the results
                Result r = (Result) receive(reply);
                nums[r.count] = r.number;
                tallyCounts[r.count]++;
            }
        }
    }
```

After the driver creates the worker threads, the driver sends to each worker an array of message passing channels; this array contains channels to all the other worker threads. Each worker is assigned one number from the array to be sorted. Each worker sends its assigned number to the other workers; receives the assigned numbers from the other workers; and then counts the number of received assigned numbers less than its own. Finally, each worker sends its assigned number and count to the driver, which puts each worker's assigned number into its proper place in the sorted array. The workers do not need to share memory. This communication pattern is suitable for a collection of workstations on a LAN and other distributed memory computing environments that are fully connected.

Program 7.11 (**FG**, **MP**, **DP**, **GR**) is the message passing version of Program 7.9. It shows how to do nearest-neighbor communication and iteration synchronization for the two-dimensional grid of threads without using a two-dimensional array of function values and a barrier in shared memory. A three-dimensional array grid of message passing channels is used instead; the first two dimensions specify the thread and the third dimension is for that thread's four nearest neighbors. This program illustrates how to set up grids or hypercubes of communication channels between threads.

```
    class LaplaceGrid implements Runnable {...
        private static MessagePassing[][][] grid;
        private static MessagePassing done;
        ...
        public void run() {                      // thread
            double value, got, total, average, correction;
            value = random(10*M*N);
            for (int iter = 0; iter < numIterations; iter++) {
                if (id < M-2 && jd > 0 && jd < N-1)
                    send(grid[id+1][jd][0], value);
                if (id > 1   && jd > 0 && jd < N-1)
                    send(grid[id-1][jd][1], value);
                if (jd < N-2 && id > 0 && id < M-1)
                    send(grid[id][jd+1][2], value);
                if (jd > 1   && id > 0 && id < M-1)
                    send(grid[id][jd-1][3], value);
                total = 0.0;
                if (id > 0 && jd > 0 && id < M-1 && jd < N-1) {
                    for (int i = 0; i < 4; i++) {
```

```
                    got = receiveDouble(grid[id][jd][i]);
                    total += got;
                }
                average = total/4.0;
                correction = average - value;
                value += correction;
            }
        }
        send(done, 0);
    }
    public static void main(String[] args) {
        grid = new MessagePassing[M][N][4];
        for (int m = 0; m < M; m++) for (int n = 0; n < N; n++)
            for (int i = 0; i < 4; i++)
                grid[m][n][i] = new AsyncMessagePassing();
        done = new PipedMessagePassing();   // start the workers
        for (int m = 0; m < M; m++) for (int n = 0; n < N; n++)
            new LaplaceGrid(m, n);
        for (int m = 0; m < M; m++) for (int n = 0; n < N; n++)
            receiveInt(done);                // wait for them to finish
    }
}
```

Each thread starts out with a random number as its current functional value. Each thread on the grid then sends its current value to its north, south, east, and west nearest neighbors (those that exist — boundary nodes do not have all four). Each interior thread on the grid then calculates its new function value, the average of the values it receives from its four nearest neighbors. A thread that has finished its step blocks on its **receive** until its nearest neighbors finish their steps.

The concurrency in both Programs 7.9 and 7.11 is fine-grained because of the extensive communication and synchronization during execution. In this version, the threads do not need to share memory since no variables are shared (the global parameters, m and n, are broadcast to all threads). This type of communication pattern is compatible with architectures in which the CPUs have local memories and are arranged in a grid with nearest-neighbor hardware communication links and a global broadcast bus.

The final matrix multiplication example, Program 7.12 (**FG, MP, DP, GR**), is based on a *heartbeat* or *systolic* algorithm for multiplying ℓ-by-m and m-by-n matrices. Refer to Figures 7.2 and 7.3, based on ([6], pages 105–107). The CPUs, equal in number to the entries in the ℓ-by-m matrix, are arranged in a rectangular array or grid, with only nearest neighbor communication links. Thus, this matrix multiplication algorithm does not need a shared-memory machine to work.

```
    class Multiply implements Runnable {...
        // the following from main()
        private MessagePassing north, east, south, west;
```

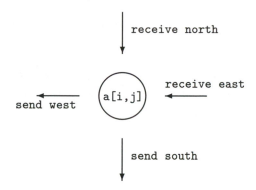

Figure 7.2: One of the Nodes, `multiply(n, i, j, a[i,j])`.

```
...
public void run() {                      // thread
    double sum, x;
    for (int i = 0; i < n; i++) {
        x = receiveDouble(north);
        send(south, x);
        sum = receiveDouble(east);
        sum += a*x;                      // a is a[l][m] from main()
        send(west, sum);
    }
}
}
class SystolicMatrixMultiply {...
    public static void main(String[] args) {
        double[][] a = new double[L][M];
        double[][] b = new double[M][N];
        double[][] c = new double[L][N];
        // create the communication channels
        MessagePassing[][] channelN =
            new MessagePassing[L+1][M+1];
        MessagePassing[][] channelW =
            new MessagePassing[L+1][M+1];
        for (int l = 0; l <= L; l++)
            for (int m = 0; m <= M; m++) {
                channelN[l][m] = new AsyncMessagePassing();
                channelW[l][m] = new AsyncMessagePassing();
            }
        // start a thread for each a[l,m]
        for (int l = 0; l < L; l++) for (int m = 0; m < M; m++) {
            new Multiply(N, l, m, a[l][m],
                channelN[l][m],    //   north
```

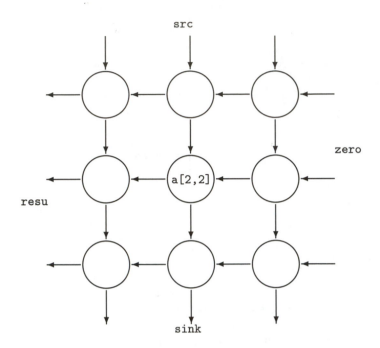

Figure 7.3: A 3-by-3 Grid.

```
            channelW[l][m+1], //    east
            channelN[l+1][m], //    south
            channelW[l][m]);  //    west
    }
    // send columns of b[][] into the source channels
    // along the top
    for (int n = 0; n < N; n++) for (int m = 0; m < M; m++)
        send(channelN[0][m], b[m][n]);
    // send zeros into the left side of the systolic array
    for (int n = 0; n < N; n++) for (int l = 0; l < L; l++)
        send(channelW[l][M], 0.0);
    // throw away the stuff coming out the bottom
    // (was put in the top)
    for (int n = 0; n < N; n++) for (int m = 0; m < M; m++)
        receiveDouble(channelN[L][m]);
    // gather the results into c[l,n]
    for (int n = 0; n < N; n++) for (int l = 0; l < L; l++)
        c[l][n] = receiveDouble(channelW[l][0]);
    }
}
```

Program	Grain	Type of Memory	Type of Synchronization	Type of Parallelism	Pattern of MP Communication
6.14	MG	SM	MP	WC	ST
7.1	FG	DM or SM	MP	DP	PI
7.2	FG	DM or SM	MP	DP	PI
7.3	CG	DM or SM	MP	DP	ST
7.4	CG	DM or SM	MP	WC	ST
7.5	CG	DM	MP	WC	ST
7.6	CG	SM	SY	DP	
7.7	CG	SM	SY	DP	
7.9	FG	SM	SY	DP	
7.8	MG	SM	SY	DP	
7.10	FG	DM or SM	MP	DP	TC
7.11	FG	DM or SM	MP	DP	GR
7.12	FG	DM or SM	MP	DP	GR

Table 7.1: Parallel Program Characteristics.

To compute $C = A \times B$, each thread (CPU) is assigned the entry from matrix A corresponding to its position in the array of CPUs. Zeros are pumped in from the right, and the rows of B are pumped in the top, one per "heartbeat" of the algorithm. The entries of C pop out the left. There are $2n$ heartbeats. In contrast to the earlier parallel matrix multiplication examples, no single CPU is assigned the job of completely computing a single element of the product matrix C. Instead the computation of each element of the product flows through the grid of CPUs.

In this program, the threads are arranged in a grid with nearest neighbor communication. The array of message passing channels sink, implemented in the main driver, absorbs the values of B falling off the bottom row of the grid; the array resu gets the results of the matrix multiplication from the left-most column of the grid. Each Multiply thread (node) in the grid receives numbers from two message passing channels, north and east, sent to the node during initialization by the main driver and connected to the node's north and east neighbors. The main driver also sends to each node during initialization the channels of its south and west neighbors. Contrast this method of nearest-neighbor communication with Program 7.11, in which each thread computes the communication channels of its neighbors by appropriate subscripting of the array grid. Program 7.12 is an example of fine-grained concurrency.

Table 7.1 summarizes the characteristics of the example programs presented in this chapter.

Summary

This chapter is a brief introduction to parallel processing with Java. The two principal architectures used are shared-memory multiprocessors and (distributed memory) clusters of workstations on a LAN. Other more specialized parallel machines exist, for example, multiprocessor machines in which each CPU has its own memory and a fast switch connects the CPUs into a grid or hypercube pattern, Cray vector supercomputers, and SIMD CM-2 Connection Machines.

Shared-memory multiprocessors are ideal for programs having multiple threads that share one address space. Some number of CPUs is allocated to the program by the operating system. The threads in the program execute on the CPUs, possibly one per CPU, depending on the relative number of threads and CPUs. Semaphores, monitors, barriers, the `join` method, and message passing are available for synchronization and communication. A program may spawn a fixed number of threads to solve a problem, based on the number of CPUs allocated to it. The threads form a crew of workers and the problem is broken up into some number of tasks, which are placed into a bag of tasks. Idle worker threads extract the next task from the bag until it is empty. Or a program may spawn some number of threads determined by the input data, regardless of the number of CPUs. The number of threads active varies during execution as threads are created dynamically and terminate.

On distributed memory machines, threads in different address spaces must use message passing to synchronize and communicate. The message passing connections between threads fall into a number of patterns: totally connected, star, grid, and pipeline. Computer scientists often disagree on which architecture, distributed or shared memory, it is easier to write parallel programs.

We looked at shared memory and distributed memory parallel algorithms that sort an array, generate prime numbers, multiply matrices, solve the N-queens problem, and compute a function iteratively over a rectangular domain.

7.6   Exercises

1. **One-Way Merge Sort.** Write a Java program that implements the merge sort using message passing. An array to be sorted is split in half and given to two threads. Each thread sorts its half of the array and then sends, one at a time and in sorted order, its part of the array to a merge thread. The merge thread takes the smaller of the two numbers (or the next number available if one of the two sorts has had all its numbers read) and places it into the next available slot of the final sorted array.

Create three threads: two sorts and a merge. To one sort, pass the first half of the unsorted array; to the other sort, pass the other half. As the sorts progress in parallel, they send to the merge thread the sorted elements in their half of the array, one-by-one as they are determined. In parallel with the sorts, the merge receives the next element from the appropriate sort and places it into the final sorted array.

You have two choices for input data: read the size of the array and the unsorted array elements from the keyboard, or parse the array size from the command line and generate that many random numbers for the unsorted array.

Test your program on a set of numbers that is already sorted and on another that is in reverse sorted order. Make sure your program properly handles requests to sort arrays of length 2, length 1, length 0, and illegal negative lengths.

The following shows one way to set up the message passing channels.

```
import Utilities.*;
import Synchronization.*;

class Worker extends MyObject implements Runnable {

    private int id = -1;
    private MessagePassing channel = null;

    public Worker(int id, MessagePassing channel) {
        this.id = id;
        this.channel = channel;
        new Thread(this).start();
    }

    public void run() {
        int item = id;
        send(channel, item);
    }
}

class MergeSort extends MyObject {

    public static void main(String[] args) {
        int numWorkers = 2;
        AsyncMessagePassing[] channel =
            new AsyncMessagePassing[numWorkers];
        for (int i = 0; i < numWorkers; i++) {
            channel[i] = new AsyncMessagePassing();
            new Worker(i, channel[i]);
        }
        for (int i = 0; i < numWorkers; i++) {
            int value = receiveInt(channel[i]);
            System.out.println("MergeSort received value " + value
                + " on channel " + i);
        }
    }
}

/* .............. Example compile and run(s)

D:\>javac meso.java

D:\>java MergeSort
MergeSort received value 0 on channel 0
MergeSort received value 1 on channel 1
                            ... end of example run(s)  */
```

2. **Multiway Merge Sort.** One-way merge sort uses two sort threads and one merge thread. Multiway merge sort organizes $N = 2^k - 1$ merge threads as a binary tree. Each leaf merge thread in the tree reads from two sort threads; each interior (nonleaf) merge thread reads from its two child merge threads in the tree. The

root merge thread in the tree collects and prints the sorted array. The original unsorted array is split up among the sort threads. Note that a one-way merge sort is a multiway merge sort with $k = 1$.

3. **Pipeline Sieve of Eratosthenes.** Write a Java program, patterned after the one in Program 7.2, that uses asynchronous message passing to implement the pipeline Sieve of Eratosthenes.

Create a thread `filter(2)` that filters out all multiples of 2. To the `filter(2)` thread, send all integers from 2 up to `MAX_NUM` (default value 1000). The `filter(2)` thread creates another thread, `filter(3)`, that filters out all multiples of 3. The `filter(2)` thread then sends to the `filter(3)` thread the integers sent to `filter(2)` that are not multiples of 2, i.e., 3, 5, 7, 9, 11, 13, 15, ... The `filter(3)` thread creates another thread, `filter(5)`, that filters out all multiples of 5. The `filter(3)` thread then sends to the `filter(5)` thread the integers sent to `filter(3)` that are not multiples of 3, i.e., 5, 7, 11, 13, 17, 19, ... And so forth.

Design the program to print out all prime numbers less than or equal to `MAX_NUM`. Note that the smallest number each filter thread gets is prime. Think about how and when to stop creating filter threads and about the minimum number of filter threads necessary to print out all prime numbers less than or equal to `MAX_NUM`.

4. **Compare/Exchange Sort.** Use asynchronous message passing to implement the compare/exchange sort. To sort N numbers (where for simplicity we assume N is even), the algorithm distributes pairs of numbers (using asynchronous message passing) to $N/2$ worker threads, i.e., the numbers are split into $N/2$ pairs and each of the $N/2$ worker threads is given one of the pairs. The worker threads are laid out in a line; each worker thread communicates only with its two neighbors (except the worker threads on the two ends, which have one neighbor each). There are $N/2$ iterations of the algorithm. On each iteration, a worker sends the smaller number of its pair to the left and the larger of its pair to the right. After all the iterations, the workers send the final pair they have back to the main driver.

Complete Program 7.13 (see page 569 of the on-line appendix), a skeleton implementation that sets up the neighbor communication links between the workers.

5. **Speedup.** On a shared-memory multiprocessor, time Programs 7.1, 7.2, and 7.3 with various numbers of CPUs if your version of Java supports allocating CPUs to threads. What conclusions do you draw?

6. **Race Conditions.** Explain why Program 7.9 is incorrect if there is no call to `b.gate` at the end of the `run` method. Discover the race condition possible if the semaphore `release` in Library Class 7.1 is a simple semaphore rather than an array.

Explain why Program 7.11 has the correct per iteration synchronization.

7. **Multithreaded "Game of Life."** Write a multithreaded version of the "Game of Life" Java program you did in Exercise 2.4. Each cell has its own dedicated thread to compute the cell's value in the next generation. This thread is embedded

in a class instantiated $M \times N$ times by the driver, once for each cell in the grid. Thread synchronization is done with semaphores.

The primary problem to solve is coordinating all the cell threads during each generation. A cell thread cannot start computing the cell's new value for the next generation until all other cells have completed their computation for the current generation. Use Java semaphores to solve this problem. You may find useful the barrier implemented in Library Class 7.1 and illustrated with Program 7.9.

8. **Message Passing "Game of Life."** Write a version of the "Game of Life" Java program you did in Exercise 7 that uses message passing in distributed memory for thread communication and synchronization instead of (barrier) semaphores in shared memory. Each cell thread sends its current cell value to its eight nearest neighbors and then reads its nearest neighbor cell values to compute its new call value for the next generation. A cell thread cannot start computing its new value for the next generation until all other cells have completed their computation for the current generation.

9. **Parallel Genetic Algorithm.** Parallelize the simple GA, Program 2.10. There are two approaches: (a) start a thread for each chromosome's fitness function evaluation and (b) split the population into subpopulations that evolve separately but every so often exchange their best members. Which approach is appropriate for a shared-memory multiprocessor? For a collection of workstations connected by a LAN? On what kinds of problems would each approach work best?

10. **Parallel Radix Sort.** Fix the duplicate input data problem in Program 7.10. In the sample run, 2 occurs twice in the input data and only once in the output whereas an extra 518 appears in the output.

11. **Are Pipes Thread-Safe?** Remove all lines

```
synchronized (sending) {
```

and

```
synchronized (receiving) {
```

and their matching closing braces from Library Classes 6.6 and 6.7. Recompile them and execute Program 6.3 with the -0 option and Program 7.4 with the -n10 option. Do you get corrupted object stream exceptions and bad integer row numbers, respectively? If so, explain why.

12. **Parallel Sieve of Eratosthenes.** Execute Program 7.1 several times to generate the first 100 prime numbers. Do you always get the same values in the `seenCount` array for the first several filter threads? If not, explain why.

13. **Algorithm Animation.** Animate the program you have written for one of the exercises above.

List of Programs/Classes

List of Library Classes

Program and Library Class Source Code

All program and library class source code is available over the Internet using the following URLs.

> http://www.mcs.drexel.edu/~shartley/ConcProgJava/
>   bookJavaExamples.tar.gz

> http://www.mcs.drexel.edu/~shartley/ConcProgJava/
>   bookJavaExamples.zip

> http://www.mcs.drexel.edu/~shartley/ConcProgJava/
>   bookJavaExamples.html

> ftp://ftp.mcs.drexel.edu/pub/shartley/bookJavaExamples.tar.gz

> ftp://ftp.mcs.drexel.edu/pub/shartley/bookJavaExamples.zip

The first in a `gzip`-compressed `tar` archive file, the second is a `zip` archive, and the third is a Web page of links to each program and library class using the book's numbering scheme. The last two are anonymous `ftp` access alternatives for the first two.

A listing of the source code (this appendix, pages 261–569), can be downloaded as a `gzip`-compressed Postscript file using the URLs

> http://www.mcs.drexel.edu/~shartley/ConcProgJava/
>   bookJavaExamples.ps.gz

> ftp://ftp.mcs.drexel.edu/pub/shartley/bookJavaExamples.ps.gz

and printed on any Postscript printer after uncompressing. The appendix was deleted from this book to keep its size manageable.

Bibliography

[1] Gregory R. Andrews, *Concurrent Programming: Principles and Practice*, Benjamin/Cummings, 1991.

[2] Ken Arnold and James Gosling, *The Java Programming Language*, Addison-Wesley, 1996.

[3] David Beasley, David R. Bull, and Ralph R. Martin, "An Overview of Genetic Algorithms: Part 1, Fundamentals," *University Computing*, Vol. 15, No. 2, 1993, pp. 58–69.

[4] David Beasley, David R. Bull, and Ralph R. Martin, "An Overview of Genetic Algorithms: Part 2, Research Topics," *University Computing*, Vol. 15, No. 4, 1993, pp. 170–181.

[5] Leland L. Beck, *System Software: An Introduction to Systems Programming*, second edition, Addison-Wesley, 1990.

[6] M. Ben-Ari, *Principles of Concurrent and Distributed Programming*, Prentice-Hall, 1990.

[7] Andrew D. Birrell, "An Introduction to Programming with Threads," Technical Report No. 35, Digital Equipment Corp. Systems Research Center, January 1989 (available by anonymous **ftp** from machine **pub/DEC/SRC/research-reports/SRC-035.ps.Z**).

[8] Grady Booch, *Object-Oriented Analysis and Design*, second edition, Benjamin/Cummings, 1994.

[9] Barry Boone, *Java Essentials for C and C++ Programmers*, Addison-Wesley, 1996.

[10] Thomas Bräunl, *Parallel Programming: An Introduction*, Prentice-Hall, 1993.

[11] Timothy Budd, *An Introduction to Object-Oriented Programming*, Addison-Wesley, 1991.

[12] Peter A. Buhr, Michel Fortier, and Michael H. Coffin, "Monitor Classification," *ACM Computing Surveys*, Vol. 27, No. 1, March 1995.

[13] Alan Burns and Geoff Davies, *Concurrent Programming*, Addison-Wesley, 1993.

[14] Gary Cornell and Cay S. Horstmann, *Core Java*, Prentice-Hall, 1996.

[15] Harvey M. Deitel, *An Introduction to Operating Systems*, second edition, Addison-Wesley, 1990.

[16] E. W. Dijkstra, "Cooperating Sequential Processes," Technological University, Eindhoven, The Netherlands, 1965 (reprinted in *Programming Languages*, F. Genuys, editor, Academic Press, 1968).

[17] David Flanagan, *Java in a Nutshell*, O'Reilly, 1996.

[18] George Gilder, "The Battle Beyond Apple," *Wall Street Journal*, Vol. CCXXX, No. 28, August 8, 1997, p. A12.

[19] David E. Goldberg, *Genetic Algorithms in Search, Optimization, and Machine Learning*, Addison-Wesley, 1989.

[20] Lee Gomes and Don Clark, "Battle Code: Java is finding niches but isn't yet living up to its early promises," *Wall Street Journal*, Vol. CCXXX, No. 41, August 27, 1997, p. A1.

[21] James Gosling, Bill Joy, and Guy Steele, *The Java Language Specification*, Addison-Wesley, 1996.

[22] Stephen J. Hartley, *Operating Systems Programming: The SR Programming Language*, Oxford University Press, 1995.

[23] David Hemmendinger, "A Correct Implementation of General Semaphores," *ACM Operating Systems Review*, Vol. 22, No. 3, 1988.

[24] C. A. R. Hoare, "Monitors: An Operating System Structuring Concept," *Communications of the ACM*, Vol. 17, No. 10, October 1974.

[25] R. C. Holt, G. S. Graham, E. D. Lazowska, M. A. Scott, *Structured Concurrent Programming with Operating Systems Applications*, Addison-Wesley, 1978.

[26] Phil Kearns, "A Correct and Unrestrictive Implementation of General Semaphores," *ACM Operating Systems Review*, Vol. 22, No. 4, 1988.

[27] Doug Lea, *Concurrent Programming in Java: Design Principles and Patterns*, Addison-Wesley, 1997.

[28] Laura Lemay and Charles L. Perkins, *Teach Yourself Java in 21 Days*, Sams.net, 1996.

[29] Ted Lewis, "Bringing Up Java," *IEEE Internet Computing*, Vol. 1, No. 4, July-August 1997, pp. 110–112.

[30] Ted Lewis and Hesham El-Rewini, *Introduction to Parallel Computing*, Prentice-Hall, 1992.

[31] Scott Oaks and Henry Wong, *Java Threads*, O'Reilly, 1997.

[32] Michael J. Quinn, *Parallel Computing: Theory and Practice*, second edition McGraw-Hill, 1994.

[33] Stuart Ritchie, "Systems Programming in Java," *IEEE Micro*, Vol. 17, No. 3, May/June 1997, pp. 30–35.

[34] Abraham Silberschatz and Peter B. Gavin, *Operating System Concepts*, fourth edition, Addison-Wesley, 1994.

[35] William Stallings, *Computer Organization and Architecture*, third edition, Prentice-Hall, 1993.

[36] William Stallings, *Operating Systems*, second edition, Prentice-Hall, 1995.

[37] John T. Stasko, "TANGO: A Framework and System for Algorithm Animation," *IEEE Computer*, Vol. 20, No. 9, Sept. 1990, pp. 27-39.

[38] John T. Stasko and Doug Hayes, "XTANGO Algorithm Animation Designer's Package," October 1992, available by anonymous `ftp` from machine `ftp.cc.gatech.edu` (from directory `pub/people/stasko`, retrieve file `xtango.tar.Z`, then uncompress and extract file `xtangodoc.ps` from directory `./xtango/doc` in the archive file `xtango.tar`).

[39] W. Richard Stevens, UNIX *Network Programming*, Prentice-Hall, 1990.

[40] Andrew S. Tanenbaum, *Structured Computer Organization*, third edition, Prentice-Hall, 1990.

[41] Andrew S. Tanenbaum, *Modern Operating Systems*, Prentice-Hall, 1992.

[42] Andrew S. Tanenbaum, *Distributed Operating Systems*, Prentice-Hall, 1995.

[43] Andrew S. Tanenbaum and Albert S. Woodhull, *Operating Systems: Design and Implementation*, second edition, Prentice-Hall, 1997.

[44] Patrick Henry Winston and Sundar Narasimhan, *On to Java*, Addison-Wesley, 1996.

Index